Game Audio Programming 5

Welcome to the fifth volume of *Game Audio Programming: Principles and Practices* – the first series of its kind dedicated to the art, science, and craft of game audio programming. In this volume, some of the top game audio programmers in the industry delve into audio programming topics from low-level subjects like oscillator techniques to high-level topics such as automated testing, reverb, and music.

Game audio programmers at all skill levels will find something to learn in this book. The methods in these pages have been used in games of all sizes and shapes, from large AAA titles down to small indie games, so they are all tried and tested and ready for you to apply in your own game audio code. There are chapters about speech systems, asynchronous multithreaded audio engine architecture, impulse responses, and more.

This collection compiles topics from a vast body of advanced knowledge and wisdom about game audio programming. Whether you are a newly minted game audio programmer or an expert, or if you're just the lucky soul who gets to do the work, this book is for you!

Guy Somberg has been programming audio engines for his entire career. From humble beginnings writing a low-level audio mixer for slot machines, he quickly transitioned to writing game audio engines for all manner of games. He has written audio engines that shipped AAA games like *Hellgate: London*, *Bioshock 2*, *The Sims 4*, and *Torchlight 3*, as well as smaller titles like *Minion Master*, *Tales from the Borderlands*, and *Game of Thrones*. Guy has also given several talks at the Game Developer Conference, the Audio Developer Conference, and CppCon. When he's not programming or writing game audio programming books, he can be found at home reading, playing video games, and playing the flute.

Game Audio Programming 5
Principles and Practices

Edited by
Guy Somberg

CRC Press
Taylor & Francis Group
Boca Raton London New York

CRC Press is an imprint of the
Taylor & Francis Group, an **Informa** business

Designed cover image: Getty Images

First edition published 2026
by CRC Press
2385 NW Executive Center Drive, Suite 320, Boca Raton FL 33431

and by CRC Press
4 Park Square, Milton Park, Abingdon, Oxon, OX14 4RN

CRC Press is an imprint of Taylor & Francis Group, LLC

ISBN: 9781032856339 (hbk)
ISBN: 9781032852850 (pbk)
ISBN: 9781003519119 (ebk)

DOI: 10.1201/9781003519119

Typeset in Minion
by KnowledgeWorks Global Ltd.

To Mila – I appreciate your offer to write a chapter for me if you could. We'll get you trained up and ready sometime in the next few volumes.

And to Emily, as always, and for all of the same reasons.

Contents

SECTION V: **Music**

Contributors

Robert Bantin has been writing audio code for an ever-expanding length of time. While at school they were an active member of the Amiga demo scene. At Salford university they studied acoustics and brought their coding experience to their studies in the form of DSP and audio-focused applications. Upon graduating they were recruited by Philips ASA Labs in Eindhoven in order to join the MPEG technology program. Robert Bantin has since worked on several AAA games for Activision, Codemasters, and Ubisoft. When they're not programming, they can be found at home cooking, attempting to shred on guitar, and playing video games when the rest of their family are asleep. The rabbit is doing well, but we're down to one cat.

Roberto Bender In 2018, Roberto transitioned from a prominent position at HP to join Ubisoft, driven by his passion for video games. Originally from Brazil, he relocated to Canada to pursue his dream job. At Ubisoft, Bender is dedicated to creating unforgettable gaming experiences, blending his enthusiasm for the industry with his expertise. He began his AAA game development career as a sound programmer on *Assassin's Creed Odyssey*. His expertise and dedication quickly led to him to take ownership of all music systems within the *Assassin's Creed* franchise, culminating in the release of *Assassin's Creed Shadows*. In 2025, Bender also shared his insights as a presenter at the Game Developers Conference, further contributing to the advancement of audio in game development.

Pablo Schwilden Diaz started off as a sound designer 10 years ago but gradually became more lazy and more interested in audio programming and tools development to spend less time doing redundant tasks. Now leading the team at Demute, he works as a full time Audio Programmer on many different titles from clients and internal tools for the rest of the team.

Mike Filion has been developing video games for more than 15 years with Ubisoft Québec, with the majority in the world of audio. When explaining his work and passion to friends and family, he often oversimplifies by stating that he is "responsible for ensuring the bleeps and bloops work in the game". He has had the opportunity to work with many talented people associated with games from around the world such as *Assassin's Creed, Tom Clancy's The Division*, and more. In between delivering amazing titles, he is known to friends and family for his multitude of different projects, from traveling the world with his daughter (of whom he's immensely proud) to earning his pilot's license to renovating his "haunted" house.

Charlie Huguenard makes creative tools, art installations, video games, music, skate parks, and a variety of other sometimes-useful things with code, electronics, wood, concrete, and a variety of other tools. He has worked on audio and music systems in *Unreal Engine* and *Fortnite* at Epic Games, built and led the multidisciplinary sound department at Meow Wolf, and shepherded the internal spatial audio middleware at Facebook. He is always learning a new skill, starting a new project, and finding more interesting uses for failed experiments. He loves all dogs.

Jon Mitchell has been working in games and game audio for long enough that he no longer likes using actual numbers to talk about it, and instead will just mumble something about his career having now attained legal drinking age in any country in the world. Despite starting out as a demoscene-style graphics effects programmer, his interests in trackers, electronic music and music visualization quickly led him to audio programming. He's worked on audio tools, systems, and gameplay code for games from sprawling open-world games like *Sleeping Dog* to small linear adventure games like *Broken Sword 3*. For the past 5 years, he's been working with the extraordinarily creative and affable folks at Blackbird Interactive on *Homeworld 3*. When not at work, he is happiest reading to his three insatiably curious kids or shuttling them around by cargo bike.

Fiach O'Donnell is an audio programmer who has worked on AAA game projects for Echtra Games and Splash Damage, Ltd. He is primarily interested in the development of runtime audio gameplay systems and tools to enhance sound designer productivity. Before pursuing a career in game audio programming, Fiach worked in several cloud computing research roles and gained experience in recording and producing audio and music for short films, orchestras, and bands. He received his BSc in Computer Science from University College Cork and his MSc in Music & Technology from Munster Technological University. When he's not programming, Fiach enjoys reading, playing guitar, and traveling with his wife.

Collin Schupman is a Senior Audio Programmer at High Moon Studios, where he recently earned his first shipped title with *Call of Duty: Black Ops 6*. His career has always revolved around sound – from nearly a decade spent building high-end audio plugins to pushing the boundaries of real time game audio. At High Moon, he works across tooling, pipeline, and runtime systems. Besides that, he writes and performs music and stays active outdoors.

David Su is a game developer, musician, audio programmer, sound designer, and researcher interested in creating new musical experiences through technology. He is currently the lead audio and systems programmer at Brass Lion Entertainment, working on *Wu-Tang: Rise of the Deceiver*. He is also an adjunct assistant professor at the University of Southern California, teaching a course on sound design for games. David's game credits include *One Hand Clapping*, *NFL Endzone*, *Trolls Music Stars*, and *Evergreen Blues*. He has also worked on music software at Output, Sunhouse, and Amper Music. David has spoken at the Game Developers Conference, GameSoundCon, and the International Computer Music Conference. He received his MS from the MIT Media Lab and his BA from Columbia University.

Colin Walder has been developing audio technology for games since 2006, with a focus on AAA games. His credits include *GTA V*, *Red Dead Redemption 2*, *The Witcher 3: Wild Hunt*, and *Cyberpunk 2077*, where he was involved in a wide range of audio topics from acoustics and ambisonics to performance and streaming. He currently works as Engineering Director, Management and Audio at CD Projekt RED, where in addition to audio topics, he provides direction for management across the technology department.

Preface

INTRODUCTION

Welcome to the fifth volume of *Game Audio Programming: Principles and Practices*! I'm so pleased to be able to share this newest edition with you. The contributors to this book and I are all passionate about game audio programming, and these books are one way that we can share our knowledge and enthusiasm both with each other and with the game developer community at large.

The depth of knowledge and skills on display from my contributors in these pages is incredible. Some of them have dived deep into topics that I've never thought about, or provided clarity where none previously existed. As with all of my books, we all build upon each other's work, and we would not be able to build the systems that we do without the inspiration, expertise, and knowhow that we learn from each other.

THIS BOOK

As authors, we strive to bring to this book ideas, techniques, and thinking that readers can take and apply directly to their work. Some chapters end up providing high-level overviews of their topics: a new way to think about the landscape or a survey of techniques. Other chapters do deep dives into practical applications and how to implement specific features.

Here are brief summaries of all the chapters in this book:

- **The Flavors of Game Audio Programming** by Pablo Schwilden Diaz: Pablo considers what it means to be a game audio programmer. He discovers that the field is sufficiently broad that there are actually three different flavors, which he likens to the members of a fantasy adventuring party. The combination of all three gives us the unicorn!

- **Oscillators for Real Time Synthesis** by Collin Schupman: This chapter discusses a number of different fundamental waveforms (noise, sine, square, sawtooth, and triangle). It presents both a mathematical description of the waveforms, and presents code on how to implement them.

- **Recording Audio Data to a Memory Buffer** by Guy Somberg: Ordinarily, audio data is just output to the operating system's sound device, but sometimes we need to insert a probe and record the data to a buffer. This chapter goes into two different methods for implementing this buffer recording: as an output plugin that records the final mix, and as a DSP that can be inserted at any point in the graph.

- **An Overview of Game Acoustics** by Mike Filion: A high-level overview of the various topics that go into game audio acoustics. This chapter first does a survey of applying several different middleware solutions and then goes into a few implementation details of how to roll your own systems.

- **Multilayered Dynamic Reverb** by Colin Walder: *Cyberpunk 2077* implemented a complex multilayered reverb system with three reverbs representing small, medium, and large spaces. This chapter describes the system and goes into some of the implementation details on how they went about it.

- **Creating Impulse Responses for Virtual Environments** by Guy Somberg: If you want to author an impulse response for a game environment, there is a lot of background knowledge that you need. This chapter starts with the fundamentals and builds up enough background and code to be able to put together an impulse response from a virtual environment.

- **Transient Driven Events from Game Parameters** by Robert Bantin: Parameters from the game will naturally come in to the audio engine at the game's framerate – typically 60 Hz. We can examine and filter this signal in exactly the same way that we would a high-sample rate audio signal (e.g. 48 kHz), just at a much lower rate. This chapter goes into an example of how to do this sort of analysis.

- **Addressing the Neglect of Sound in Reused Animations** by Roberto Bender: Animations are frequently reused between characters in games, which means that audio that is applied to those animations is also reused. By applying knowledge of animation sequencers and build tables, this chapter describes a system that creates an intermediate layer to provide more audio variety in the face of animation reuse.

- **Rule Systems and Context Aware Speech in** *Homeworld 3* by Jon Mitchell: When faced with the challenge of implementing a system to play audio for characters speaking in a dynamic game world, one good tool is the Event-Condition-Action pattern. This chapter goes into the details of how they implemented this pattern in *Homeworld 3*.

- **Updates to the Sound Engine State Machine** by Guy Somberg: In *Game Audio Programming Principles and Practices Volume 1*, Chapter 2, I presented a state machine to represent the lifecycle of a playing sound. This chapter updates that state machine slightly by removing two of the states, and explains why we can do that and under what circumstances.

- **Asynchronous Multithreaded Audio Engine Architecture** by Guy Somberg: The classic audio engine can be thought of as a loop over all of the playing sounds. By taking advantage of two observations – called the steady state and the one-way pipeline – we can create an asynchronous and multithreaded audio engine that is much more performant, at the cost of some code complexity.

- **Asynchronous Multithreaded Audio Engine Code** by Guy Somberg: This chapter is a follow-up to the previous one. It dives into the code for how to implement an asynchronous multithreaded audio engine.

- **Automated Testing for Game Audio Systems** by Charlie Huguenard: Automated tests are a great way to catch bugs early, either as you're writing new code or as you're modifying old code. It can sometimes be difficult to think about how to apply automated testing techniques to game audio code, so this chapter explains the how and the why of automated testing for audio.

- **An Algorithmic Approach to "Max Within Radius" Virtualization** by Guy Somberg: Max Within Radius is the application of Walter Murch's Law of Two and a Half to game audio. On the surface, it can seem simple, but there are subtleties into how to implement it. This chapter explains the technique, finds an algorithm to make it work, and presents code on how to implement it.

- **Synchronizing Music to Gameplay to Create Music Moments** by Fiach O'Donnell: In *Game Audio Programming Principles and Practices Volume 2*, Chapter 21, Colin Walder presents a system to synchronize game state to music. This chapter thinks about it from the other perspective: how do we synchronize music to gameplay? The answer involves using a time-invariant pitch shift effect to subtly time-stretch the music so that important beats happen on forthcoming game moments.

- **Remixing Musical Loops in RealTime** by David Su: One way to create musical variation is by taking small music loops and playing them on top of each other. This chapter examines systems on how to author a system that can automatically beat-match and transpose loops so that they can be combined in exciting ways.

PARTING THOUGHTS

This series of books has become influential in the game audio community. After nearly a decade since the first volume, there are now people whose audio programming careers have started and flourished, and who cannot imagine a world without these books in it. Although it is a point of pride for me that I am the shepherd of this series of books, I am also a student of them. Hardly a week goes by that I don't pull one out for reference or inspiration. This volume is no exception – I hope that you, dear reader, get as much out of this book as I have.

Acknowledgments

Wow, I'm at volume 5 now! The list of people who have made it possible for me to get this far grows longer every year, and I can't believe how lucky I am to have had all of you in my path. Most of the names here have been in most or all of my Game Audio Programming books, and that's because they deserve it.

As always, my contributors are what make these books possible. Every time I do one of these books, I discover at least one chapter that I just *have* to go implement immediately. Thanks to all of you, both old and new!

Everybody who is in the videogame industry has a different origin story. Mine is filled with people from whom I have learned and grown, and who nurtured my journey: Tyler Thompson, David Brevik, Brian Fitzgerald, and Justin Miller.

My first job out of college involved writing an audio engine for a slot machine, under the guidance of Thomas Buckeyne. It's entirely likely that without that experience, I never would have discovered my love of audio programming.

The first big game that I worked on was Hellgate: London, along with David Steinwedel, from whom I learned how to work with sound designers.

The sound designers whom I've worked with over the years have had a hugely positive impact on me: David Steinwedel, Jordan Stock, Andy Martin, Pam Aranoff, Michael Kamper, Michael Csurics, and Erika Escamez.

Fiach O'Donnell is not just the first audio programmer I've ever worked with, he's now a contributor to the book! Thanks also to Tomas Neumann, who has been my audio programming companion from afar from early days.

Thanks to Rick Adams from CRC Press, who got me started writing the first volume of this series, and thanks to Will Bateman, Alyss Barraza, and the rest of the team at CRC Press, who are working on this volume. I appreciate all of your hard work on my behalf in making this book a reality.

This book is already dedicated to my wife Emily, but she also goes in the acknowledgments section because I wouldn't be able to do this without her.

CHAPTER 1

The Flavors of Game Audio Programming

Pablo Schwilden Diaz

1.1 THE NEED FOR SPECIALTIES

Over the past years, one of the most recurrent questions students or sound designers have asked about my role is: "How do you become a Game Audio Programmer?" I am sure many fellow Game Audio Programmers had to answer the same question, and each had their own answer.

However, as I have come to know more people with the title (official or not) of Game Audio Programmer, I have realized that each of them had a different trajectory and learning experience before they accepted their role. There is not one common standardized path to becoming a Game Audio Programmer. For the longest of times, I would just shrug at the question and answer, "Well, it really depends on what you like".

Eventually, I discovered that there is a pattern, and once I saw it, I realized that the hints of it were everywhere. This pattern is visible in the sections that separate the chapters of the previous volume of *Game Audio Programming: Principles and Practices* (Somberg 2024). Stéphane Beauchemin hints at it in Beauchemin (2019). It all made sense.

The pattern turns out to be that there are distinct types of Game Audio Programmers. It might sound obvious, but this was the key to understanding how to become a Game Audio Programmer. In game development, game programmers specialized and became gameplay programmers, animation programmers, engine programmers, etc. The exact same thing happened to Game Audio Programmers without me realizing.

From there started the quest to discover, understand, and define what the different specialties are: the different flavors of Game Audio Programming.

1.2 THE ENDURING MYTH

Let us start with the fundamentals: What is a Game Audio Programmer?

We can first look at it semantically. The word "game" tells us that it is someone working in video games, "audio" indicates that it is someone working with content in the form of sound, and "programmer" says that it is someone working with code. That gives us a person who works on code and sound for video games.

At first glance, this semantic description seems sufficient. However, when we start to dig a bit deeper, we realize that these concepts are too broad to give an accurate picture. People working in video games can be doing vastly different things, from creating games, developing tools, selling those games, or managing the legal aspects of things. Similarly, audio encompasses many disciplines: sound design, music, voice, mixing, etc. And programming is also a huge world with several different aspects: web, software, hardware, etc.

Therefore, this semantic view of the role is incomplete because it can encompass people who do wildly different things and have truly little in common on a more practical level. Two people under this definition of Game Audio Programmer could share barely any skills, tools, and concepts. We need to give more detail to this definition.

A more detailed definition of this elusive role was given in Beauchemin (2019). There, Stéphane does an excellent job at describing more precisely what the job of a Game Audio Programmer is and how it relates to video game development. He goes over concepts like audio tools, audio integration, middleware integration, low-level systems, DSP, and plugins. If you have not had the chance to read it yet, I would be tempted to advise you to pause this chapter and go read Beauchemin's one, before continuing here.

With that chapter, we get a good grasp of an array of tasks and skills the Game Audio Programmer can have. However, if you compile all the tasks described, the amount and depth of skills required is daunting. Beauchemin mentions it: "Because audio programmers have to juggle so many different specialized aspects of development, it's not hard to see why many generalist programmers shy away from audio programming tasks" (Beauchemin 2019). In a sense, this definition of Game Audio Programmer is so detailed and specific that only a few exceptionally talented and experienced people would fit into such a definition.

I, for one, do not have some of the skills mentioned in the chapter and cannot execute some of the tasks laid out. Am I, therefore, not a Game Audio Programmer? I would argue that the answer is that I am a Game Audio Programmer despite not having the entire depth of skills, and that statement applies broadly to a large number of people who are doing the work.

Ultimately, we are left with either too broad or too specific of a definition. Beauchemin dispelled the myth of a very particular kind of Game Audio Programmer, but not all of them. However, along the way, he left a hint for us. In this quote: "Contrariwise, as an audio programmer, I often find myself doing the job of a tools programmer, a gameplay programmer, or a systems programmer", we can see that he is summing the work of three titles into one (Beauchemin 2019). So, what if there were more than one kind of Game Audio Programmer? That would explain why that role is so hard to define.

1.3 THE HOLY TRINITY

As I started trying to classify Game Audio Programmers into distinct groups, I felt close to biologists. I kept going back and forth, starting with five groups, then finding a person that did not fit any of those, creating more groups, having too many groups, scrapping everything, and starting again.

The solution was in front of me. In Beauchemin's quote, we saw that he specifically mentioned three titles. Incidentally, the previous volume of *Game Audio Programming: Principles and Practices* (Somberg 2024) is also divided into three sections: Game Integration, Low-Level Topics, and Tools. So, I started aligning the people, skills, and tasks I knew into three categories, following this logic.

- A group for systems, engines, and anything low-level (as in, close to hardware and computer language).

- A group for tooling, workflows, and pipelines.

- A group for gameplay, integration, and game scripting.

With these three groups, I could easily classify different tasks and skillsets. DSP-related tasks proved a bit more difficult because they could equally be a part of all three groups or be their own separate group. To keep things easy, I decided to put DSP as part of the low-level group, but I accept that this might be the subject of further discussion.

When it comes to people, this grouping matched everyone I knew in the Game Audio Programming field. A few rare people encompass all three groups, but less experienced people like me would only be a part of one or two groups.

Finally, we come to our definition: a Game Audio Programmer is someone who does the tasks contained in at least one of these three groups.

Now came that challenging task of naming those three categories of work,[1] the specializations of Game Audio Programming. It was important for me that these names feel right for the people they represent and are easy enough to understand. The whole point is to make things clearer! GDC 2024 was for me the occasion to ask other Game Audio Programmers their opinion, collect feedback, discuss, and argue about semantics. After some iterations (and some beers), I finally landed on the following three names (Figure 1.1):

- Audio Rendering Programming

- Audio Tools Programming

- Gameplay Audio Programming

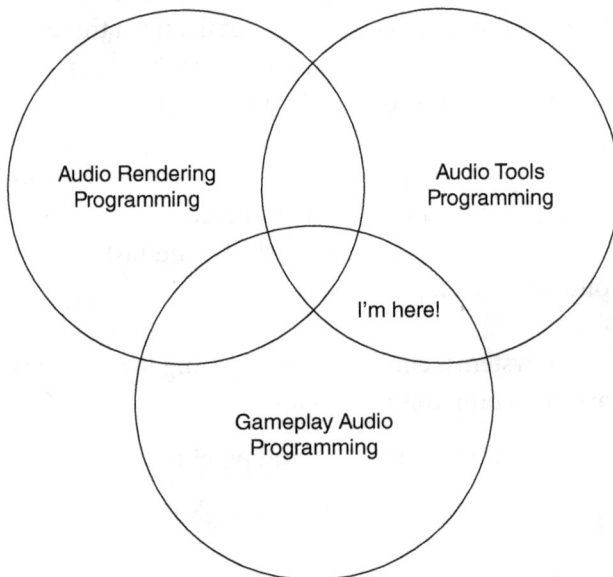

FIGURE 1.1 Venn diagram illustrating the three fields of Game Audio Programming.

Hopefully, these names communicate clearly enough what these different flavors of Game Audio Programming contain. Now let us see in more detail what they are.

1.4 AUDIO RENDERING PROGRAMMING

One day, the Audio Rendering Programmer woke up from its slumber, looked at a computer and said, "Let there be sound." The computer replied with a joyous "beep" and the Audio Rendering Programmer was happy.

Audio rendering in the context of video game development is a huge topic, and one that I am less knowledgeable about. What globally defines this flavor of Game Audio Programming is the idea that we are working at the level of audio samples. We are taking numbers and commanding the CPU to do operations on these numbers to produce new numbers that describe sound. Or reading numbers from a disk or the network and storing them somewhere to use later. Or giving numbers to an operating system so they can do some more math on it.

It might be easier to grasp with an example. This example is the only piece of DSP code I have ever produced. The goal of this code is to swap the left and right channels of a stereo audio stream. I wrote in C# for the Unity game engine, but the concept around it can apply to different setups.

```
void OnAudioFilterRead (float[] data, int channels)
{
    if(channels != 2) return; //early exit if data isn't stereo

    int bufferLength = data.Length / channels;
    for (int i = 0; i < bufferLength; i++)
    {
        (data[i * channels], data[i * channels + 1]) =
            (data[i * channels + 1], data[i * channels]);
    }
}
```

OnAudioFilterRead() is called by the Unity system each audio frame. It provides a list of numbers representing an audio signal and the number of channels in that signal. One important concept that is not immediately obvious in the code is that audio data is interleaved, which means that the audio samples of each channel are weaved together. In the case of a stereo file, we are given one sample of audio from the left channel, then one sample from the right channel, then we repeat.

Therefore, to swap the left and right channels, we must swap the samples two by two. We can see this in the code, where we take the value at `i * channels` and put it in `i * channels + 1` and inversely take the value at `i * channels + 1` and put it in `i * channels`. Even such a simple piece of code requires knowledge about how multichannel audio formats are described in digital form and how we manipulate them.

However, this kind of work is only the beginning. The tasks included in Audio Rendering Programming also generally include the following:

- Communicating with the platform audio interface to pass the audio of the game to the operating system (and every platform has a different interface).

- Retrieving audio data on the disk to load it in RAM or stream it on the fly.

- Decoding compressed audio formats.

- Creating modular systems to apply operations of audio data like volume, frequency filtering, delaying, reverberation, etc.

- Accessing hardware specific features like decoding acceleration or parallel processing.

- Handling threading and scheduling of audio operations.

Even having listed those, I am sure I missed tasks included in Audio Rendering Programming, but hopefully we can get a grasp of their general nature and domain.

The reason I know so little about this specific field is that it is very closely related to game or audio engine development. When we are using tools like Unity, Unreal Engine, Wwise, or FMOD, all this groundwork has already been done for us by other Audio Rendering Programmers. Nowadays, game developers that develop their own game engine and/or audio engine are becoming rare, meaning that the work of Audio Rendering Programmers is getting centralized in a handful of companies.

This does not mean that this specialty is not useful outside of the domain of game engine development. After all, I did still have to write that little piece of audio rendering code. Examples like these where there is a specific feature that requires going deep into the system are a regular occurrence because every game is unique, and new games often try to go further than what was done before.

To be a competent Audio Rendering Programmer, two fields of knowledge are important: digital audio and software development (preferably multi-platform). These two fields are very deep and old, so they might not be easily approachable due to the sheer amount of prerequisite knowledge. C++ is going to come up quite often and concepts like threading, I/O, DSP, and buffers are going to be common.

Without going into too much detail, let us look at some more examples of Audio Rendering Programming taken from previous volumes of *Game Audio Programming: Principles and Practices.*

- **Flexible Delay Lines: Practical Methods for Varying Sample-Rate Delays During Playback by Robert Bantin** (Bantin 2024)

  This is a very good example because even though Robert's team uses Wwise, they needed to add specific audio features to achieve what they wanted for their game. In this chapter we can see how they went into detail on how to manage audio samples to create a delay that can change size and provides the math behind the acoustic representation of echoes in closed spaces.

- **Multithreading for Game Audio by Dan Murray** (Murray 2019)

  This chapter provides a good example of the software development side of Audio Rendering Programming. It is all about multithreading, communicating with hardware, and handling buffers. The chapter even contains nice search-engine friendly terms to further deepen the understanding of the concepts used.

To finish off our description of this specific flavor of Game Audio Programming, I would say that the Audio Rendering Programmer is a bit like a mage in a traditional tabletop roleplaying adventure (Figure 1.2). They are usually wise and are experts in indecipherable texts written across generations. They understand complex formulas and minute details about the fabric of digital audio. Their work is sometimes obscure to other people, but lays foundations on which the rest

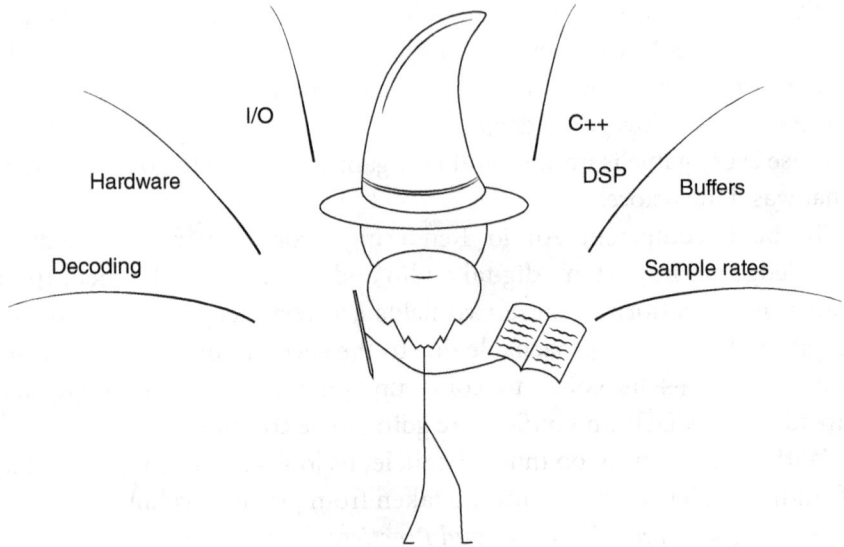

FIGURE 1.2   Magician Audio Rendering Programmer.

of the game audio world relies. Their spells are very powerful, but they might require a lot of setup to work.

1.5 AUDIO TOOLS PROGRAMMING

One day, the Audio Tools Programmer woke up from its slumber, looked at the computer and said, "Work seven days and seven nights and when you're done, wake me up." The computer started working and the Audio Tools Programmer went back to sleep.

Audio Tools Programming is one of my favorite disciplines in Game Audio Programming. It is all about making people's lives easier. Whenever an audio task is boring, uncreative, or takes too long (or all the above), that is the perfect moment for the Audio Tools Programmer to come in and save the day. This flavor of Game Audio Programming is all about creating systems that turn computers into tools that other people can use to create game audio. When the tools work right, we are going to be celebrated by all our colleagues.

Let us take an example to illustrate. The following script is a Python script that I wrote to automatically recognize lines recorded by an actor using Reaper. Bear with me, this is going to be a bit of a trek.

First, we are going to need a user interface. In this case, we want a window with several input fields where the user can specify information we need, like where to locate the Excel file listing the lines recorded, the language spoken, etc. In this example, we are going to use `tkinter` a Python library that already does the work for us. I will not go into too much detail of its implementation, but you can easily find its documentation online if you wish.

```python
root = Tk()
root.title("Import voice lines csv parameters")

mainframe = ttk.Frame(root, padding="3 3 12 12")
mainframe.grid(column=0, row=0, sticky=(N,W,E,S))
root.columnconfigure(0,weight=1)
root.rowconfigure(0,weight=1)

ttk.Label(mainframe, text="Folder with CSVs").grid(
  column=1, row=1, sticky=E)
csv_folder = StringVar(root, "Enter folder path...")
folder_entry = ttk.Entry(mainframe, textvariable=csv_folder)
folder_entry.grid(column=2, row=1, sticky=(W,E))

ttk.Label(
  mainframe, text="Dialogue text header").grid(
    column=1, row=3, sticky=E)
csv_textrowname = StringVar(
  root, "Enter text column header...")
text_entry = ttk.Entry(mainframe,
textvariable=csv_textrowname)
text_entry.grid(column=2, row=3, sticky=(W,E))

ttk.Label(mainframe, text="Line key header").grid(
  column=1, row=4, sticky=E)
csv_keyrowname =
  StringVar(root, "Enter line key column header...")
key_entry = ttk.Entry(mainframe, textvariable=csv_keyrowname)
key_entry.grid(column=2, row=4, sticky=(W,E))

ttk.Label(mainframe, text="Language code").grid(
  column=1, row=5, sticky=E)
csv_language = StringVar(root, "Enter language spoken...")
language_entry = ttk.Entry(mainframe,
  textvariable=csv_language)
```

```
language_entry.grid(column=2, row=5, sticky=(W,E))

ttk.Button(mainframe, text="Detect takes from CSV",
command=ImportCSVs).grid(column=2, row=6, sticky=W)

for child in mainframe.winfo_children():
  child.grid_configure(padx=5, pady=5)

root.bind("<Return>", ImportCSVs)
root.mainloop()
```

This code is populating a window with labels and entry fields where the user can input strings that we are storing for later use. One thing to note here is that it is more important to have practical tools that people want to use, rather than pretty and efficient code. In this case, the first demand I had from the sound designers was that the script remembers their past inputs, so they do not have to type everything again every time they run the tool. We could have searched for a proper way to store data in the Reaper session file format but that would have taken a lot of time and could potentially break the whole Reaper session file. Instead, we hacked our way around it by using the Reaper project notes. Project notes are not intended to be used for this functionality, but our team did not use the notes for anything else, so it was a convenient way to save data in the project. We would just write our data in a formatted string in the project notes and retrieve them when needed.

```
projectNotes = RPR_GetSetProjectNotes(0, False, "", 200)[2]

saved_folder = ""
saved_textrow = ""
saved_keyrow = ""
saved_language = ""

#Detect saved values in project notes
if projectNotes.split(",").__len__() >= 4:
  DM_Log("Found saved values in project notes")
  saved_folder = projectNotes.split(",")[0]
  saved_textrow = projectNotes.split(",")[1]
  saved_keyrow = projectNotes.split(",")[2]
  saved_language = projectNotes.split(",")[3]
```

With this user-facing part done, we can now focus on the actual functionality of the tool: recognizing lines recorded in a Reaper session. We could have decided to program our own speech-to-text system but instead opted to use an already existing library called `speech_recognition`. This library can communicate with different cloud speech-to-text providers with a common interface. In our case, we chose to use Microsoft Azure, but other providers would also work.

```
RPR_Undo_BeginBlock()
DM_Log("Start import")
  try:
    global azure_key
    azure_key = os.getenv("AZUREKEY")

    if azure_key == None:
      DM_Log("No Azure key found.
  Please set the environment variable AZUREKEY to your key.")
      return
    else:
      DM_Log("Azure key found.")

    CSVFiles = GetCSVFilesInFolder(Path(saved_folder))
    for filepath, csvname in CSVFiles:
      DetectLines(filepath)
    root.destroy()
  except Exception as e:
    DM_Log(e)
    root.destroy()
RPR_Undo_EndBlock("Detect Takes from CSV", 0)
```

There are a couple of things specific to Audio Tools Programming that are worth mentioning here:

1. The undo blocks (`RPR_Undo_BeginBlock()` and `RPR_Undo_EndBlock()`), which add the resulting actions to Reaper's undo stack. Most audio tools (and, in fact, most tools in general) are going to require a system that lets users undo their changes.

2. The use of `try/except` and very frequent logging. Although these techniques could apply to all programming, in tooling it is crucial for a user to not have their program crash in front of them. Even if

the program doesn't crash, if nothing changes when they perform an action, it can give the impression that nothing has happened at all.

We can already see the specific kind of tasks included in Audio Tools Programming. It usually requires thinking not only about audio but also about interfaces, user experience, saving and loading data, and communicating information in a comprehensible way. It very often involves connecting different libraries, systems, and software together. People specializing in this field tend to be particularly good jacks-of-all-trades, mixing programming languages and technologies easily.

People who do this as their main work will usually fall into two categories: either they develop commercial tools for a greater audience, or they develop tools for their own internal team. The important part is that they are always working for someone else. Audio tools are only valuable in the hands of someone who uses those tools, which means that on top of the technical skills, Audio Tools Programming usually requires the ability to communicate with users, understand their problems, and find the path of least resistance to a solution.

Sometimes we will need to extract the right information to find the right solution. As Guy Somberg very rightfully said at the GDC in 2014: "Sound designers will create wonderful content, even with trash" (Somberg 2014). It is up to us to make sure they are not using trash, and that they are happy sound designers.

Let us look again at a couple of examples of Audio Tools Programming from the previous volumes.

- **Optimizing Audio Designer Workflows by Matias Lizana García** (Lizana García 2024)

  This chapter gives a very good overview of all the different things Audio Tools Programming can do to help audio designer workflows. Matias mentions technical considerations like visualization and validation but starts by giving tips on communication with the users of the tools.

- **Software Engineering Principles of Voice Pipelines by Michael Filion** (Filion 2021)

  This chapter goes into more detail of one specific but very commonly found pipeline: voice lines. It shows in good detail how a

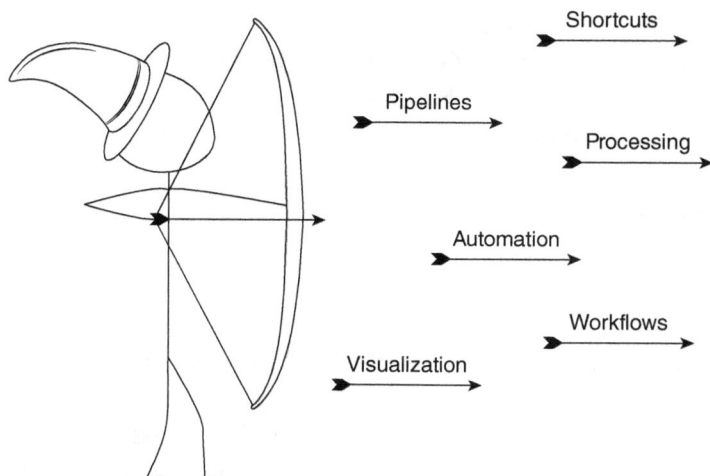

FIGURE 1.3   Archer Audio Tools Programmer.

singular workflow pipeline can touch different programs and how important it is to consider other things than just the process itself.

To go back to our roleplaying campaign, the Audio Tools Programmer is the ranger or archer of the party (Figure 1.3). Alone, they are going to have a challenging time progressing through battles. However, once they are in a varied group, they can become the most useful ally and completely turn the tides of a situation. They will be handy in many different disciplines and usually be the ones finding a shortcut to save everyone from a very tedious battle.

1.6 GAMEPLAY AUDIO PROGRAMMING

One day, the Gameplay Audio Programmer woke up from its slumber, looked at the computer and sighed, for the menu buttons didn't have any sound. The Gameplay Audio Programmer sat at the desk and started working.

Gameplay Audio Programming is all about making the game audio work, and my personal feeling about it is that it is equally rewarding and frustrating. Building systems tied to gameplay, finding creative ways to solve audio challenges, and fitting all the pieces of the audio puzzle are some of the coolest moments of Gameplay Audio Programming. Debugging missing sounds, profiling hardware usage on consoles, or tackling multiplayer replication issues are some of the most challenging moments of Gameplay Audio Programming.

Let us see a simple example of this new flavor of Game Audio Programming. In this case, I programmed a system to play announcer voice lines in a game. This was a non-diegetic voice triggered by specific game events such as capturing an enemy objective. The main objective behind this system was to manage the fact that different events could happen in very quick succession. We needed to find a way for the messages to only play one at a time to avoid hearing a garbled mess. This project was done in Unreal Engine using Wwise, but the concepts can easily be translated to any game engine.

First, we need to have a definition of each announcement.

```
USTRUCT(BlueprintType)
struct FCMessageData
{
  GENERATED_BODY()
public:
  UPROPERTY(EditDefaultsOnly)
  FName Key;

  UPROPERTY(EditDefaultsOnly)
  FText Text;

  UPROPERTY(EditDefaultsOnly)
  UAkAudioEvent* AkEvent;

  /**
  * @brief Priority of this message. Higher priority messages
  * will interrupt lower ones.
  */
  UPROPERTY(EditDefaultsOnly)
  int Priority = 0;

  UPROPERTY(EditDefaultsOnly)
  EMessageCategory Category = EMessageCategory::NonQueued;
};
```

This data includes basic elements like the text of the announcement, a unique key identifier, and the audio event that needs to play. Additionally, it also contains a priority value and a message category that will define how the system should act when this announcement is played. The categories are NonQueued, Queued, and Critical. We will see how these categories interact in the following code.

```
bool playingMessage = false;
FCMessageData lastPlayedMessage;
TQueue<FCMessageData> queuedMessages;

void UCAudioSubsystem::PostMessageAudio(
  const FCMessageData& MessageData)
{
  if(playingMessage)
  {
    //A message is already playing
    if (MessageData.Priority > lastPlayedMessage.Priority)
    {
      //Interrupt playing message and start the new one
      StopGlobalEvent(lastPlayedMessage.AkEvent, 0,
        EAkCurveInterpolation::Log3);
      PostGlobalEventWithCallback(MessageData.AkEvent,
        AkCallbackType::AK_EndOfEvent, MessageAudioCallback);
      lastPlayedMessage = MessageData;
    }
    else
    {
      //New message is lower priority, check type
      switch (MessageData.Category) {
        case EMessageCategory::NonQueued:
          //Just cull new message
          return;
        case EMessageCategory::Queued:
          //Queue new message
          queuedMessages.Enqueue(MessageData);
          break;
        case EMessageCategory::Critical:
          //Still interrupt and play new message
          StopGlobalEvent(lastPlayedMessage.AkEvent, 0,
```

```
                EAkCurveInterpolation::Log3);
            PostGlobalEventWithCallback(MessageData.AkEvent,
                AkCallbackType::AK_EndOfEvent,
                MessageAudioCallback);
            lastPlayedMessage = MessageData;
            break;
        }
      }
    }
    else
    {
      PostGlobalEventWithCallback(MessageData.AkEvent,
        AkCallbackType::AK_EndOfEvent, MessageAudioCallback);
      lastPlayedMessage = MessageData;
      playingMessage = true;
    }
}
```

This method is called every time the game requests to play the voice line of a new message. We first check if another voice line is currently playing. If not, then we play this new message and store it. We also set the Boolean playingMessage to true, so we know that we are now playing a message. If the method is triggered while a message is playing, we check the priority of the new message. If it is of higher priority than the currently playing message, we consider that this message is important and cannot be delayed, so we will stop the message that is currently playing and start the new one. If the new message is of lower priority, then we will need to look at its category. NonQueued messages will simply never play, intended for messages that do not contain game-critical information. Queued messages will be kept in a queue and played whenever possible, for messages that need to be heard but where timing is not critical. Finally, Critical messages will always be played, even if they are of lower priority. This category lets designer set messages to always play without having to worry about the priority of other messages.

For this code to work, we also need to catch the moment voice lines finish playing. For that, we use a callback that we passed to Wwise when playing a voice line.

```
void UCAudioSubsystem::OnMessageAudioFinished(
  EAkCallbackType CallbackType,
```

```
    UAkCallbackInfo* CallbackInfo)
{
  //UE_LOG(LogTemp, Warning, TEXT("OnMessageAudioFinished"));
  if(CallbackType == EAkCallbackType::EndOfEvent)
  {
    UAkEventCallbackInfo* EventCallbackInfo =
      Cast<UAkEventCallbackInfo>(CallbackInfo);
    if(EventCallbackInfo)
    {
      if (lastPlayedMessage.AkEvent->GetShortID() ==
          EventCallbackInfo->EventID)
      {
        //Last played message has finished
        if (!queuedMessages.IsEmpty())
        {
          FCMessageData nextMessage;
          queuedMessages.Dequeue(nextMessage);
          PostGlobalEventWithCallback(nextMessage.AkEvent,
            AkCallbackType::AK_EndOfEvent,
            MessageAudioCallback);
        }
        else
        {
          playingMessage = false;
        }
      }
    }
  }
}
```

This method will be called whenever a voice line stops playing. We will check if that line is the last one that was triggered and if there are any messages queued up. If there are messages in the queue, we play the next one. If there are not, then we set playingMessage to false so that we know that we are not playing messages anymore.

With this simple example, we get an idea of the mindset around Gameplay Audio Programming. The tasks are about making specific game systems and audio features work. This flavor of Game Audio Programming revolves around creating behaviors and data that will help achieve the game's vision. For that, we need to hook up and interact with different game systems like animation, particles, UI, AI, etc. Usually, this work happens inside a game engine and requires general knowledge of the game engine used to build the game.

However, there is also a whole other part that we did not see in the example: debugging and optimizing. Gameplay Audio Programming also includes making sure the game can run correctly and play sounds correctly, so monitoring performance and finding creative ways to make more with less are also part of the responsibilities. Depending on the schedule and production of the video game, we might end up being firefighters, trying to stabilize the audio of the game as it continues growing and evolving constantly.

Every game ever developed (unless it is specifically silent) will require someone to tackle the Gameplay Audio Programming. Sometimes, it is not a person dedicated solely to this role and this work falls on another more generalist programmer. What is the difference between having someone specialized in Gameplay Audio Programming compared to someone with general Gameplay Programming knowledge handling audio?

It probably sounds obvious to you reading a book about Game Audio Programming, but sound does not behave the same way as the rest of the content in a video game. For example, showing an image every frame is not an issue per se, as we would just see a fixed image. However, playing a sound every frame is a completely dissimilar experience, closer to an electronic explosion glitching through the loudspeakers. Another example is optimization, which needs to be managed differently for audio than for graphics. Visually, we tend to prefer showing as many objects as possible and reducing the cost of each object so thousands of them can be rendered at the same time, creating a vast landscape. But with audio, good optimization would be the opposite: we would first try to reduce the number of objects playing because having too many sounds playing at the same time is useless and turns to noise very quickly.

Therefore, it is usually more important for someone in this role to have knowledge and experience about audio than about gameplay programming. Without basic knowledge about sound and its behavior, a generalist programmer might create more problems than solutions.

Let us look at a couple of examples of chapters talking about Gameplay Audio Programming in the previous volumes.

- **State-Based Dynamic Mixing by Colin Walder** (Walder 2024)
  This chapter showcases a very good example of Gameplay Audio Programming, where data from the game will drive the audio mix.

Audio sources   Event system

Music system

Dynamic mixing

Dialogue system

Memory management

Debugging

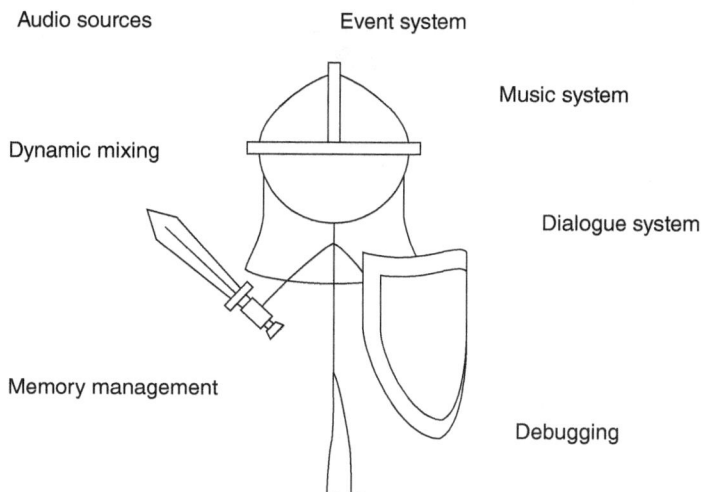

FIGURE 1.4   Warrior Gameplay Audio Programmer.

Colin demonstrates how it is important that audio is aware of the gameplay to create the best experience for the player.

- **Audio Object Management Techniques by Christian Tronhjem** (Tronhjem 2024)

    This chapter shows the other side of Gameplay Audio Programming I mentioned: performance. In this chapter, we see how we can manage audio objects to faithfully represent digital environment with many audio sources without completely breaking the performance of the game.

To finish off our roleplaying party, the Gameplay Audio Programmer would be the warrior (Figure 1.4). They are on the front line, dealing with the bulk of the encounters and pulling the group forward. They might not always have the efficiency of the archer or the precision of the mage, but they get things done, which is especially important. Without them, the party would not have gotten out of the tavern and started any game development adventure anyway.

1.7 BLURRY LINES

It is important to note that the three specialties I described above are tendencies, not fixed and solidly delimited roles or skillsets. Some tasks might be fit for two or even three roles depending on the situation.

FIGURE 1.5   Unicorn Multiclass Audio Programmer and friends.

Is multithreading audio behavior more tied to the engine or the game? Who is responsible for making a full audio profiler work?

The goal of having defined these different flavors of Game Audio Programming is to describe more accurately the day-to-day of different Game Audio Programmers and help people navigate this still-foggy field of work. Hopefully, people can resonate with these descriptions better than with the high-level and abstract concept of Game Audio Programmer. These descriptions are not intended to be used as a ground for exclusion or segregation. The video game industry needs quite the opposite: building bridges by understanding better what our colleagues do, whatever their department.

Also, remember that people might have more than one set of skills. A few rare people are of that rarest of breeds, the mythical Game Audio Programmers who combine all three classes into a superpowered multi-class unicorn capable of yielding the strengths of all specialties. Figure 1.5 shows our full RPG party, complete with unicorn.

1.8 CONCLUSION

We have seen how Game Audio Programming is a diverse and complex field, and how it can be divided into three distinct categories (or flavors). We then defined and studied these three specialties: Audio Rendering

Programming, Audio Tools Programming, and Gameplay Audio Programming. With this framework in mind, hopefully you will be able to make more sense of what being a Game Audio Programmer entails on a practical level and what are the skills and knowledge required for each of these categories. A good exercise would be to try to see for each following chapter of this book if it falls neatly into one of the three categories we have seen.

But more importantly, let us go back to our original question: "How do you become a Game Audio Programmer?" Now, armed with new knowledge and concepts, we can finally give a better answer.

If you want to be an Audio Rendering Programmer, start by learning about audio rendering on computers and game engine development. Tutorials on systems like OpenAL or SDL are a good place to gather basic knowledge that will help get you started.

If you want to be an Audio Tools Programmer, start by learning Python or Lua and doing simple scripts in whichever tool you already use. Reaper scripting is an effective way to start as there is a lot of online content and it is a central tool for audio creation.

If you want to be a Gameplay Audio Programmer, start by learning about generalist game development. Pick up a Unity, Unreal, or Godot tutorial off the internet and build your first games. From there, you will then be able to get the basic knowledge about game development that you can apply to audio specifically as you go further.

If you want to become a unicorn, well...

Whatever your choice and your path, if you are interested in Game Audio Programming and have made it all the way to here, you might want to consider our little community on Discord where we discuss things like what you just read, and many other topics related to this really cool field of making computers go "beep boop". Scan the QR code in Figure 1.6.

FIGURE 1.6   Game Audio Programmers Discord QR code.

NOTE

1. Here Pablo is trying to solve one of the two hard problems in computer science, according to Phil Karlton: cache invalidation and naming things. –Ed

REFERENCES

Bantin, Robert. 2024. "Flexible Delay Lines: Practical Methods for Varying Sample-Rate Delays During Playback." In *Game Audio Programming 4: Principles and Practices*, edited by Guy Somberg, 215–237. Boca Raton, FL: CRC Press.

Beauchemin, Stéphane. 2019. "A Rare Breed: The Audio Programmer." In *Game Audio Programming 2: Principles and Practices*, edited by Guy Somberg, 17–29. Boca Raton, FL: CRC Press.

Filion, Michael. 2021. "Software Engineering Principles of Voice Pipelines." In *Game Audio Programming 3: Principles and Practices*, edited by Guy Somberg, 71–80. Boca Raton, FL: CRC Press.

Lizana García, Matias. 2024. "Optimizing Audio Designer Workflows." In *Game Audio Programming 4: Principles and Practices*, edited by Guy Somberg, 265–278. Boca Raton, FL: CRC Press.

Murray, Dan. 2019. "Multithreading for Game Audio." In *Game Audio Programming 2: Principles and Practices*, edited by Guy Somberg, 33–60. Boca Raton, FL: CRC Press.

Somberg, Guy. 2014. *Lessons Learned from a Decade of Audio Programming*. www.gdcvault.com/play/1020452/Lessons-Learned-from-a-Decade

Somberg, Guy, ed. 2024. *Game Audio Programming 4: Principles and Practices*. Boca Raton, FL: CRC Press.

Tronhjem, Christian. 2024. "Audio Object Management Techniques." In *Game Audio Programming 4: Principles and Practices*, edited by Guy Somberg, 3–23. Boca Raton, FL: CRC Press.

Walder, Colin. 2024. "State-Based Dynamic Mixing." In *Game Audio Programming 4: Principles and Practices*, edited by Guy Somberg, 24–39. Boca Raton, FL: CRC Press.

I

Low-Level Topics

CHAPTER 2

Oscillators for Real Time Synthesis

Collin Schupman

2.1 BACKGROUND

In the before times (up to the early 1980s), video game sound design and music composition relied on on-device synthesis, with chips like the Ricoh RP2A03 used in the NES, the MOS Technology 6581 used in the Commodore 64 SID, and Yamaha's YM2151 generating audio through tone generation, subtractive, and FM synthesis methods. By the mid-1980s the industry had shifted toward the playback of pre-recorded analog waveforms. Chips like the Amiga's Paula, the SNES's S-DSP, and the PlayStation's SPU[1] laid the foundation for today's sample-based audio systems. Subsequent advances in these technologies have continued to enable richer, more detailed soundscapes.

Sample-based audio has trade-offs though. Creatively, it requires working with discrete audio data. Tasks such as making tempo changes, key shifts, subtle timbre shifts, and re-orchestration are often more complex, unintuitive, and require extra computation or storage. Also, as a practical matter, uncompressed audio inflates game sizes. Modern games exceeding the 100–200 GB range lead to long installs and high storage demands.

Moving game audio tasks to real time synthesis methods offers potential solutions to these issues. Fortunately, modern advances in processing power, RAM, and middleware technology are making real time synthesis increasingly feasible in today's game engines.

DOI: 10.1201/9781003519119-3

2.1.1 Examples

Many modern games use synthesis creatively and practically. *Cocoon* (2023) features fully synthesized sound design with no recorded audio, generating loop-free sound unique to each player (Schmid 2023). *Rise of the Tomb Raider* (2015) dynamically varies percussion patterns in real time, adapting to gameplay for musical variety (Lamperski 2016). *Grand Theft Auto V* (2013) employed granular synthesis for ambient sounds like air conditioning and bicycle movement, saving RAM and storage while preserving audio quality (MacGregor 2014). *Spore* (2008) used a custom version of the Pure Data software to generate its fully dynamic score (Jolly 2011).

2.1.2 Let's Make Some Oscillators

Real time audio synthesis holds immense potential for modern game music and sound design. While developing a fully featured synthesizer is beyond this chapter's scope, we'll start with something basic: a set of oscillators.

We'll implement noise, sine, saw, square, and triangle waves, focusing on strict algorithmic methods for simplicity to build a solid foundation, as these fundamentals underpin many other implementations. By the end, you'll have functional software oscillators and the knowledge to explore other methods tailored to your needs.

2.1.3 Assumptions

This chapter assumes you are familiar with the basics of digital audio, real time audio rendering, C++, and trigonometry.

2.2 NOISE

We will begin with a noise signal, which we define as a signal without a dominant frequency, and therefore no noticeable pitch.

2.2.1 Applications

Noise signals have diverse applications across synthesis and sound design. In synthesis, they are essential for creating non-pitched sounds such as snares, hi-hats, cymbals, and crashes. The NES and Commodore 64 chips mentioned in Section 2.1 even featured dedicated channels for noise. Combined with filters and high resonance, they can be used to simulate environmental effects such as wind, ocean waves, and rustling leaves. In synthesizers, they can add texture, grit, or natural distortion when blended with other sounds, making synthesized tones feel more organic.

2.2.2 Physical Definition

For our purposes, we will create a white noise oscillator, defined as having equal energy across the entire frequency spectrum. Other noise signals, such as pink, brown, and blue noise, have different energy distributions, typically characterized by changes in decibel energy per octave. These other noise types are useful and can be found in synthesizers, but white noise is the most common implementation, so that will be our focus. Figure 2.1 shows an amplitude and frequency plot of white noise.

2.2.3 Pseudo-Random Number Generators

To generate our white noise, we will use a **pseudo-random number generator (PRNG)** – a deterministic algorithm that approximates randomness. PRNGs are widely applied across many fields and are evaluated under different criteria. For real time audio rendering, the two most important considerations are **perceptual quality** (how much we can audibly tell how "random" the signal sounds) and **efficiency** (ensuring the generator is fast enough for real time rendering). We will focus on a simple and commonly used PRNG algorithm, the Linear Congruential Generator.

2.2.4 The Linear Congruential Generator

While not state-of-the-art, the **Linear Congruential Generator (LCG)** is a deterministic, fast, memory-efficient, and random-enough algorithm for our use case. While some implementations of the C standard library's rand() function use this algorithm, this is not guaranteed, and the quality and efficiency of the randomness can vary.[2,3] Therefore, we will code our own. Let's start by looking at the math.

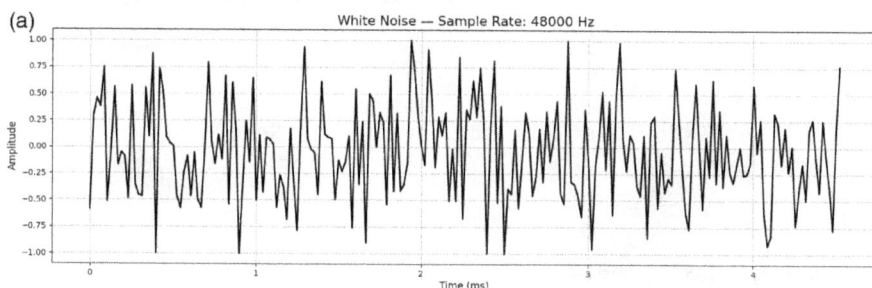

FIGURE 2.1 (a) An amplitude graph of white noise values over time. (b) A frequency plot of white noise. (*Continued*)

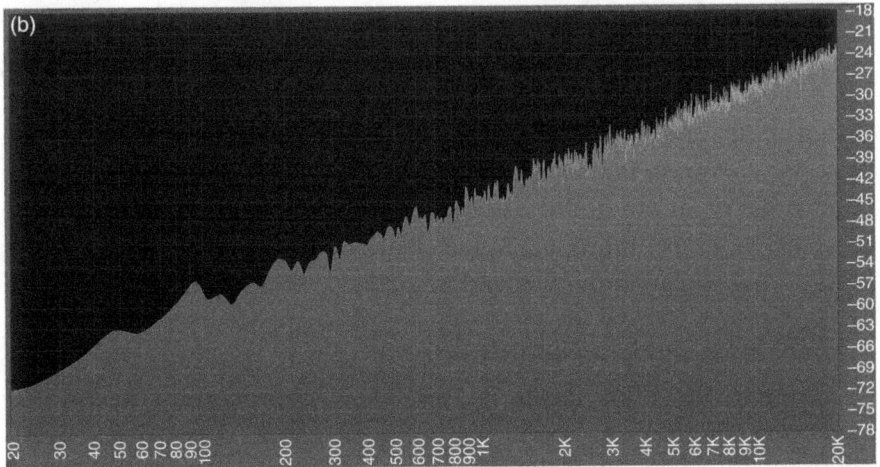

FIGURE 2.1 *(Continued)*

The LCG is defined as:

$$X_{n+1} = (a \cdot X_n + c) \ mod \ M$$

where X_n is the current random number, X_{n+1} is the next random number in the sequence, a is the multiplier (a carefully chosen constant), c is the increment (another carefully chosen constant), M is the modulus, which defines the range of random numbers, and X_0 is the seed value for the sequence.

Our code will be a mostly straightforward translation of this formula, followed by a refinement step to improve the quality of the randomness and a normalization step to make the values suitable for use in a real time audio rendering context. Here is a full implementation in C++:

```cpp
class NoiseOscillator
{
public:
  NoiseOscillator(uint32_t seed = kDefaultSeed)
  : mCurrentState(seed)
  {
  }
  float getNextValue()
  {
    mCurrentState = mCurrentState * kMultiplier + kIncrement;
    const int32_t shiftedState =
```

```
      static_cast<int32_t>(mCurrentState >> kBitShift) -
      kIntNormalizationFactor;
    return static_cast<float>(shiftedState) /
      kFloatNormalizationFactor;
  }
private:
  static constexpr uint32_t kDefaultSeed = 42;
  static constexpr uint32_t kMultiplier = 1664525;
  static constexpr uint32_t kIncrement = 1013904223;
  static constexpr int kBitShift = 7;
  static constexpr int32_t kIntNormalizationFactor =
    (1 << (31 - kBitShift));
  static constexpr float kFloatNormalizationFactor =
    static_cast<float>(kIntNormalizationFactor);
  uint32_t mCurrentState;
};
```

The algorithm is known to produce less-quality randomness in the lower bits, so we shift them out. Finally, we normalize the return value to a usable range in real time audio rendering. The constants for the default seed, multiplier, and increment are taken from Numerical Recipes in C.[4]

2.2.5 Other Methods: Pros and Cons

Apart from the pros of this algorithm listed in Section 2.2.4, its cons are that it is still considered low-quality in terms of randomness when compared to more advanced alternatives such as **Mersenne Twister** or **Xorshift generators** and would not be an optimal choice for other applications. All that said, it remains effective for many real time audio programming use cases under the given criteria; it is efficient and random-enough for our ears. Unreal Engine's `NoiseNode` utilizes LCG as do countless other software synthesizers. Michaels (2022) presents an interesting deep dive into the details of random number generation, and the different approaches one might take given different audio applications.

2.3 THE SINE WAVE

Let us move on to the most fundamental waveform: the sine wave. A sine wave is a signal with a single fundamental frequency, meaning it has no harmonics or overtones – just a pure tone. Figure 2.2 shows an amplitude and frequency plot of a sine wave. Note the presence of only a single tone in the frequency plot.

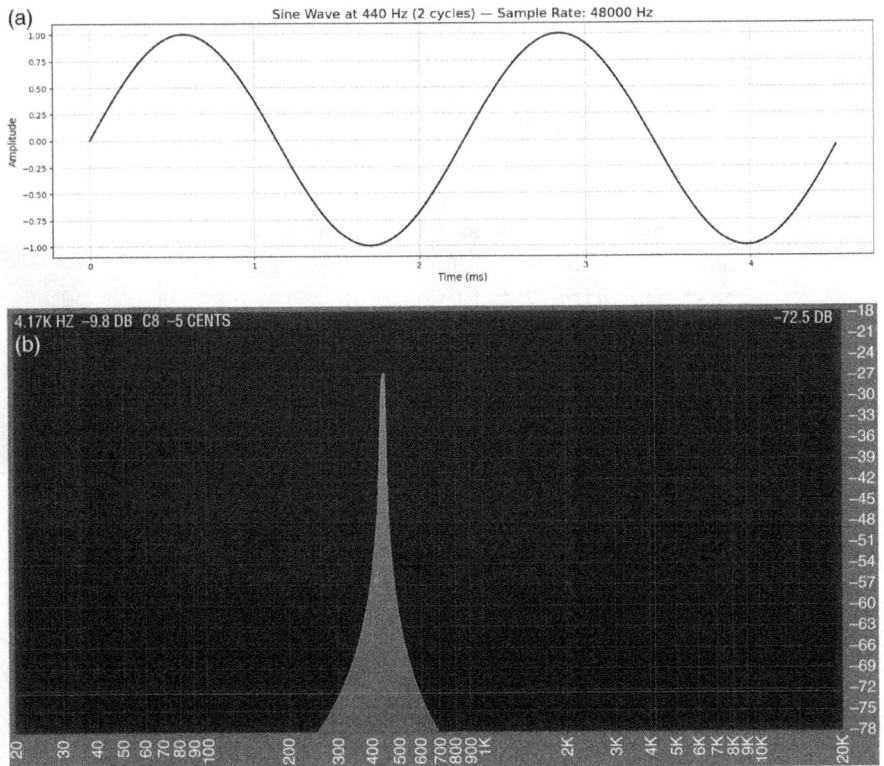

FIGURE 2.2 (a) A sine wave amplitude plotted over time. (b) A frequency plot of a sine wave over time.

2.3.1 Applications

In the early days of analog synthesizers, which mostly focused on subtractive synthesis, it was uncommon to use sine waves as sound sources. Lacking any frequencies beyond the fundamental, there is nothing to filter, and they are more difficult to create in analog settings. However, sine waves as sources have become much more common in the digital age because they are perfect for creating clean, uncolored tones. A few examples of use cases are:

- Low-frequency sine waves are great for emphasizing sub-bass frequencies.

- High-pitched, modulated sine waves are ideal for sounds such as laser beams and energy blasts.

- Pitch sweeps simulate sliding objects or ricochets.

- By layering or detuning sine waves, one can create ethereal sound-scapes or unsettling drones.

- Sine waves are frequently employed to mimic resonances in vibrating strings or pipes, as well as to simulate water bubbling or dripping effects.

Sine waves are also crucial in various synthesis techniques, including physical modeling, additive modulation, granular modulation, amplitude modulation, and frequency modulation. In addition, they are an essential tool for audio programmers working on rendering systems. Because they produce a pure tone with no harmonics, they serve as ideal test signals for verifying that an audio rendering pipeline is free of discontinuities or artifacts before introducing more complex sound sources.

2.3.2 The Discrete-Time Sinusoidal Function

To generate a sine wave suitable for real time audio rendering applications, we start with the discrete-time sinusoidal equation:

$$y(n) = \sin\left(2\pi \cdot freq \cdot \frac{n}{fs}\right)$$

where *freq* is the desired frequency in Hz, *n* is the current sample index, and *fs* is the sample rate in samples per second.

We are leaving out any amplitude calculations because in a synthesizer the gain is handled through a separate step. Unlike our noise oscillator, we will not be translating this equation directly for two reasons:

1. **Accuracy**: As the current sample index grows large, the input to the sine function can become very large. Due to limitations of the IEEE floating-point standard, precision decreases for larger values, potentially causing inaccuracies that make the output unusable for real time audio.

2. **Performance**: We can simplify the number of calculations per buffer required.

2.3.3 Numerically Controlled Oscillators

To address these issues, we will develop a reusable prototype known as a Numerically Controlled Oscillator (NCO). An NCO generates cyclical waveforms in discrete systems by maintaining a normalized phase value and incrementing it by a specific amount per sample based on the desired frequency and the sample rate. Once the phase exceeds the normalized maximum, it wraps around to maintain continuity (Wikipedia contributors 2024b).

By modifying how we interpret the normalized phase, we can generate various waveforms such as sine, sawtooth, square, and triangle waves. This flexibility allows us to encapsulate the shared data and functionality into a generic, templated `Oscillator` class, which can be adapted to different waveform types.

```cpp
template<typename Waveform>
class Oscillator
{
public:
  void setFrequency(float frequency)
  {
    mFrequency = frequency;
    _resetPhaseInc();
  }
  void setSampleRate(float sampleRate)
  {
    mSampleRate = sampleRate;
    _resetPhaseInc();
  }
  float getNextValue()
  {
    float value = mWaveform.generate(
      mCurrentPhase, mPhaseInc);
    _updateCurrentPhase();
    return value;
  }
private:
  void _updateCurrentPhase()
  {
    mCurrentPhase += mPhaseInc;
    if (mCurrentPhase >= 1.f)
    {
      mCurrentPhase -= 1.f;
    }
  }
  void _resetPhaseInc()
```

```
  {
     mPhaseInc = mFrequency / mSampleRate;
  }
  float mFrequency = 440.f;
  float mSampleRate = 44100.f;
  float mPhaseInc = 0.f;
  float mCurrentPhase = 0.f;
  Waveform mWaveform;
};
```

Geometrically speaking, the sine wave is the projection of a point rotating around a unit circle. The frequency of the wave determines how quickly the point rotates around the circle and the position of this point is determined by the phase of the wave, which represents the angle of rotation around the circle. Since our sine functions work in radians, we can use our normalized phase accumulator value, convert it to radians, and pass it as the input to the sine function:

$$y(n) = \sin(2\pi \cdot currentPhase)$$

Turning to the code, we can encapsulate our sine wave calculation and plug it in with a simple **struct**:

```
static float generateSinValue(float currentPhase)
{
  return std::sin(
    2.f * std::numbers::pi_v<float> * currentPhase);
}
struct SineWave
{
  float generate(float currentPhase, float /*phaseInc*/)
  {
    return generateSinValue(currentPhase);
  }
};
```

And with that, we have solved our two original issues. Our input is now restricted to a [0..2π] range and we have reduced the number of calculations required per buffer. All of this results in a much more efficient and better sounding sine wave.

2.3.4 Other Methods: Pros and Cons

The implementation above works well for real time audio rendering, particularly in cases requiring highly accurate sine waves, but it is by far not the only method. Some other common techniques include:

- **Wavetables:** Wavetables are a technique where pre-computed wave values are stored in memory and iterated through, rather than calculated on the fly. In this approach, a table is populated with sine values at an oversampled rate, and the phase accumulator is used as the read index into the table, with interpolation applied as needed. This method trades memory usage for computational efficiency, which becomes increasingly important when building more complex, layered instruments. Algorithmic methods may still be preferable when higher precision sine waves are required, such as in cases like virtual analog synthesis or certain forms of FM and additive synthesis.

- **Alternate Approximation Techniques:** Libraries like JUCE implement alternative approximations for the sine function, such as the Padé approximant (Weisstein n.d.) or the Bhaskara approximant (Wikipedia contributors 2024a). These methods provide faster computations while maintaining acceptable accuracy, particularly when inputs are constrained to a limited range.

- **Coupled Form Oscillator:** This method utilizes Euler's formula, particularly the Coupled Form (using the real and imaginary parts of an imaginary number) to rotate around a circle and avoid expensive calls to trigonometric functions. This method is efficient, but unsuitable for certain applications such as FM modulation.

- **Digital Resonator:** The Direct Form Digital Resonator leverages DSP properties of the z-plane to generate sine waves using a recursive difference equation efficiently. This method settles on a stable sine wave after a warmup period and can potentially be more efficient with certain inputs.

2.4 SAWTOOTH, SQUARE, AND TRIANGLE WAVES

We now turn our attention to a family of signals characterized by their harmonic content in relation to a fundamental frequency: the **sawtooth**, **square**, and **triangle** waves. Figure 2.3 shows examples of these waveforms. The sawtooth wave (Figure 2.3a) contains integer even and odd

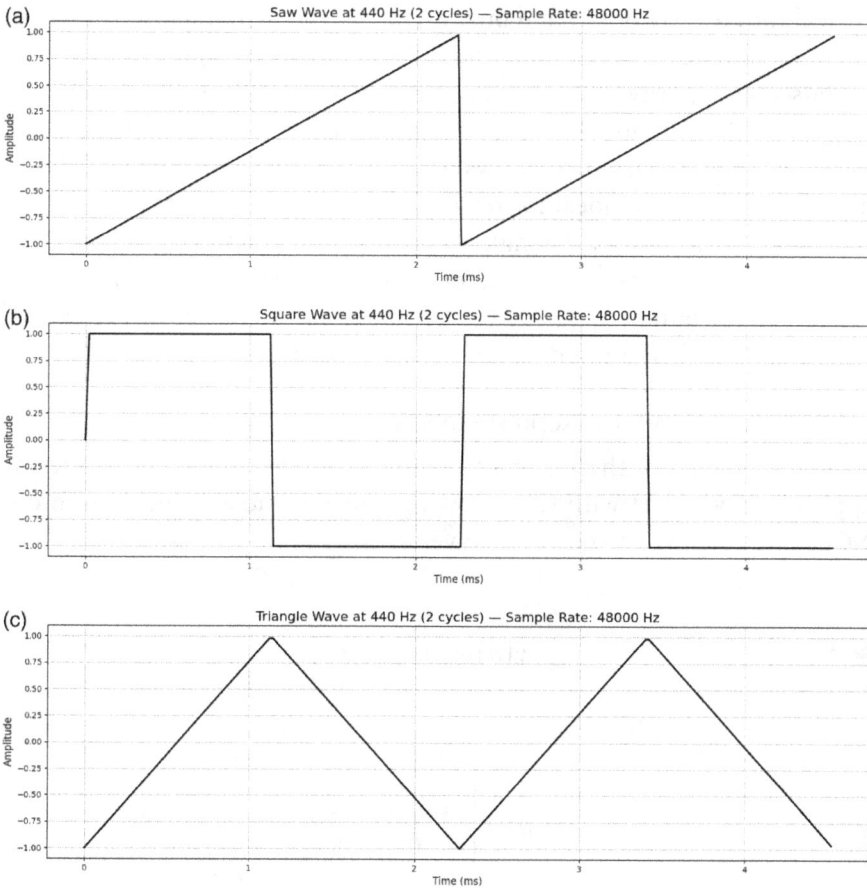

FIGURE 2.3   (a) The waveform of a sawtooth wave. (b) The waveform of a square wave. (c) The waveform of a triangle wave.

harmonics of the fundamental frequency, producing bright and aggressive tones. The square wave (Figure 2.3b) contains only odd harmonics and produces a hollow tone. Finally, the triangle wave (Figure 2.3c) shares the odd harmonics of the square wave but with amplitudes that are proportional to the inverse square of the harmonic number, giving it a softer and more mellow quality.

2.4.1 Applications

Sawtooth, square, and triangle waves are fundamental to subtractive synthesis, serving as the foundational content to filter. The sawtooth wave, with its rich harmonic content including both even and odd harmonics, is ideal for creating bright and buzzy textures that lend themselves well to dynamic and aggressive tones. One could imagine designing machinery soundscapes, energy effects or aggressive drones. Square waves, characterized by their hollow sound and odd harmonics, excel in pulse-width modulation (PWM), which allows for dynamic tonal shaping and rhythmic effects. These are ideal for retro/chiptune sounds, alarm sounds, and classic beeps and boops. Triangle waves, with their smooth, mellow quality, are perfect for crafting softer, more delicate tones. They could be used to generate certain percussive sounds, or add harmonic content to natural soft sounds, such as air and water.

2.4.2 Naïve Waveform Representations

To generate each of these signals for use in a real time audio rendering application, we start with the following naïve formulas which, given our NCOs, we could use to generate waveforms.

Sawtooth:

$$y(n) = 2.0n - 1.0$$

Square:

$$y(n) = \begin{cases} 1.0, \ n < 0.5 \\ -1.0, \ n \geq 0.5 \end{cases}$$

Triangle:

$$y(n) = 4.0 \cdot abs(n - 0.5) - 1.0$$

However, there's a reason these are called naïve. If we implemented these functions directly and rendered them, we would get a significant issue: aliasing. Aliasing in real time audio is the result of trying to render frequencies which exceed the Nyquist limit of the system, which is one-half of the sampling rate. These out-of-bounds frequencies fold back into the audible range, ruining the sound of our beautiful oscillators. Figure 2.4 displays the frequency spectrum for a naïve-square waveform with visible aliasing.

To understand why this aliasing happens, we have to look to Fourier Analysis, which tells us that any signal can be represented as the sum of sine waves at different frequencies. The naïve implementations contain

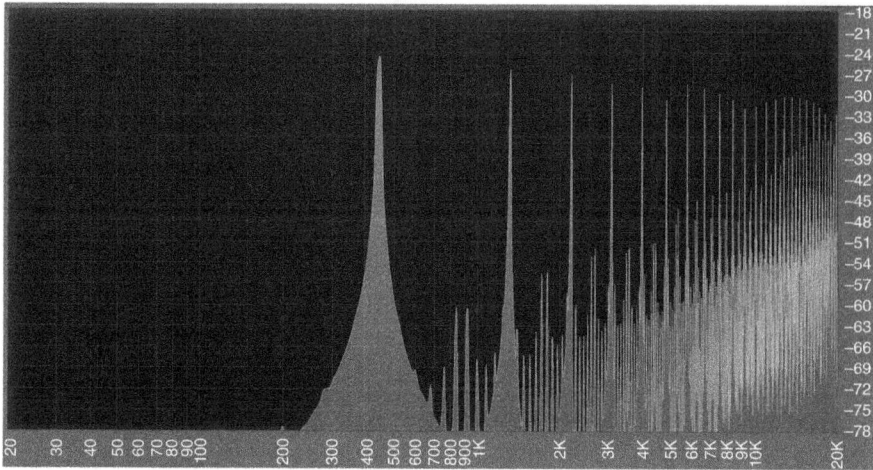

FIGURE 2.4 The frequency spectrum for a square waveform rendered using the naïve formulas.

sharp transitions, which require very high-frequency sine wave components to reproduce accurately. During rendering, these high-frequency components exceed the Nyquist limit and thus are folded back into the audio signal range, causing the waves to sound terrible.

To address this, various techniques have been developed to generate bandlimited signals that reduce or eliminate aliasing. In many real time applications, completely eliminating aliasing isn't necessary. Instead, it's often sufficient to minimize it to the point where any remaining artifacts are pushed above the audible range or rendered perceptually insignificant.

2.4.3 Polynomial Band-Limited Step Function (PolyBLEP)

We will implement our band-limited oscillators using a Polynomial Band-Limited Step function (PolyBLEP). I chose this technique because it is a popular, modern, and well-documented choice for software synthesizers that generate waveforms algorithmically. PolyBLEP can be intuitively understood as a method to band-limit naïve waveforms based on the assumption that aliasing is created by sharp discontinuities in waveforms. To fix this, we do a bit of math to calculate a residual based on our current distance from a discontinuity in the waveform and apply that to the naïve waveform to smooth out any discontinuities. A complete explanation of the theory behind PolyBLEP is outside the scope of this chapter, but you can refer to the original paper (Välimäki et al. 2010) for a good explanation of how it works.

Here is our implementation which we will use to calculate the residuals to apply to the naïve waveforms, based on a blog post by Martin Finke (Finke 2013) with adjustments:

```
static float polyBlepResidual(
  float currentPhase, float phaseIncrement)
{
  float t = currentPhase;
  const float dt = phaseIncrement;
  if (t < dt)
  {
    t /= dt;
    return t+t - t*t - 1.0;
  }
  else if (t > 1.0 - dt)
  {
    t = (t - 1.0) / dt;
    return t*t + t+t + 1.0;
  }
  else
  {
    return 0.0;
  }
}
```

This function detects when the waveform is near a discontinuity and calculates the residual to be applied to the original waveform. Here is how we can use it to generate a band-limited sawtooth wave:

```
static float generateSawValue(
  float currentPhase, float phaseIncrement)
{
  float value = (2.0 * currentPhase) - 1.0; // Naïve saw
  value -= polyBlepResidual (currentPhase, phaseIncrement);
  return value;
}
```

For a square wave the residual is calculated for two transitions: one at the start and one at 50% phase:

```
static float generateSquareValue(
  float currentPhase, float phaseIncrement)
```

```cpp
{
  // Naive square
  float value = (currentPhase < 0.5f) ?  1.0f : -1.0f;
  value += polyBlepResidual(currentPhase, phaseIncrement);
  value -= polyBlepResidual(
    fmod(currentPhase + 0.5, 1.0), phaseIncrement);
  return value;
}
```

The triangle wave uses the square wave implementation as its foundation:

```cpp
static float generateTriangleValue(
  float currentPhase, float phaseIncrement,
  float previousOutput)
{
  float value = generateSquareValue(
    currentPhase, phaseIncrement);
  value = phaseIncrement * value +
    (1 - phaseIncrement) * previousOutput;
  return value;
}
```

With these functions in place, we can wrap them up in simple structs and plug them into our templated **Oscillator** class:

```cpp
struct SawtoothWave
{
  float generate(float currentPhase, float phaseInc)
  {
    return generateSawValue(currentPhase, phaseInc);
  }
};
struct SquareWave
{
  float generate(float currentPhase, float phaseInc)
  {
    return generateSquareValue(currentPhase, phaseInc);
  }
}
struct TriangleWave
{
  float generate(float currentPhase, float phaseInc)
  {
```

```
    float value = generateTriangleValue(
      currentPhase, phaseInc, mPreviousValue);
    mPreviousValue = value;
    return value;
  }
private:
  float mPreviousValue;
};
```

And there we have it! Useful oscillators with severely reduced aliasing. Figure 2.5 shows our new square wave.

As you can see, our PolyBLEP oscillator produces a much cleaner harmonic spectrum compared to when using naïve waveforms. While some residual aliasing can still occur at higher frequencies, it's far less pronounced.

2.4.4 Other Methods: Pros and Cons

While PolyBLEP is a popular method for generating band-limited waveforms in real time synthesis, other techniques may be better suited for specific use cases. Here are some common alternatives:

- **Wavetables:** Like sine waves, wavetables may also be used to generate these more complex waveforms by manually calculating the known "shape" of the harmonic content. Another benefit of wavetables is that they allow more flexibility for tasks such as morphing waveforms.

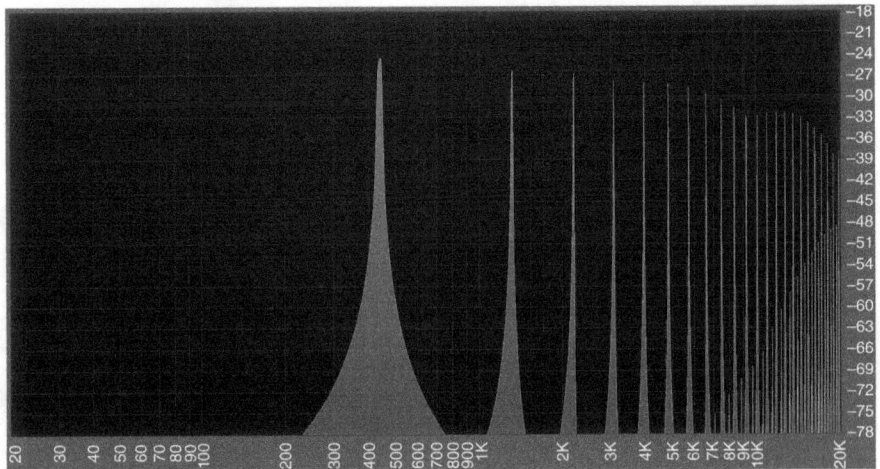

FIGURE 2.5 The frequency spectrum for a square wave rendered with the PolyBLEP method.

- **MinBLEP (Minimum Band-Limited Step):** Like PolyBLEP, the MinBLEP method (Brandt 2001) uses precomputed correction signals stored in a look-up table. It is more expensive both in terms of space and time compared to PolyBLEP due to the storage of correction signals and convolution, but results in higher quality, lower-aliased rendered output.

Given the emphasis on minimizing computational cost, PolyBLEP is particularly useful in resource-constrained environments, such as writing a synthesizer for a mobile game or an embedded system. MinBLEP is a better choice when resources can be traded for higher-quality waveforms, while wavetables provide greater scalability at the expense of storage and strict waveform quality.

2.5 RENDERING

These oscillators are designed to be driven by a real time audio rendering system. Almost every real time system you work with will have some kind of prepare-to-play stage, which is invoked whenever parameters like the sampling rate or block size change. This is where we set those parameters on our oscillators:

```
void prepareToPlay (double sampleRate, int samplesPerBlock)
{
  mCurrentOscillator.setSampleRate(
    static_cast<float>(sampleRate));
}
```

For playback, we'll assume that we're inside the main audio callback function of such a system, which typically provides an array of buffers to write to and a channel count. To set the frequency at this point, you can imagine doing so at the start of the block – for example, by reading an RTPC value or a State Switch indicating a frequency change that we can apply to our oscillators.

```
mCurrentOscillator.setFrequency(frequency);
```

Finally, for each sample we need to render for the block size, we'll render the output given our previous implementation and run it through a quick

gain stage to control the volume and a simple sine-law panning solution
to distribute the signal across a stereo channel setup (Hack Audio 2011):

```
void Render(
  float* leftChannelWriteBuffer,
  float* rightChannelWriteBuffer, int blockSize)
{
  for (int sample = 0; sample < blockSize; ++sample)
  {
    float val = mCurrentOscillator.getNextValue();

    // Simple gain stage to not make our ears explode
    val *= 0.1f;

    // Panning Stage: Sine-Law Panning
    constexpr float pan = 0.5f;
    const float rightGain =
      std::sin(pan * (std::numbers::pi / 2.0f));
    const float leftGain =
      std::sin((1.0f - pan) * (std::numbers::pi / 2.0f));

    leftChannelWriteBuffer[sample] = val * leftGain;
    rightChannelWriteBuffer[sample] = val * rightGain;
  }
}
```

2.6 CONCLUSION

In this chapter, we investigated the fundamental challenges of implementing oscillators for real time audio synthesis. Along the way, we've built a
set of oscillators that sound great, showcase minimal aliasing, and serve
as foundational building blocks for larger synthesis projects. We've also
gained an understanding of implementation trade-offs, learning the
strengths and weaknesses of each approach.

With these tools in hand, we're ready to dive into more advanced synthesis concepts. Next steps include exploring other oscillator techniques mentioned, adding envelopes to shape amplitude over time, enabling polyphony
to playback multiple oscillators simultaneously, incorporating filters to sculpt
timbre, and creating modulators to enable dynamic movement and variations. Hollemans (2024) is an excellent resource for these topics.

We are entering an exciting new era in video game music and sound design. Incorporating more real time synthesis techniques can not only help solve practical challenges, such as memory and storage constraints, but also open new creative possibilities. By mastering these foundational techniques, we're well-positioned to contribute to this evolving landscape and craft innovative, expressive audio software for interactive experiences.

NOTES

1. Goodwin (2019, pp. 11–33).
2. Standard library implementations should always be treated cautiously with real time audio rendering.
3. Also, you should not be using `rand()` for anything anyway. –Ed
4. Press et al. (2002, pp. 275–278).

REFERENCES

Brandt, Eli. 2001. "Hard Sync without Aliasing." *School of Computer Science, Carnegie Mellon University.*

Finke, Martin. 2013. *Making Audio Plugins Part 18: PolyBLEP Oscillator.* Accessed April 1, 2025. https://www.martin-finke.de/articles/audio-plugins-018-polyblep-oscillator/

Goodwin, Simon N. 2019. *Beep to Boom: The Development of Advanced Runtime Sound Systems for Games and Extended Reality.* New York, NY: Routledge.

Hack Audio. 2016. *Hack Audio: Sine-Law Panning.* Accessed April 1, 2025. https://www.youtube.com/watch?v=diWriCFHXx0

Hollemans, Matthijs. 2024. *Creating Synthesizer Plug-Ins with C++ and JUCE.* London: The Audio Programmer Ltd. https://www.theaudioprogrammer.com/books/synth-plugin-book

Jolly, Kent. 2011. "Usage of Pd in Spore and Darkspore." Pure Data Convention, 36–39. Weimar, Germany. https://www.uni-weimar.de/kunst-und-gestaltung/wiki/images/Usage_of_Pd_in_Spore_and_Darkspore.pdf

Lamperski, Philip. 2016. "Real-Time Procedural Percussion Scoring in 'Tomb Raider's' Stealth Combat." GDC16. San Francisco. https://gdcvault.com/play/1023215/Real-time-Procedural-Percussion-Scoring

MacGregor, Alastair. 2014. "The Sounds of GTA V." GDC14. San Francisco. https://www.youtube.com/watch?v=tGmgydjM06Y

Michaels, Roth. 2022. "Fast, High-quality Pseudo-random Numbers for Audio Developers." *ADC22.* https://www.youtube.com/watch?v=N2AM6ixC6LI

Press, William H, Saul A Teukolsky, William T Vetterling, and Brian P Flannery. 2002. *Numerical Recipes in C: The Art of Scientific Computing.* 2nd ed. New York, NY: Cambridge University Press. https://s3.amazonaws.com/nrbook.com/book_C210.html

Schmid, Jakob. 2023. "Realtime Synthesis and Dynamic Music in Games." *schmid.dk*. https://www.schmid.dk/talks/2023-03-01-sonic/schmid-Sonic_College_2023-Realtime.pdf

Välimäki, Vesa, Juhan Nam, Julius O Smith, and Jonathan S Abel. 2010. "Alias-Suppressed Oscillators Based on Differentiated Polynomial Waveforms." *IEEE Transactions on Audio, Speech, and Language Processing* 18(4): 786–798.

Weisstein, Eric W. n.d. "Padé Approximant." *MathWorld–A Wolfram Web Resource*. Accessed April 8, 2025. https://mathworld.wolfram.com/PadeApproximant.html

Wikipedia contributors. 2024a. "Bhāskara I's sine approximation formula." *Wikipedia, The Free Encyclopedia*. October 28. Accessed April 8, 2025. https://en.wikipedia.org/w/index.php?title=Bh%C4%81skara_I%27s_sine_approximation_formula&oldid=1253961121

Wikipedia contributors. 2024b. *Numerically controlled oscillator*. December 20. Accessed April 1, 2025. https://en.wikipedia.org/w/index.php?title=Numerically_controlled_oscillator&oldid=1264120773

CHAPTER 3

Recording Audio Data to a Memory Buffer

Guy Somberg

3.1 INTRODUCTION

Typically, audio data that is mixed by audio middleware is sent to an audio device – this is hopefully an unremarkable and fairly obvious statement. The middleware starts up a high priority mixer thread, which communicates with (or is driven by) an operating system API that requests a buffer of audio data, and then it is up to the middleware to fill that buffer with audio data. The operating system then mixes that data with audio coming from other programs, and finally sends it off to the audio device, where it eventually comes out of your speakers. This is the normal flow of audio data.

Sometimes, though, we need to subvert the normal flow. It is not uncommon to need to either change the target of the output or to intercept the audio data for any number of purposes. If you're using FMOD, the easiest way to do this is by using the NOSOUND or WAVWRITER output types or their non-realtime _NRT versions. However, these output modes are limited in scope. The NOSOUND output provides no way to access the resulting wav data, and the WAVWRITER output will write to a wav file, but you have to process that wav file separately. Additionally, neither of them provides a mechanism to intercept a particular point in the DSP chain.

In this chapter, we'll go over two different mechanisms to record audio data from the mixer into a memory buffer so that it can be used inline.

DOI: 10.1201/9781003519119-4

This code is all intended to be used in a non-realtime context, but can be adapted to a realtime context with relatively minor changes. We'll be using FMOD Studio as our middleware, but the principles should apply to other audio middleware engines as well.

3.2 RECORD USING AN OUTPUT PLUGIN

3.2.1 Output Plugins

In FMOD Studio, the drivers for playing audio are all driven through output plugins. FMOD comes with a large selection of built-in output plugins: at least one (sometimes more) for each supported device type. The list of output plugins per platform is shown in Table 3.1. In order to support new platforms and APIs, FMOD supports authoring your own output plugins. The plugin API requires us to fill out a structure and provide some callbacks.

Using an output plugin to record to a buffer is useful in cases where you know that you only need the final mix of the system. One great example of this is in Chapter 6, where we may want to record the impulse response to a memory buffer instead of a wav file. If we know that our output buffer will be used for this purpose, then we can make some optimizations in that space, which we'll dive into as a part of this section.

3.2.2 Plugin Description and Basics

We will model our output plugin after the behavior of the `WAVWRITER_NRT` built-in, but instead of writing to a wav file, we will write to a `std::vector`. For simplicity, we'll define everything inline, so all of the functions that we'll be looking at will be members of this class:

```
class RecordToBufferOutput
{
    // Functions in this section go here...
};
```

TABLE 3.1   List of Supported Output Plugins in FMOD Studio as of the Writing of This Book

Platform	Supported APIs
Windows	WASAPI, ASIO, Windows Sonic
Linux	PluseAudio, ALSA
MacOS	CoreAudio
Game Consoles	Console-specific APIs

The first thing we'll need to do is provide a description that we can give to FMOD:

```
// Get the description of the output driver for FMOD.
static FMOD_OUTPUT_DESCRIPTION* GetOutputDescription()
{
    static FMOD_OUTPUT_DESCRIPTION OutputDescription = {};

    // Plugin information
    OutputDescription.apiversion = FMOD_OUTPUT_PLUGIN_VERSION;
    OutputDescription.name = "Record to buffer";
    OutputDescription.version = 0x00010000;

    // We use Mix Direct because we're running a non-realtime
    // context.  Use Mix Buffered for realtime output.
    OutputDescription.method = FMOD_OUTPUT_METHOD_MIX_DIRECT;

    // Callbacks that describe the functionality.
    OutputDescription.getnumdrivers = GetNumDriversCallback;
    OutputDescription.init = InitCallback;
    OutputDescription.close = CloseCallback;
    OutputDescription.update = UpdateCallback;

    return &OutputDescription;
}
```

Now that we have this description, we can register it with our FMOD System object and select it as our output device. We'll have to inject code that looks like this somewhere in the initialization of the audio engine:

```
unsigned int OutputHandle = 0;
pSystem->registerOutput(
    RecordToBufferOutput::GetOutputDescription(),
    &OutputHandle);
pSystem->setOutputByPlugin(OutputHandle);
```

Now that we have this output plugin set up, we need to start implementing the callbacks that we've defined. We'll start with the simplest, which is the GetNumDriversCallback:

```
// How many drivers this output supports. Outputs that map to
// hardware may have more than one device available, so they
```

```
// will return more than one. For our purposes, we just fill
// in the output with a value of 1.
static FMOD_RESULT F_CALL GetNumDriversCallback(
  [[maybe_unused]] FMOD_OUTPUT_STATE* OutputState,
  int* NumDrivers)
{
  *NumDrivers = 1;
  return FMOD_OK;
}
```

3.2.3 Initialization and Shutdown

Our next callbacks will all require some member data. We need to know the DSP buffer size (that is, the unit of mixing), and have a location to store our audio data. We will store them in **private** member variables:

```
// The number of samples in each buffer.  This is the
// unit of mixing.
unsigned int mDspBufferLengthSamples = 0;
// Our actual sample data.
std::vector<short> mSampleData;
```

We'll also provide a **private** helper function to get the instance from the plugin data:

```
// Cast the Output State's plugin data to the appropriate
// type
static RecordToBufferOutput& Get(
  FMOD_OUTPUT_STATE& OutputState)
{
  return *static_cast<RecordToBufferOutput*>(
    OutputState.plugindata);
}
```

We're now ready for the **Init** callback, which is called from System::init(). We allocate the memory, then initialize the plugin. For this example, we'll only support 16-bit mono output, but this code can be modified easily to support other output formats.

```
// Initialize this object
FMOD_RESULT Init(
```

```
  FMOD_SPEAKERMODE& SpeakerMode,
  int& SpeakerModeChannels,
  FMOD_SOUND_FORMAT& OutputFormat,
  int DspBufferLength,
  void* ExtraDriverData)
{
  // We are required to pass in a pointer to the
  // RecordToBufferOutput in the ExtraDriverData.
  // Otherwise the user of this class has no way to get
  // access to it!
  if (ExtraDriverData == nullptr)
    return FMOD_ERR_INVALID_PARAM;

  // Fill in the output pointer.
  auto** OutputPointer = static_cast<RecordToBufferOutput**>(
    ExtraDriverData);
  *OutputPointer = this;

  // We're going to hard-code 16-bit mono here, but more
  // generic code could parameterize this.
  OutputFormat = FMOD_SOUND_FORMAT_PCM16;
  SpeakerMode = FMOD_SPEAKERMODE_MONO;
  SpeakerModeChannels = 1;

  // Cache the DSP buffer length.
  mDspBufferLengthSamples = DspBufferLength;

  return FMOD_OK;
}


// Callback for initializing the output plugin
static FMOD_RESULT F_CALL InitCallback(
  FMOD_OUTPUT_STATE* OutputState,
  [[maybe_unused]] int SelectedDriver,
  [[maybe_unused]] FMOD_INITFLAGS Flags,
  [[maybe_unused]] int* OutputRate,
  FMOD_SPEAKERMODE* SpeakerMode, int* SpeakerModeChannels,
  FMOD_SOUND_FORMAT* OutputFormat,
  int DspBufferLength,
  [[maybe_unused]] int* DspNumBuffers,
  [[maybe_unused]] int* DspNumAdditionalBuffers,
```

```
  void* ExtraDriverData)
{
  // See if we need to allocate.
  if (OutputState->plugindata == nullptr)
  {
    // Allocate the memory for our class.
    OutputState->plugindata =
      FMOD_OUTPUT_ALLOC(
        OutputState,
        sizeof(RecordToBufferOutput),
        alignof(RecordToBufferOutput));

    // Error check
    if (OutputState->plugindata == nullptr)
      return FMOD_ERR_MEMORY;

    // Initialize the class.
    new (OutputState->plugindata) RecordToBufferOutput;
  }

  // Call the Init() function on our newly-allocated class.
  return Get(*OutputState).Init(
    *SpeakerMode, *SpeakerModeChannels,
    *OutputFormat,
    DspBufferLength,
    ExtraDriverData);
}
```

With this input callback, we can see that we need to pass in a pointer to a `RecordToBufferOutput` class in the extra driver data. We do that in our call to `System::init()`:

```
RecordToBufferOutput* Output = nullptr;
pSystem->init(128, FMOD_INIT_NORMAL, &Output);
```

The `Init` callback allocates the memory and initializes the object, so the `Close` callback is where we clean everything up:

```
// Called when the system is shut down
static FMOD_RESULT F_CALL CloseCallback(
  FMOD_OUTPUT_STATE* OutputState)
```

```cpp
{
  // Destruct our object
  Get(*OutputState).~RecordToBufferOutput();

  // Free the memory and null out the pointer.
  FMOD_OUTPUT_FREE(OutputState, OutputState->plugindata);
  OutputState->plugindata = nullptr;
  return FMOD_OK;
}
```

3.2.4 Update and Mixing

Finally, our mix is driven by the **Update** callback. Because this is a non-realtime plugin, this callback is called from the **System::update()** call. We are free to ignore the hard real time rules of the mixer thread and allocate in this function because we know that we're going to be run in a non-realtime context.

```cpp
// Do the actual mixing
FMOD_RESULT Update(FMOD_OUTPUT_STATE& OutputState)
{
  // Allocate room for the new buffer
  mSampleData.resize(
    mSampleData.size() + mDspBufferLengthSamples);

  // Figure out where to write our buffer
  auto CurrentLocation =
    mSampleData.end() - mDspBufferLengthSamples;
  void* WriteBuffer = &(*CurrentLocation);

  // Read from the mixer into the buffer.
  return FMOD_OUTPUT_READFROMMIXER(
    &OutputState, WriteBuffer, mDspBufferLengthSamples);
}

// Callback from the System::update() call
static FMOD_RESULT F_CALL UpdateCallback(
  FMOD_OUTPUT_STATE* OutputState)
{
  // Forward to the member function
  return Get(*OutputState).Update(*OutputState);
}
```

The only thing that is left is a `public` function to access the underlying mixing buffer:

```
// Get the actual audio data
const std::vector<short>& GetSampleData() const
{
  return mSampleData;
}
```

3.2.5 Optimizations

The above code will work fine if you're recording for an indeterminate amount of time. The `std::vector` will grow in amortized constant time, so we won't even have that many allocations to contend with. However, if we know both the expected length of our recording and how it will be used, then we can make some tweaks to the above code to make it even more performant.

First, if we know how long we expect the output to be, then we can pre-allocate exactly that much space, and relegate any future mixing to a garbage buffer. To implement this, we'll first add a couple of `private` members:

```
// Once we've filled our sample data, the mixer may still
// run, so we store a buffer to mix into that we can just
// ignore.
std::vector<short> mGarbageBuffer;
// Where in our sample data we are currently writing to.
std::vector<short>::iterator mCurrentLocation;
```

Next, we'll need to pre-allocate the garbage buffer so that we can have a place to write to. We'll need to add this one line to the member `Init()` function:

```
mGarbageBuffer.resize(mDspBufferLengthSamples);
```

And then our member `Update()` function needs to change so that we can write to the appropriate location within our buffer:

```
// Do the actual mixing
FMOD_RESULT Update(FMOD_OUTPUT_STATE& OutputState)
{
```

```
  // Figure out where to write our buffer
  void* WriteBuffer;
  if (mCurrentLocation == mSampleData.end())
  {
    // If we've filled up our sample data buffer, then
    // go ahead and write to the garbage buffer.
    WriteBuffer = &mGarbageBuffer[0];
  }
  else
  {
    // Find and increment the current write location
    WriteBuffer = &(*mCurrentLocation);
    mCurrentLocation += mDspBufferLengthSamples;
  }

  // Read from the mixer into the buffer.
  return FMOD_OUTPUT_READFROMMIXER(
    &OutputState, WriteBuffer, mDspBufferLengthSamples);
}
```

The last piece of this puzzle is that we need to both pre-allocate the sample buffer and initialize the current location. We'll add a `public` member function that the user will have to call to set the expected length:

```
// Set the expected buffer length to at least the given
// number of samples.
void SetBufferLengthSamples(
  unsigned long long ExpectedSamples)
{
  // We round up to the nearest multiple of the buffer length
  auto ModifiedExpectedSamples =
    ((ExpectedSamples + mDspBufferLengthSamples - 1) /
      mDspBufferLengthSamples) * mDspBufferLengthSamples;
  // One extra buffer to make sure that the output has
  // settled and we're all at zeroes
  ModifiedExpectedSamples += mDspBufferLengthSamples;

  // Allocate the memory and set our current buffer.
  mSampleData.resize(ModifiedExpectedSamples);
  mCurrentLocation = mSampleData.begin();
}
```

Using this mechanism, if we know what our expected buffer length is ahead of time, then we can avoid allocations entirely and just write into memory.

If we know that the buffered audio data is going to be sent to FMOD's convolution reverb DSP[1] (as in Chapter 6), we can make one simple tweak to optimize that use case. The buffer that is sent as the impulse response file is expected to be prepended with a single 16-bit value containing the number of channels in the input. To implement this, all we need to do is change the last two lines in `SetBufferLengthSamples()` to the following:

```
// We plan to use this for FMOD's convolution reverb, so
// we will need one extra sample prepended and the value
// set to the number of channels. (We're in mono, so the
// number of channels is one.)
mSampleData.resize(ModifiedExpectedSamples + 1);
mSampleData[0] = 1;
mCurrentLocation = mSampleData.begin() + 1;
```

3.3 RECORDING USING A DSP PLUGIN

3.3.1 DSP Plugins

An output plugin is a great choice if you explicitly want to catch the final mix, but it has a few disadvantages as well. Output plugins can't intercept the mix at any point in the DSP graph – they only work for the final output, so you cannot simply place a probe into your mix to record. Also, because it drives the entire mix, it can't be used along with an existing playback mechanism.

If these disadvantages of the output plugin make it undesirable or unusable for your use case, then a more flexible alternative is to record to a DSP, which can then be placed as a "probe" at just about any point in the DSP graph. In FMOD, DSPs can be waveform generators (such as a synth) or they can affect the signal (such as a multiband EQ filter). In our case, we will implement a passthrough effect that will intercept the audio data and copy it off to a buffer.

3.3.2 Plugin Description and Basics

As with the output plugin, we'll put everything into a single class:

```
class RecordToBufferDsp
{
  // Functions in this section go here...
};
```

And also similar to the output plugin, the first thing that we need to do is to provide a data structure describing our plugin:

```
static FMOD_DSP_DESCRIPTION* GetDspDescription()
{
  // Description structure for our parameter, which will
  // just be a pointer to the 'this' object.
  static FMOD_DSP_PARAMETER_DESC ParameterDescription;
  FMOD_DSP_INIT_PARAMDESC_DATA(
    ParameterDescription, "This", "", "Dsp Object", 0);

  // Array of parameters to pass into the DSP Description
  static FMOD_DSP_PARAMETER_DESC* Parameters[] =
    {&ParameterDescription};

  static FMOD_DSP_DESCRIPTION DspDescription = {};
  // Plugin information
  DspDescription.pluginsdkversion = FMOD_PLUGIN_SDK_VERSION;
  strcpy_s(DspDescription.name, "RecordToBuffer");
  DspDescription.version = 0x00010000;
  DspDescription.numinputbuffers = 1;
  DspDescription.numoutputbuffers = 1;
  DspDescription.numparameters = 1;
  DspDescription.paramdesc = Parameters;

  // Callbacks
  DspDescription.create = &RecordToBufferDsp::Create;
  DspDescription.release = &RecordToBufferDsp::Release;
  DspDescription.reset = &RecordToBufferDsp::Reset;
  DspDescription.read = &RecordToBufferDsp::Read;
  DspDescription.getparameterdata =
    &RecordToBufferDsp::GetParameterData;

  return &DspDescription;
}
```

Once we have this structure in place, we can register it with FMOD and create an instance of this DSP with the following code:

```
unsigned int RecordDspHandle = 0;
pSystem->registerDSP(
```

```
    RecordToBufferDsp::GetDspDescription(), &RecordDspHandle);

FMOD::DSP* pDSP = nullptr;
pSystem->createDSPByPlugin(RecordDspHandle, &pDSP);
```

With the DSP created, we can now attach it anywhere that we want to place a recording probe. In practice, given any `Channel` or `ChannelGroup` (or, more broadly, a `ChannelControl`), we can attach this DSP and get a recording:

```
void Record(FMOD::ChannelControl* ChannelControl)
{
  FMOD::DSP* pDSP = nullptr;
  pSystem->createDSPByPlugin(RecordDspHandle, &pDSP);
  ChannelControl->addDSP(FMOD_CHANNELCONTROL_DSP_HEAD, pDSP);
}
```

3.3.3 Initialization and Shutdown

In order to make all of this work, however, we must implement the callbacks. This is all very similar to the Output plugin mechanism: `private` data for the buffer with a `public` accessor, a `private` `Get()` function, and allocation/deallocation functions that use FMOD's allocation routines.

Despite the similarity in principle, it's still worthwhile to see the details. We'll start with private data and some helper functions:

```
public:
  const std::vector<float>& GetSampleData() const
  { return Buffer; }

private:
  // Current sample data
  std::vector<float> Buffer;

  // Get the RecordToBufferDsp object from the DSP State
  static RecordToBufferDsp* Get(FMOD_DSP_STATE& DspState)
  {
    return static_cast<RecordToBufferDsp*>(
      DspState.plugindata);
  }
```

Now we are ready to start implementing the callbacks. We'll start with the basics. Memory allocation is relatively straightforward, although we do have to use placement new in order to initialize the object and explicitly call the destructor in order to destroy it, similar to the output plugin.

```cpp
static FMOD_RESULT F_CALL Create(FMOD_DSP_STATE* DspState)
{
  // Allocate memory
  DspState->plugindata =
    FMOD_DSP_ALLOC(DspState, sizeof(RecordToBufferDsp));
  if (DspState->plugindata == nullptr)
    return FMOD_ERR_MEMORY;

  // Initialize the object
  new (DspState->plugindata) RecordToBufferDsp;

  return FMOD_OK;
}


static FMOD_RESULT F_CALL Release(FMOD_DSP_STATE* DspState)
{
  auto* Dsp = Get(*DspState);

  // Run the destructor
  Dsp->~RecordToBufferDsp();

  // Free the memory
  FMOD_DSP_FREE(DspState, DspState->plugindata);
  DspState->plugindata = nullptr;

  return FMOD_OK;
}
```

DSPs can be expensive to create, so oftentimes they are cached and reused. In order to support this process, FMOD supports a reset() function call, which we will hook into:

```cpp
static FMOD_RESULT F_CALL Reset(FMOD_DSP_STATE* DspState)
{
  // Reset is called before the first time a DSP is used, or
```

```
// explicitly by calling DSP::reset().  We will just clear
// out the sample buffer.
auto* This = Get(*DspState);
This->Buffer.clear();
return FMOD_OK;
}
```

3.3.4 DSP Parameter Access Patterns

The actual functionality of this DSP will be implemented through the Read callback, but we have one other simple callback to implement beforehand: the GetParameter callback. There are some subtleties to how this is implemented here that we will discuss after we show the code:

```
static FMOD_RESULT F_CALL GetParameterData(
  FMOD_DSP_STATE* DspState,
  int ParameterIndex,
  void** Data,
  unsigned int* Length,
  [[maybe_unused]] char* ValueStr)
{
  // We have requested a data parameter, which we support
  // exactly one of at index zero.
  if (ParameterIndex == 0)
  {
    // Fill in the data with our 'this' pointer and set
    // the length to the size of a pointer.
    *Data = Get(*DspState);
    *Length = sizeof(RecordToBufferDsp*);
    return FMOD_OK;
  }

  // Any other parameter is invalid.
  return FMOD_ERR_INVALID_PARAM;
}
```

The way that we have implemented this DSP is that the user asks for the This parameter (or gets the parameter at index 0), then calls GetSampleData() on the object. This pattern will work fine so long as the DSP is not currently running – or, more generally, is attached to the DSP graph. If the DSP is attached, then we will have the DSP graph potentially writing to the buffer in the mixer thread, while trying to read the buffer from the main thread. Therefore, in order to use this mechanism as presented in this chapter, we must provide a guarantee that it is not running by doing one of a number of options:

- Detach the DSP from the graph by calling `ChannelControl::removeDSP()`.

- Run the system in a non-realtime mode such as `NOSOUND_NRT`, `WAVWRITER_NRT`, or by using the output plugin described in Section 3.2.

- Pause the mixer by calling `System::lockDSP()` (along with a matching `System::unlockDSP()` to resume) in order to make sure that the mixer is not running while the main thread is accessing the DSP.

Alternatively, if we want to be able to support reading and manipulating the recorded buffer while it is running, we will have to implement a larger collection of DSP parameters that make copies of the data and manipulate. Doing so is not particularly complex, but is outside the scope of this chapter.

3.3.5 Read Callback Basics

The actual recording functionality falls to the **Read** callback, which provides an input memory buffer, an output memory buffer, and expects that the DSP will manipulate the sample data in the middle. We'll start with a simple no-operation DSP that just copies the input to the output. (If we don't do this copy, then the output will be silent.)

```
static FMOD_RESULT F_CALL Read(
  [[maybe_unused]] FMOD_DSP_STATE* DspState,
  float* Inbuffer,
  float* Outbuffer,
  unsigned int LengthSamples,
  int InChannels,
  int* OutChannels)
{
  // Copy (passthrough) the input to the output.
  memcpy(Outbuffer, Inbuffer,
    LengthSamples * InChannels * sizeof(float));
  *OutChannels = InChannels;
  return FMOD_OK;
}
```

Of course, this doesn't actually do any recording. Let's take a first pass at recording by copying the data off to a buffer. We'll add these lines to the `Read()` function:

```
// Copy off the data into the buffer
auto* This = Get(*DspState);
This->Buffer.insert(This->Buffer.end(), Inbuffer,
  Inbuffer + (LengthSamples * InChannels));
```

This is correct as far as it goes, but it won't actually work right in practice. The fundamental problem is the number of channels in the input buffer. This code assumes that the number of channels remains constant from call to call. It turns out that this assumption does not hold. For example, if we take a mono sound source and play it,

```
FMOD::Channel* pChannel = nullptr;
pSystem->playDSP(pSound, nullptr, false, &pChannel);
```

the resulting `Channel` will be mixed as mono and have one channel. However, if we then set the `Channel` to be partially panned to the right,

```
pChannel->setPan(0.125f);
```

the `Channel` will now be mixed as stereo and have two channels. This is a runtime property and can, in fact, change from one frame to the next. We have to do some extra work in order to unify the mixing into a consistent channel count.

3.3.6 Mix Matrices

Under the hood, FMOD does this sort of mixing by applying a mix matrix to the channel. A mix matrix is a buffer that can be interpreted as a two-dimensional array where each row represents an output channel, and each column represents an input channel. The values in the matrix are the amount of the input channel that gets summed into that output channel.

A couple of examples:

- A constant power panning matrix from mono to stereo will split the single input channel into two channels, where each channel gets 0.707 (or, more precisely, $\sqrt{2}/2$) of the input channel. The mix matrix

TABLE 3.2   A Constant Power Mono-to-Stereo Panning Matrix

Output Channel	Input Channel 1
0	0.707
1	0.707

TABLE 3.3   A 5.1 Unit Matrix

Output	Input 1	Input 2	Input 3	Input 4	Input 5	Input 6
0	1	0	0	0	0	0
1	0	1	0	0	0	0
2	0	0	1	0	0	0
3	0	0	0	1	0	0
4	0	0	0	0	1	0
5	0	0	0	0	0	1

is therefore $\{0.707\ 0.707\}$, which we can interpret as Table 3.2. In this case, our left and right channels will each be $0.707 * Input$.

- A unit matrix allows a signal to pass through unchanged, and has the same pattern as a standard linear algebra identity matrix – that is, all zeroes, with ones on the diagonals. A 5.1 unit matrix is shown in Table 3.3, which will end up being the buffer $\{1\ 0\ 0\ 0\ 0\ 0\ 0\ 1\ 0\ 0\ 0\ 0\ 0\ 0\ 1\ 0\ 0\ 0\ 0\ 0\ 0\ 1\ 0\ 0\ 0\ 0\ 0\ 0\ 1\ 0\ 0\ 0\ 0\ 0\ 0\ 1\}$.

More generally, this matrix is really a matrix in the mathematical sense, and can be described and implemented using linear algebra:

$$\begin{bmatrix} Output_0 \\ \vdots \\ Output_N \end{bmatrix} = \begin{bmatrix} Input_0 \\ \vdots \\ Input_N \end{bmatrix} \begin{bmatrix} M_{00} & \cdots & M_{0j} \\ \vdots & \ddots & \vdots \\ M_{i0} & \cdots & M_{ij} \end{bmatrix}$$

We will write a simple function to do the math for us. Production code may want to expand this using SIMD instructions, but this will do for the purposes of this chapter:

```
static void ApplyMatrix(
  std::span<float> InputSample,
  std::span<float> OutputSample,
  std::span<float> MixMatrix)
```

```
{
  auto InputChannels = InputSample.size();
  auto OutputChannels = OutputSample.size();

  // Iterate over each output channel
  for (size_t i = 0; i < OutputChannels; i++)
  {
    // Each output channel sums up its matrix entry with the
    // matching entry from the input channel.
    for (size_t j = 0; j < InputChannels; j++)
    {
      OutputSample[i] +=
        MixMatrix[i * InputChannels + j] * InputSample[j];
    }
  }
}
```

Now the question is how to calculate the appropriate mix matrix. Fortunately, for standard up- and downmixing, FMOD provides functions to fill in a buffer with the matrix data. These functions (summarized in Table 3.4) are very powerful, and you can create very complex matrices using them – or you can just do standard mixing, which is what we will be doing.

For our purposes, we will be leaving the pan centered and leaving the mix at full volume, so the thing that we will need is to select the input and output channel count. We will record to a stereo buffer in this chapter, which means that we will use the FMOD_DSP_PAN_SUMSTEREOMATRIX macro. A more general solution may choose to make this output configurable, which would add some more complexity to the following functions.

TABLE 3.4 Summary of FMOD Matrix Macros

Macro Name	Input Channels	Output Channels
FMOD_DSP_PAN_SUMMONOMATRIX	Variable	1
FMOD_DSP_PAN_SUMSTEREOMATRIX	Variable	2
FMOD_DSP_PAN_SUMSURROUNDMATRIX	Variable	Variable
FMOD_DSP_PAN_SUMMONOTOSURROUNDMATRIX	1	Variable
FMOD_DSP_PAN_SUMSTEREOTOSURROUNDMATRIX	2	Variable

3.3.7 Read Callback with Speaker Redistribution

The FMOD macros take as input a speaker configuration rather than a channel count, so we will need a function to perform this mapping for us:

```
static FMOD_SPEAKERMODE GetSpeakerModeFromChannelCount(
  int Channels)
{
  switch (Channels)
  {
  case 1: return FMOD_SPEAKERMODE_MONO;
  case 2: return FMOD_SPEAKERMODE_STEREO;
  case 4: return FMOD_SPEAKERMODE_QUAD;
  case 5: return FMOD_SPEAKERMODE_SURROUND;
  case 6: return FMOD_SPEAKERMODE_5POINT1;
  case 8: return FMOD_SPEAKERMODE_7POINT1;
  case 12: return FMOD_SPEAKERMODE_7POINT1POINT4;
  default: return FMOD_SPEAKERMODE_RAW;
  }
}
```

The `FMOD_SPEAKERMODE_RAW` value will not actually work properly with the macros, but:

- The macros will return an error in those cases, which can be detected and handled.

- For most game scenarios, we will be dealing with standard speaker modes, so it's not something that we will be handling here.

All of this discussion of mix matrices gets us to where we've been wanting to go, which is code that can do a simple memory copy if the input channel count matches our desired channel count (two in our case, for stereo), and which can either up- or downmix appropriately otherwise:

```
static FMOD_RESULT F_CALL Read(
  FMOD_DSP_STATE* DspState,
  float* InBuffer, float* OutBuffer,
  unsigned int LengthSamples,
  int InChannels, int* OutChannels)
{
  auto* This = Get(*DspState);
```

```cpp
// We're hard-coding to stereo here.   More generic code
// might make this configurable.
constexpr int StereoChannelCount = 2;

if (InChannels == StereoChannelCount)
{
  // Optimal case: our input channel matches our
  // output channel, so we can just copy the data over.
  This->Buffer.insert(
    This->Buffer.end(),
    InBuffer, InBuffer + (LengthSamples * InChannels));
}
else
{
  // Otherwise, our input channel count does not match
  // the desired channel count, so we have to ask FMOD
  // for the appropriate mix matrix to either upmix or
  // downmix to stereo from the input.
  std::array<float,
    StereoChannelCount * FMOD_MAX_CHANNEL_WIDTH> MixMatrix
      = {};
  FMOD_DSP_PAN_SUMSTEREOMATRIX(
    DspState, GetSpeakerModeFromChannelCount(InChannels),
    0.0f, 1.0f, 1.0f, InChannels, MixMatrix.data());

  // Reserve memory for our new samples.
  This->Buffer.reserve(
    This->Buffer.size() +
      (LengthSamples * StereoChannelCount));

  // Go through each sample
  for (unsigned int i = 0; i < LengthSamples; i++)
  {
    // Add new zero entries for the output
    auto NewEntry = This->Buffer.insert(
      This->Buffer.end(), StereoChannelCount, 0.0f);

    // Apply our mix matrix to the input and output
    // samples.
    std::span<float> OutputSample{
      NewEntry, This->Buffer.end() };
```

```
    std::span<float> InputSample{
      &InBuffer[i * InChannels],
      &InBuffer[i * InChannels + InChannels] };
    ApplyMatrix(InputSample, OutputSample, MixMatrix);
  }
}


// Copy (passthrough) the input to the output.
memcpy(OutBuffer, InBuffer,
       LengthSamples * InChannels * sizeof(float));
*OutChannels = InChannels;
return FMOD_OK;
}
```

3.3.8 Optimizations

The only optimization that we will be making to this setup is to cache the mix matrix. We're very likely to have long stretches of data where the number of input channels does not change, so it is a waste to recalculate it every time. Instead, we will cache it in private member variables:

```
// Cached mix matrix
static constexpr int StereoChannelCount = 2;
std::array<
  float, StereoChannelCount * FMOD_MAX_CHANNEL_WIDTH>
    MixMatrix = {};

// Cached number of channels in the mix matrix
int MixMatrixChannels = 0;
```

And then we can change the code to use the new cache:

```
if (This->MixMatrixChannels != InChannels)
{
  This->MixMatrix.fill(0.0f);
  FMOD_DSP_PAN_SUMSTEREOMATRIX(
    DspState, GetSpeakerModeFromChannelCount(InChannels),
    0.0f, 1.0f, 1.0f, InChannels, This->MixMatrix.data());
  This->MixMatrixChannels = InChannels;
}
```

As with the output plugin, we can save on memory allocations if we know ahead of time approximately how long our buffer is expected to be. We won't show the code here, but it is not particularly complex to add a function and do a **reserve()** on the underlying **vector**.

3.4 WHERE TO GO FROM HERE

Both of these recording mechanisms are powerful and effective for various use cases. I use the output plugin for working with FMOD's convolution reverb, but the DSP plugin is in many ways more flexible. Missing from this chapter is any sort of configuration for both of these plugins. If you need to be able to configure the output format, then the hooks are there to do so, but this chapter is long enough already. Hopefully if you need this functionality, then this chapter has provided a good starting point to work from.

NOTE

1. In fact, this is why we have selected 16-bit mono as the output format.

II

Acoustics

CHAPTER 4

An Overview of Game Acoustics

Mike Filion

4.1 INTRODUCTION

Environmental audio realism can be challenging to implement because the audio engine often needs to do a lot of work with very little resources. Audio is just one element of the entire puzzle for immersive 3D game worlds, competing for processing resources with animation, physics, rendering, AI, and others. With the ninth generation of consoles (PlayStation 5 and Xbox Series X|S), investment from the manufacturers has pushed forward audio as a part of the overall gaming experience. We see investment on the hardware side to allow for coprocessors to offload some work from the main CPU for audio-specific tasks. With consoles being a limiting performance factor because of their fixed hardware and feature set, we are limited to what we can achieve on these machines.

In the last several years, a number of different middleware products have emerged that can be used either as a full solution for acoustics, or as inspiration on how to implement full-fledged custom systems. In this chapter we'll review a few of these middleware options and discuss some simple examples of implementing different acoustics phenomenon.

4.2 CONCEPTS

We'll use "acoustics" as an umbrella term to describe a multitude of different aural phenomenon, and "listener" to represent the movable position in the world where the sound is being perceived. Generally, this will be the player or camera, but can be different depending on the style of game.

DOI: 10.1201/9781003519119-6

Before delving into the questions about middleware and implementations, we first need to define obstruction, occlusion, propagation, early reflection, and reverb.

4.2.1 Obstruction

When discussing obstruction, there are two examples I like to think of. The first is standing on one side of a rock and having the sound on the opposite site, a distance away from the rock. In this case we will still hear the sound from the sides of the rock, the same way that water would spill around it. The other example is being able to see a sound through a door, where not all of the sound will be able to reach the player. Figure 4.1 shows both of these examples in the abstract.

In a real-world model of obstruction, there are several components to the behavior of how sound is obstructed. These include deflection and absorption by the obstacle, and transmission through the obstacle. However, for the purposes of this chapter, we'll limit the definition of obstruction to deflection and separate the modeling of transmission through obstacles to occlusion. In addition, we'll ignore the reflections that could be generated by obstruction because many DSP reverb effects allow for the modeling of these reflections.

4.2.2 Occlusion

When thinking about occlusion as it relates to game audio, I can't help but think of the example of the thin walls in an apartment building that has seen better days. If you were to place the spawn point of your main character in a room in this building, what would be the first thing he would hear

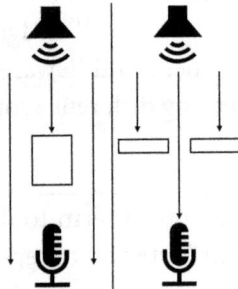

FIGURE 4.1 Two different examples of sound source and listener placement. (Left) A listener with an obstacle directly between the source and the listener's position. (Right) A listener with a direct line of sight through an opening.

from outside of the room? If we were in a busy apartment block, the sound of the neighbor's TV with the higher frequencies attenuated from the wall could be present. We would also hear the argument of the neighbors on the floor above, with a deeper voice being easier to hear through the ceiling than a higher-pitched voice.

Occlusion can be defined as the effect of a sound being modified by being perceived exclusively through an object, such as a wall. These sounds usually have a volume attenuation and/or a low-pass filter affecting them.

To determine the volume attenuation of your sound, we can use a chart of mean attenuation through a mass to determine what the attenuation would be based on the density of the object. For example, if we have a concrete floor with a density of 2300 kg/m³ and thickness 0.15 m, we can calculate the mass m as:

$$m = 2300 \frac{\text{kg}}{\text{m}^3} \times 0.15\text{m}$$

$$= 345 \frac{\text{kg}}{\text{m}^2}$$

From the chart in Figure 4.2, we can estimate that the attenuation is 48 dB. In the real world, the different frequencies of a sound would attenuate differently: lower frequencies would attenuate less than higher frequencies.

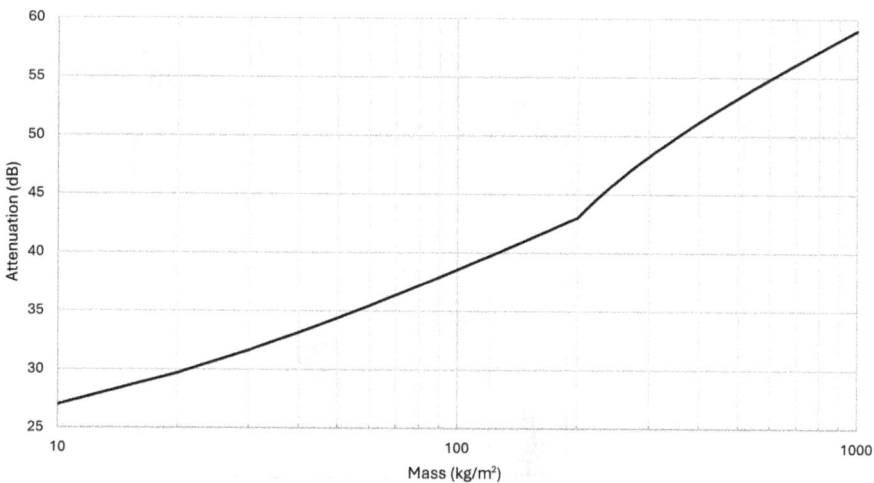

FIGURE 4.2   A graph showing mean attenuation through a mass.

In my opinion, the same results can be achieved through an artistic choice of how the low-pass filter and the volumes are reduced, depending on the nature of sound that you are occluding. The Engineering Toolbox (2008) has more details on how to calculate attenuation through surfaces.

4.2.3 Propagation

We'll define propagation as the relocation of the dry signal of a sound affected only by volume attenuation that would normally occur. In Figure 4.3, we can see that a direct line of sight to the original sound (the black speaker) doesn't exist. However, there is a point where we can expect some of the original sound to propagate from: the grey speaker. Given the wave like properties of sound, the propagation location would not be omnidirectional. Rather, in a fully realized simulation, the greater the angle from the propagation point (using a forward vector created from the difference between the original position and the new propagation point), the more volume attenuation and low pass would be applied to the sound. While a realistic simulation would demand this additional level of detail, it is an artistic and/or performance question whether or not to implement it.

A broader definition of propagation can include how the sound is modified as it travels from one given location to another. Some middleware provides extensive modeling for this element of sound propagation, including some of the software that we'll look at in this chapter.

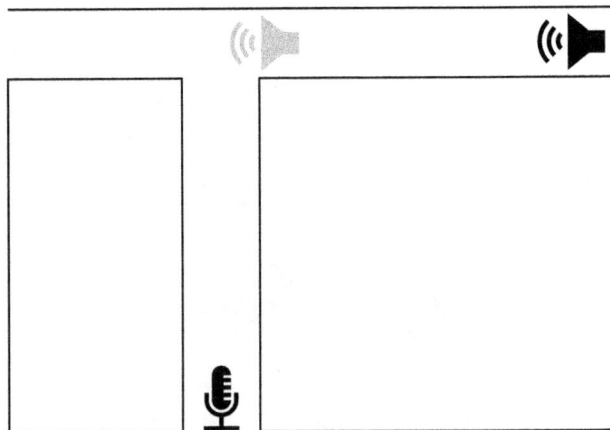

FIGURE 4.3   An example of sound propagation in a corridor.

4.2.4 Early Reflections

Early reflections enhance the feeling of physical space in a virtual environment by simulating sounds bouncing off of surfaces like walls or objects: the closer you are to an object, the faster the reflected sound reaches the player.

4.2.5 Reverb

Reverb is the persistence of sound after it is produced, caused by multiple reflections from surfaces in an environment. It occurs when sound waves bounce off walls, ceilings, and other objects, blending together to create an ambient effect. In video games, this effect allows the player to have an auditory cue of the characteristics of the space they find themselves in. When discussing the combination of reverb and early reflections, we tend to discuss late reverb, which is purely the non-dynamic elements of the reverb that are combined with early reflections to give both a dynamic and static auditory cue of the environment.

4.3 MIDDLEWARE

There are many acoustics middleware options that are free, or at least free to evaluate. Determining whether or which solution to integrate into a game can therefore be as simple as investing the time to evaluate the software. When using a popular commercialized engine such as Unity or Unreal, there is often an integration already available, which means that all that is required is for audio artists to take time to play around with the offering. In this section we'll explore a number of different options that are available.

4.3.1 Microsoft Project Acoustics

Microsoft Project Acoustics was a spatial audio simulation technology that modeled real time physics-based sound propagation in 3D environments. It precomputed acoustic data using wave-based simulation, which enabled realistic sound occlusion, diffraction, and reverberation effects without high runtime CPU costs. Unfortunately, Project Acoustics was discontinued on July 1, 2024.

It might seem an odd choice to include a discontinued option, but it is worth mentioning and examining its usage given that its offering was unique compared to other solutions.

```
#include <ProjectAcousticsRuntime.h>

bool initAcoustics(IAcoustics*& acoustics)
```

```cpp
{
  // Create acoustics runtime instance
  acoustics = CreateAcousticsInstance();
  if (!acoustics) return false;

  // Load baked acoustics data (replace with actual path)
  const char* filePath = "path/to/baked_acoustics_data.acd";
  if (!acoustics->LoadBakedData(filePath)) return false;

  return true;
}

void getOccObs(IAcoustics* acousticsSystem,
  const Vector3& posA, const Vector3& posB,
  float& occlusion, float& obstruction)
{
  if (!AcousticsSystem) return false;

  AcousticsQueryInput input;
  input.SourcePosition = posA;
  input.ListenerPosition = posB;

  AcousticsQueryOutput out;
  if (AcousticsSystem->QueryAcoustics(input, output))
  {
    occlusion = output.Occlusion;
    obstruction = output.Obstruction;
    return true;
  }

  return false;
}

int main()
{
  IAcoustics* acoustics = nullptr;
  if (!initAcoustics(acoustics)) return -1;

  Vector3 sourcePosition;
  Vector3 listenerPosition;
```

```
float occ;
float obs;
if (getOccObs(sourcePos, listenerPos, occ, obs))
{
  // Use occlusion and obstruction here
}

return 0;
}
```

Using Microsoft Project Acoustics was quite straightforward: create an instance of IAcoustics, load the pre-baked data, and then query the information. Pre-baking the data required voxelization of the game environment, and then preprocessing of that data in a separate computationally-heavy step to generate the pre-baked acoustics data that would be loaded. Unfortunately, one of the limiting factors for Microsoft Project Acoustics was the size of the precomputed data required for the game.

4.3.2 Wwise Spatial Audio

Wwise Spatial Audio provides real time simulation of sound propagation in 3D environments. It models reflection, diffraction, transmission, and reverb, enabling dynamic soundscapes based on scene geometry. It supports early reflections, diffraction, transmission, and reverberation zones for spatialized ambient effects. It integrates with game engines via geometric API support and optimizes performance through adaptive computation.

```
#include <AK/SpatialAudio/Common/AkSpatialAudio.h>

int main()
{
  // Step 1: Init Wwise
  if (!initWwise()) return -1;

  // Step 2: Init Wwise Spatial Audio
  AkSpatialAudioInitSettings settings;
  const AKRESULT res = AK::SpatialAudio::Init(settings);
  if (res != AK_Success) return -1;

  // Step 3: Add Listener & Emitter
```

```
    const AkGameObjectID listenerID = registerListener();
    const AkGameObjectID emitterID = registerEmitter();

    // Step 4: Add world geometry
    addGeometry();

    // Step 5: Process and apply spatial audio effects
    // This is called once per frame
    AK::SoundEngine::RenderAudio();

    // Step 6: Teardown
    // We could unregsiter the emitter, listener, and geometry
    shutdownWwise();

    return 0;
}
```

As Wwise offers a complete middleware solution, on the programming side there is nothing to do once we provide the geometry, listener, and emitter positions. As we update these throughout the game session, Wwise will calculate and apply the data. Sound designers can modify multiple parameters inside of the Wwise editor to tweak everything to their liking. Because Wwise is a complete solution, it is effectively a bit of a black box and there is little programmer intervention beyond the simple example shown above.

4.3.3 Google Resonance Audio

Google Resonance Audio is an open-source spatial audio SDK designed for immersive 3D sound in VR, AR, and 360-degree experiences. It supports real time binaural rendering, ambisonics, and environmental sound occlusion. While it does not provide any methods for computing acoustics parameters (obstruction, occlusion, propagation), it provides methods for using those parameters for rendering. It was initially released as part of the discontinued Daydream VR platform, but it remains available for general spatial audio applications.

```
#include <resonance_audio/api/resonance_audio_api.h>

int main()
{
```

```cpp
// Step 1: Create an instance of ResonanceAudioApi
constexpr int sampleRate = 48000; // Sample rate in Hz
constexpr int framesPerBuffer = 512;
constexpr int numChannels = 2; // Stereo output

vraudio::ResonanceAudioApi* audioEngine =
  vraudio::CreateResonanceAudioApi(
    numChannels, framesPerBuffer, sampleRate);

// Step 2: Create a sound source
const int source_id =
  audioEngine->CreateStereoSource(numChannels);

// Step 3: Set the source position
audioEngine->SetSourcePosition(
  source_id, 5.0f, 0.0f, 2.0f);

// Step 4: Set listener position
audioEngine->SetHeadPosition(0.0f, 0.0f, 0.0f);

// Step 5: Compute occlusion based on a simulated obstacle
const float occlusion_factor = 0.8f; // between 0.0 & 1.0
audioEngine->SetSoundObjectOcclusionIntensity(
  source_id, occlusion_factor);

// Step 6: Process audio rendering (simulation)
// Stereo buffer
float outputBuffer[framesPerBuffer * numChannels];
audioEngine->FillInterleavedOutputBuffer(
  numChannels, framesPerBuffer, outputBuffer);

delete audioEngine;

return 0;
}
```

After computing the acoustics parameters, the program passes the occlusion information to the SDK to render sound with the parameters. With the simple examples in Section 4.4, we can combine the Resonance SDK to create a full-fledged rendering solution.

4.3.4 Steam Audio

Steam Audio is a spatial audio middleware designed for realistic 3D sound propagation in games and VR applications. It simulates occlusion, reflection, and reverb based on scene geometry and materials, enhancing immersion. It uses ray tracing and convolution techniques for accurate acoustics, with support for real time and baked processing.

```cpp
#include <phonon.h>

int main()
{
  // Step 1: Init Steam Audio
  IPLContext context = initializeSteamAudio();
  if (!context) return -1;

  // Step 2: Create scene
  IPLScene scene = createScene(context);
  if (!scene) return -1;

  // Step 3: Create simulator
  IPLSimulator simulator = createSimulator(context);
  if (!simulator) return -1;

  // Step 4: Add world geometry
  // To be replaced with proper logic to provide
  // all scene geometry
  addStaticMesh(scene);

  Vector3 source, listener;
  const float occlusion =
    computeOcclusion(
      scene, context, simulator, source, listener);

  // Use occlusion here

  // Step 5: Teardown
  iplSimulatorRelease(&simulator);
  iplSceneRelease(&scene);
  iplContextRelease(&context);

  return 0;
}
```

This is a basic example of using Steam Audio to compute occlusion. In this example, we initialize Steam Audio, create a scene, create the simulator, and then add scene geometry. After this, we compute the occlusion for the scene with two positions and return the occlusion. The simulation provided by Steam Audio provides a plethora of information that we can use to affect the audio render.

4.4 CODE EXAMPLES

While using middleware can provide a full implementation for a game, sometimes it can be too complicated for a particular use case or overkill for simpler games and/or use cases. We will create some simple implementations of different acoustics elements that were previously discussed. We'll use Wwise as the sound engine middleware but the various function calls and types should be easily translated to other sound engines.

4.4.1 Occlusion

```
struct OcclusionCastResult
{
  float intersectionAmount;
  short material;
};

class OcclusionCaster
{
public:
  static std::vector<OcclusionCastResult> Cast(
    const Vector3& start, const Vector3& end);
};

void ApplyOcclusion(AkGameObjectID gameObjectID,
  const Vector3& soundPos, AkGameObjectID listenerID,
  const Vector3& listenerPos)
{
  std::vector<OcclusionCastResult> occlusionResults =
    OcclusionCaster::Cast(soundPos, listenerPos);
  float totalOcclusion = 0.f;
  for(const OcclusionCastResult& result: occlusionResults)
  {
    const float occlusionPerUnit =
      OcclusionSettings::GetOcclusionForMaterial(
```

```
        result.material);
    totalOcclusion +=
        result.intersectionAmount * occlusionPerUnit;
  }

  AK::SoundEngine::SetObjectObstructionAndOcclusion(
    gameObjectID, listenerID, 0.f, totalOcclusion);
}
```

This code is a simple example that shows how to calculate occlusion based on a pair of positions and then send the information to Wwise. The implementation details related to the casting are not provided as these will vary depending on the engine. Raycasting with a physics middleware would be a simple and efficient option.

Given the simplicity of the code example, there are several limitations to this simple occlusion computation, which are demonstrated in Figure 4.4. Sound A and Sound B are approximately at the same distance from the listener, and in a physically accurate simulation we would expect to hear A and B at different volume levels and filtering depending on the material. In this example, assuming that the material would be something like concrete or rock with a high occlusion per unit, A would be audible while B would be completely inaudible. Providing a more nuanced solution would require more complexity than this simple single-raycast solution.

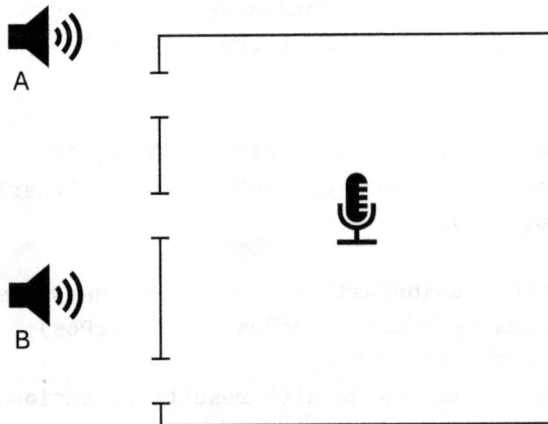

FIGURE 4.4 An example of potential problems with occlusion with two sources.

4.4.2 Obstruction

```cpp
class ObstructionCaster
{
public:
  static float Cast(const Vector3& start, const Vector3& end,
    float distance = 5.f, float res = 1.f)
  {
    Vector3 perpVec = Math::ComputeCrossProduct(start, end);
    for (float i = res; i < distance; i += res)
    {
      if (!OcclusionCaster::Cast(start,
            end + perpVec * i).empty() &&
          !OcclusionCaster::Cast(start,
            end + perpVec * -i).empty())
        continue;

      const float distA = (end - start).Length();
      const float distB =
        ((end + perpVec * i) - start).Length();

      return static_cast<float>(
        sqrt(pow(distA, 2) + pow(distB, 2))) - distA;
    }

    return 100.f;
  }
};


void ApplyObstructionAndOcclusion(
  AkGameObjectID gameObjectID, const Vector3& soundPos,
  AkGameObjectID listenerID, const Vector3& listenerPos)
{
  float totalOcclusion = ...;
  float totalObstruction =
    ObstructionCaster::Cast(start, end);

  AK::SoundEngine::SetObjectObstructionAndOcclusion(
    gameObjectID, listenerID, totalObstruction,
    totalOcclusion);
}
```

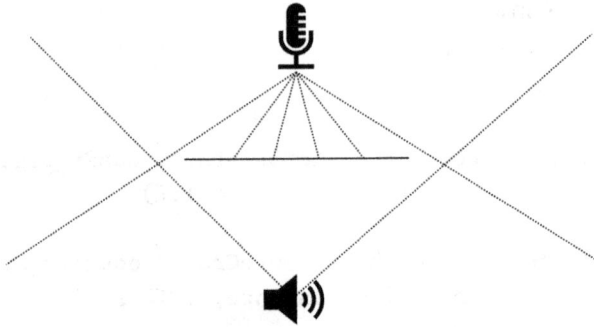

FIGURE 4.5   Visual representation of the obstruction algorithm.

The obstruction calculation builds upon the occlusion computation. The difference is that we are looking for the first pair of positions that doesn't collide with any geometry. There are two parameters for the obstruction casting: the distance from one position that we will search and the granularity of the search. The higher the granularity, the more accurate the obstruction value will be, but also the more rays that will be cast (and thus the more expensive in terms of CPU usage). The second optional parameter is the distance from the end position to search, which will also affect the CPU usage.

In Figure 4.5, we can see the rays (represented as dotted lines) and their collision with the wall which will not be used for the obstruction computation. In this example, the last set of rays would provide the same value because of the wall in the example. We use some simple trigonometry to determine the difference between the direct path and the obstructed path, which allows us to compute an obstruction value.

One thing to take into consideration is how the value of occlusion versus obstruction is used. When providing the pair of values to a single position, it would be important to apply a reduction of the occlusion with the obstruction value. Otherwise, the obstruction path would have little appreciable impact in many situations, particularly in Figure 4.5 where the material was concrete.

4.4.3 Propagation

In the simple example of Figure 4.5, we would be able to provide a propagation position in addition to the occlusion and obstruction information, which would be the intersection of the two rays. However, a more general solution will require some more work.

```cpp
struct PathPoint
{
  Vector3 position;
  std::vector<PathPoint*> linkedPoints;
};


PropagationPathFinder
{
public:
  static std::vector<Vector3> FindPath(
    const Vector3& start, const Vector3& end);

private:
  static std::vector<PathPoint> pathPoints;
};

void ApplyObsOccAndPropagation(AkGameObjectID gameObjectID,
  const Vector3& soundPos, AkGameObjectID listenerID,
  const Vector3& listenerPos)
{
  // This value can be used from the previous example
  // on computing occlusion
  float totalOcclusion = ...;

  std::vector<Vector3> pathPoints =
    PropagationPathFinder::FindPath(soundPos, listenerPos);
  float totalPathLength = 0.f;
  for (int i = 0; i < pathPoints.size() - 1; ++i)
  {
    totalPathLength +=
      (pathPoints[i] - pathPoints[i + 1]).Length();
  }
  // Value between 0 and 100 for obstruction
  float totalObstruction =
    (1.f - ((soundPos - listenerPos).Length() /
    totalPathLength)) * 100.f;

  Vector3 positions[] =
    { soundPos, pathPoints[pathPoints.size() - 1] };
  AK::SoundEngine::SetMultiplePositions(
    gameObjectID, 2, positions);
```

```
Vector3 obsOccValues[2];
obsOccValues[0].occlusion = totalOcclusion;
obsOccValues[0].obstruction = 0.f;

obsOccValues[1].occlusion = 0.f;
obsOccValues[1].obstruction = totalObstruction;

AK::SoundEngine::SetMultipleObstructionAndOcclusion(
    gameObjectID, listenerID, obsOccValues, 2);
}
```

The implementation of the pathfinding algorithm and its associated data structures other than PathPoint are outside the scope of this chapter. The PathPoint would need to be predetermined before calling FindPath(), and would contain an entry for each of the path points in the world in addition to their link/visibility to other path points. Otherwise, the implementation details of FindPath() would be a standard A* implementation. In Figure 4.6, we can see a visual example of the path finding nodes. The algorithm could provide either of the two paths around the large square. The path points that are directly visible to each other would be linked neighbors.

Using the code provided higher combined with this example, we would have the propagation position at the door. With the Wwise API, we set up the emitter with multiple positions. The first position is the original location of the sound with the occlusion value applied and without any

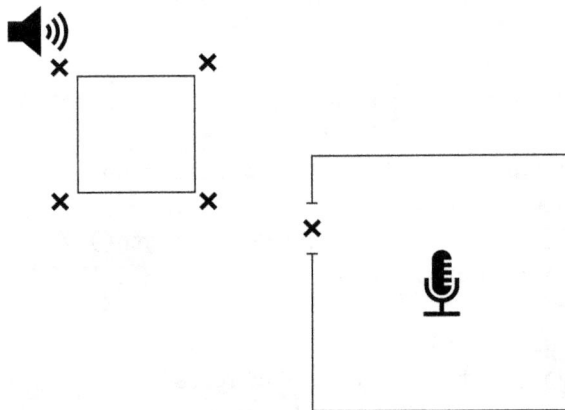

FIGURE 4.6   Propagation example with path nodes shown as crosses.

obstruction; the second position is the calculated propagation location configured with the obstruction value and no occlusion. This combination allows us to have the direct path at the original location with the propagated path being affected by the obstruction. The propagated position doesn't have any distance attenuation applied, but it could be added to the obstruction value or in another method.

The computed value for obstruction in this case is the direct path length divided by the propagated path length. This number doesn't translate to any direct real-world measurement – it is simply a preference.

4.4.4 Early Reflection and Reverb

Because of the complexity associated with both of these topics, it's difficult to provide a simple example similar to those provided for occlusion, obstruction, and propagation. There is a multitude of materials available on reverbs, their design, and their implementation. Several of the different middleware solutions discussed in this chapter provide an early reverb solution.

4.5 CONCLUSION

In this chapter we looked at different middleware solutions for realizing an acoustics model to aid immersion in the game world. We saw some usages of a few of the available middleware solutions and how to use some of their basic features. We explored some simple implementations of different acoustic phenomenon and discussed their limitations. With these tools in hand, implementing a full acoustics simulation with middleware, a custom solution, or a mix of the two should be a bit easier with the knowledge gained in this chapter.

REFERENCE

The Engineering Toolbox. 2008. "Sound Transmission through Massive Walls or Floors." *The Engineering Toolbox.* Accessed April 27, 2025. https://www. engineeringtoolbox.com/sound-transmission-massive-walls-d_1409.html

CHAPTER 5

Multilayered Dynamic Reverb

Colin Walder

5.1 INTRODUCTION

When attempting to immerse the player in the virtual worlds that we create, reverb is perhaps our most powerful tool for creating a sense of the space that the player is in. Providing a simulation or representation of the physical process of sounds reflecting off the surfaces surrounding a listener provides important information about the location of the sound through the balance of direct sound and reflected sound.

When a source is closer to the listener, the direct sound is more prominent since sound energy dissipates with distance. When the sound source is further away, the difference between direct and reflected source distances becomes smaller and the reflected sound is comparatively louder. Perhaps even the direct signal is obstructed, giving the listener information that the source is in the same or a connected space but hidden from lines of sight.

Beyond this balance, the reflected sound is also giving the listener a wealth of information about the shape, size, and geometric properties of the space. Each time a sound is reflected, it is affected by the surface it bounces off. These countless reflections then combine together to form the distinctive reverb character of a space. If we want to immerse the player, then it makes sense for us to use reverb to reinforce the impression and experience of the virtual space.

A straightforward (and traditional) approach is to assign a reverb effect to virtual spaces – probably set manually by a sound designer using area

 DOI: 10.1201/9781003519119-7

or volume shapes or triggers – which will then be applied to individual sounds with different amounts based on their position relative to the listener. It's a pretty effective system. We're supporting both the sense of position of the sound and the sense of space. We can perhaps get by with even just one reverb for the listener space if CPU power is limited and still get a lot of benefit. However, this system's granularity is limited. Players will feel the coarse changing of spaces as they move between rooms, and it's unlikely that the sound designers will have the time to craft out every nook and cranny, especially in the large worlds of contemporary games.

A natural progression, then, is to consider approaches of simulation for the reverb. Hardware capability has improved with successive generations, and it's now feasible to consider raycasting solutions, either as an offline or a runtime process. Using this type of system means that we can have reverb that matches very closely to the geometry of the virtual world. The reverb will support immersion into the game space with smooth and dynamic variation even as a player moves through a detailed environment. Plus, it's removing a lot of manual work from sound designers' hands, freeing them up to do creative work.

However, here we hit a snag. Part of that creative work is to choose which reverb to place in each space. They might choose something that matches the physical space, but they also might not. Subverting the game space with a reverb that doesn't support it might be a path to evoke emotions such as claustrophobia with a very close reverb or isolation by exaggerating the size. Either way the sound designer is almost certainly going to choose a reverb character that sounds good and in practice real spaces do not always sound acoustically good. If the sound designer wants to craft the sound of the reverb, perhaps they need to start setting up geometry with acoustic materials or otherwise manipulating the physical properties of the space. Given this discussion, this model turns out not to be such an improvement over the original workflow...if anything it got worse.

When we consider the often fantastical, hyper-realistic, or even alien environments that we create in games, we can start to question just how realistic we need to be? Or should we rather take a more cinematic approach, using reverb to both create a physical anchor and support the narrative.

The answer, of course, depends on the game you're making and even on your personal preference. When faced with these questions on Cyberpunk 2077, we decided we wanted to have something of both – which led to the development of our multilayered dynamic reverb.

5.2 LAYERED REVERB APPROACH

The central idea of our approach is to have several reverbs of different sizes layered on top of each other and then dynamically mix them based on the geometry around the player position (or, more precisely, the listener position). Each area in the game can be assigned a set of small, medium, and large reverbs which represent a different blend of acoustics in that space, along with the distances at which to crossfade between them. For example, there can be a large variance between the length of the large reverb from one area to another, but a small room is still going to have a short reverb tail in its large reverb. Of course, this isn't how real acoustics works, but the effect is that as the player moves around the level, they will hear bigger reverbs coming from directions where there is more space and smaller reverbs from directions that are more closed-in.

For directionality, we chose to use 4 horizontal directions of reverb, as shown in Figure 5.1. This is primarily a practical decision as it matches conveniently with the main 4-speaker square of a 5.0 setup and allows us to represent each layer with a standard reverb bus in Wwise that then has custom mixing applied to the speaker volumes to achieve the blending. There are some inherent performance advantages in being able to represent many different combinations of physical spaces with only three reverbs; it helps that by default the reverbs in Wwise premix the input signals and then output a multichannel signal for the sake of optimization. This was a feature that turned out to be important to us, especially on

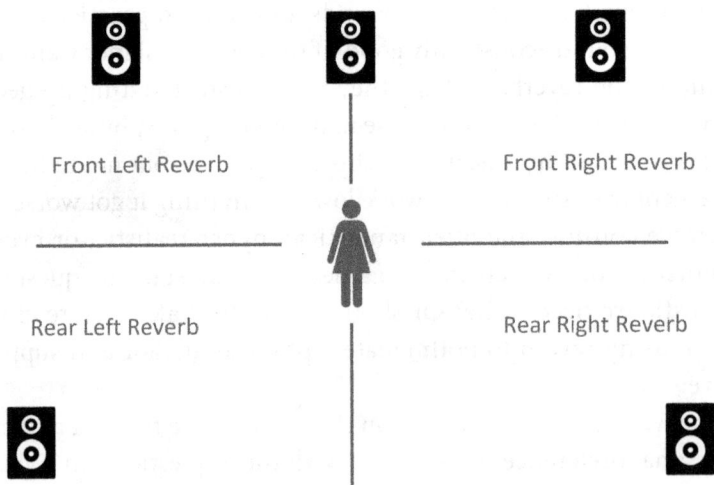

FIGURE 5.1   Reverb quadrants as they map to physical speakers in a 5.1 setup.

the PlayStation4 and Xbox One consoles, although it does mean that the directionality of the source is lost as part of the process. This loss isn't generally an issue, since the largely diffuse nature of reverb reduces the importance of direction, but there were some cases which required special handling because of that. We'll get to those later.

The sound designers have a lot of creative control here. They can select the reverb set from both algorithmic and convolution reverbs and tune those reverbs exactly as they traditionally have. The reverbs are then set on the same areas that the editor uses to trigger ambience, meaning they are mapped out in a way and with the kind of details that the sound designers are already thinking about for the spaces in the game. At the same time, the geometric detail of the level is being represented acoustically without any additional markup needed on the part of the sound designers.

In addition, as we were developing the game we found it made sense to provide multiple configurations of reverb. For example, in some spaces the sound designers would choose to only use two dynamic layers or even just to have a single static reverb in the traditional style. Which configuration to use is a purely aesthetic choice. We also provided options for a custom reverb layer for VO that would be used in place of the dynamic layers. It is important in our game that the VO is clear and understandable, so taking a more cinematic and simple approach made it easier to ensure the consistency and clarity of spoken lines. Similarly, for vehicles we wanted to have convolution reverb for the interiors of the cars, so this sits as an additional layer for those sounds in the car interior.

5.3 CREATING THE HEDGEHOG

In order to blend the reverbs directionally based on geometry, our first step is to build a picture of the geometry around the player. Since our reverb is listener-based, we chose to use a "hedgehog" of raycasts,[1] where raycasts are incrementally describing a sphere around the listener position. When approaching this system, we considered both runtime and offline approaches. Some of our acoustic systems were processed offline, such as the computation-heavy acoustic graph. In the case of reverb, though, we wanted a smooth blend of reverb layers as the player moves around the world. At the same time, we knew that the end result would be rather low resolution, since it effectively boils down to four directions of a latency-friendly signal. This low resolution gave us plenty of opportunities to simplify and optimize, making runtime the better option.

The first step in creating the hedgehog is to decide on the density of the raycasts. Since Cyberpunk is in the first person perspective, we put a priority on the density in the horizontal plane. When we think about how the player moves around and explores the world, the majority of navigation, geometry detail, and action will be happening in this plane. Even though Cyberpunk has been designed with a lot of verticality in the city, we still want to have some bias here. For some games, a single plane of horizontal raycasts might be enough. However, we do have those vertical spaces and wanted to have some feeling of changing acoustic between, for example, moving between a narrow tunnel and a narrow alley with an open ceiling. Notice how here the thinking is focused first on the experience of the player, rather than physical accuracy.

Following this principle, we settled on a horizontal density of 36 slices and a vertical density of 7 planes,[2,3] firing raycasts horizontally from the listener position every 10 degrees and then from those raycasts at elevations of ±20, 40, and 60 degrees. Figure 5.2 shows a visualization of how these rays are distributed.

In our implementation, while the center of the hedgehog follows the listener position, the raycast angles are decoupled from the listener rotation. We don't want the hedgehog results to change as the player moves the camera, only as they change position. I don't think that this is necessarily the only way to approach it, but for Cyberpunk our feeling was that it gave

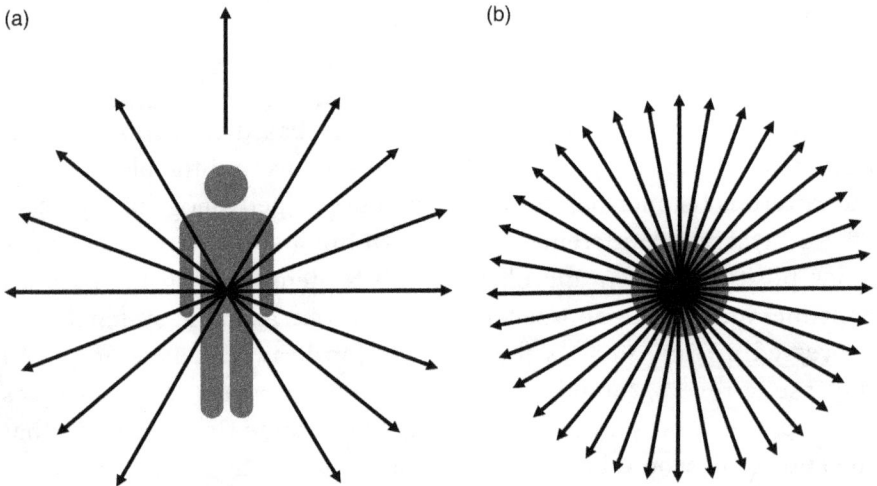

FIGURE 5.2   Representations of rays in the hedgehog. (a) Face-on cross-section. (b) Top-down cross-section.

more stability and consistency. When we think about the reverb, it makes more sense that it's a function of the position of geometry relative to the player. We could also argue that it helps with the latency of the raycasts, since when the player is stationary, the hedgehog will quickly stabilize and looking around won't result in any additional lag from changing results.

This describes our sphere but leaves notable blind spots directly up and down from the listener position. Directly down from the listener is not so important since our player will almost always be standing on something and any extreme edge cases can always be fixed manually (though to my knowledge we never had that situation). Upward, however, is rather more important since we really would like to feel the difference when the space opens up above us, and it is much more common than the counter case. Solving this problem is simple, of course: in addition to the sphere rays, we added one that fires directly up. It's an important enough case that we store this separately from the rest of the sphere so that it can be conveniently queried.

All in all, this gives us 253 raycasts to generate our hedgehog. This was too much for us to consider in a single frame on our launch platforms of PlayStation4 and Xbox One, so we processed one plane of the hedgehog plus the upward raycast every frame, giving us a grand total of 37 raycasts. In addition, the raycasts are performed async, so we may need to wait for a couple of frames before we have the result. When the game is running at 30 fps, this means we might have as much as 3 seconds of latency responding to changes in the geometry surrounding the player in the vertical direction. But since we update a full plane each frame, we still have some reaction horizontally much faster than that, and for the important vertical result, it will be as fast as reasonably possible. For us the audible result worked; it felt dynamic enough when mapped to the reverb.

```
void Hedgehog::Init()
{
  //Start at the bottom angle
  float verticalAngle =
    -1.f * k_verticalDirAngle * (k_numberOfPlanes - 1u) / 2;

  for( int i = 0; i < k_numPlanes; i++)
  {
    for( int j = 0; j < k_numSlices; j++)
    {
      Vector raycastVector = Vector::Forward();
      raycastVector.RotatePitch(
```

```
            verticalAngle + k_verticalAngle * i );
        raycastVector.RotateYaw( k_horizontalDirAngle * j );
        planes[i].slices[j] = raycastVector;
    }
  }
}

void Hedgehog::Tick( const Transform &origin )
{
  isEvenTick = !isEvenTick;

  ProcessRaycastResults();

  for( int j = 0; j < k_numSlices; j++ )
  {
    ScheduleAsyncRaycast(
      origin.Position(),
      origin.Position() + planes[currentPlane][j] );
  }

  ++currentPlane;

  Vector verticalStartPos =
    isEvenTick ?
      origin.Position :
      origin.Position + origin.Up() * 6.f;

  ScheduleAsyncRaycast(
    verticalStartPos,
    verticalStartPos + origin.Up() * raycastLength );
}
```

On more recent systems with more powerful CPUs, there would perhaps be less pressure for these kinds of optimizations. Another possibility is to perform these raycasts on the GPU, which would allow for orders of magnitude more detail but brings with it its own complexities, so it would be important to balance those against how much gain there would be.

After creating the hedgehog for our dynamic reverb, we then found it useful for other audio systems such as placing specific reflections and a rudimentary roof detection. We implemented the roof detection by alternating the standard upward raycast with a "far up" raycast that started from an offset 6 m higher. If the standard raycast hits geometry but the far up raycast doesn't, it means there is a sky-facing roof above the player. We even found the hedgehog useful for some gameplay systems such as detecting obstacles in front of the player. Coupling many such functionalities does introduce some complexity and requires some refactoring in order to make the system more broadly usable, but it can potentially save on duplicate raycasts. As part of extending the system, we added several helper function getters including:

- `GetPlaneRawResults()`/`GetPlaneRawDistances()`: Simple, but useful when you're only interested in floors or ceilings.

- `GetUpDistance()`: Knowing what's directly above the player can be handy.

- `GetHitDistance()`: Provide pitch and yaw angles and get the hedgehog distance. We also provided a helper to compute it from a world position.

- `GetFittingNeighbour()`: Provide pitch, yaw, and a `std::function<bool()>`.[4] Returns a neighboring result that satisfies the function if possible. Useful for detecting if there are flat surfaces in a given direction.

- `GetClosestDistance()`: Also available in forward, left, and right flavors.

The final thing to consider for the hedgehog is a special case for the orientation of "up". When the player was walking around the level, up was always the world-up as mentioned above. When the player was driving, we found that this setup didn't work as well. We had cases where the player would be driving up a steep road and the hedgehog would report blocking geometry in front of the player. That might be technically true, considering the position of the camera, but it doesn't really make sense in terms of the experience. So, when the player is driving, we instead rotate the hedgehog to align to player-up.

The function that we're most interested in for the dynamic reverb is `GetHitDistance()`. Because the orientations of our hedgehog and listener aren't tightly bound, we include some helper functions to find the closest aligned raycast results based on an input pitch and yaw, mapping from the "raycast hedgehog" to the "listener hedgehog". Potentially this could be done using interpolation, but for the reverb we found that it wasn't necessary.

```
uint GetSliceIndexForYaw( const float yaw )
{
  float normalizedAngle = yaw;
  while( normalizedAngle < 0.f )
  {
    normalizedAngle += 360.f;
  }
  return static_cast<uint>(
    Floor( normalizedAngle /
        k_horizontalDirAngle + 0.5f )) % k_numberOfSlices;
}

uint GetPlaneIndexForPitch( const float pitch )
{
  constexpr verticalAngOffset =
    -1.f * k_verticalDirAngle * ( k_numberOfPlanes - 1 ) / 2;
  const float normalizedAngle = pitch - verticalAngOffset;
  const int underflowIndex =
    static_cast<int>( Floor( (
      normalizedAngle / k_verticalDirAngle ) + 0.5f ) );
  return static_cast< uint >( Floor(
    normalizedAngle / k_horizontalDirAngle + 0.5f ) ) %
    k_numberOfSlices;
}

void GetHitDistance(
  const float pitch, const float yaw, float &distance )
{
  if( pitch > 90.f - k_verticalDirAngle * 0.5f )
  {
    distance = GetUpRaycastResult().distance;
  }

  distance =
    GetRaycastResult(GetSliceIndexForPitch(),
      GetSliceIndexForYaw() ).distance;
}
```

5.4 RESOLVING MEANINGFUL VALUES FROM THE HEDGEHOG

Now we have a picture of the geometry around the listener, we'll need to process it into some metrics that we can use to drive our reverb. Since we wanted to use 4-way directional reverb (both for convenience and effect… we'll get to that), we needed to resolve the sphere into quadrants.

For each vertical slice in the quadrant, we take a weighted average of the distances from each result in the slice, and then take a mean average of the results for all the slices in the quadrant. It is possible to specify the weights in the settings in case a sound designer wants to accentuate a particular vertical element in an environment, though in practice I don't believe we ever deviated from the default weightings of 0.05, 0.1, 0.15, 0.4, 0.15, 0.1, 0.05. We placed a strong bias on the results at and around the horizontal plane; while Night City is a world designed with vertical exploration in mind, the majority of traversal, focus, and navigation of the player is nevertheless in the horizontal plane. We wanted to build that into the experience from the audio side too. It's also the plane on which we have the most accurate positional audio representation, both from the point of view of humans having better horizontal auditory localization, and the likelihood that speakers or headphones will be physically positioned in this plane. By itself that might not be a particularly strong case to go in this direction, but it might provide some support and strengthen the experience.

```
float CalculateReverbFactorForChannel(
  ReverbQuadrant quadrant, ReverbSize reverbSize)
{
  float reverbFactor = 0.f;
  uint sliceCount = 0;

  for ( int i = 0; i < k_numReverbDir; i++ )
  {
    for ( int j = 0; j < k_numVerticalReverbDir; j++ )
    {
      if ( IndexIsInQuadrant( i, quadrant )
      {
        float distance = GetDistanceFromHedgehog( i, j );
        reverbFactor +=
          CalculateDistanceXFade( distance, reverbSize ) *
            settings.verticalWeightings[j];
        if ( i == 0 ) sliceCount++;
```

```
        }
      }
   }

   if ( sliceCount != 0 )
   {
      reverbFactor /= sliceCount;
   }

   return reverbFactor;
}
```

Now that we have the resolved distances for our four reverb quadrants (front left, front right, rear left, rear right), we need to map this to a reverb factor for each of our small, medium, and large reverbs. To help with this, we use a three-section crossfade utility class. The crossfade is initialized with two crossover distances, provided by the reverb settings on the area, which denote the transition points from small to medium reverbs and from medium to large. Each crossover point is paired with a fade value that gives the distance over which to perform a linear crossfade.

```
float CalculateXFade(
   Point point1, Point point2, float xVal )
{
   if( x >= point2.x ) return point2.y;
   if( x <= point1.x ) return point1.y;

   return point1.y +
      (point2.y - point1.y) * (xVal - point1.x) /
         (point2.x - point1.x);
}

float CalculateDistanceXFade(
   float distance, ReverbSize reverbSize )
{
   float x1 = settings.crossoverPoint1;
   float x2 = settings.crossoverPoint2;
   float fade1 = settings.crossFade1;
   float fade2 = settings.crossFade2;

   switch( reverbSize )
```

```
{
case ReverbSize::Small:
  return CalculateXFade(
    { x1, 1.f }, { x1 + fade1, 0.f }, distance );
case ReverbSize::Medium:
  return distance <= x2 ?
    CalculateXFade(
      { x1, 0.f }, { x1 + fade1, 1.f }, distance ) :
    CalculateXFade(
      { x2, 1.f }, { x2 + fade2, 0.f ), distance );
case ReverbSize::Large:
default:
  return CalculateXFade(
    { x2, 0.f }, { x2 + fade2, 1.f }, distance );
}
```

5.5 MIXING THE LAYERS IN WWISE

Now we have the dynamic values that we will use to drive our reverbs, but before we can apply them in Wwise, we need to connect our sounds to the appropriate reverbs using game object aux send values. Which reverbs we want to use will be determined by our reverb settings, so when we move into a trigger volume, we call our `ApplySettings()` function with the name of the new settings and a transition time. Here we store the current settings as the transition settings, set the current settings to the new settings, and reset the transition timer. We also register our callbacks to the reverb buses in Wwise at this point, but we'll come back to that later.

Transitions between settings is something that we added in an iteration after it became apparent that the changes in reverb when the listener moved between very different areas were too abrupt. There is a potential problem in the current code that it's not handling the case where a transition to new reverb settings happens while a transition is currently in progress. For Cyberpunk, we agreed with the sound designers that the transitions would be short enough (transition times can be adjusted by the sound designer on the Trigger Volume) that in practice it should not be an issue, and indeed we never came up against it.

With the settings applied, we can now apply the reverb to our sound game objects as part of our update each frame. Here we will first select the type of reverb to apply; let's look first at the full `Dynamic` type.

For each reverb we want to apply to the object, we need to fill out an `AkAuxSendValue` struct and apply it using `AK::SoundEngine::SetGameObjectAuxSendValues()`:

```
AkAuxSendValue auxVal;
//We want to use the default listener
auxVal.listenerID = AK_INVALID_GAME_OBJECT;
//The id we resolve from our settings
auxVal.auxBusID = reverbBusId;
//Per-object attenuation
auxVal.fControlValue = reverbLevel;

AK::SoundEngine::SetGameObjectAuxSendValues(
  soundGameObjectID, &auxVal, 1);
```

For the `reverbBusID`, we have the name of the bus in the settings (this is the same name that the bus has set in Wwise), and then have a lookup where we've mapped the name to ID. If you don't have a pipeline in place to store the IDs, then you can also compute the ID at runtime by forcing the name to lowercase and running an FNV hash on it. In general, I think it's worthwhile to store a map for IDs and other data from Wwise, as it's useful in various circumstances on top of saving a small amount of CPU.

The `reverbLevel` is an attenuation value that we'll use to perform per-object adjustments to the reverb. Importantly this is *not* the reverb factor that we resolved from the hedgehog; we'll use that later. The two cases that we do use it for are for fixing a problem that arises with having a globally applied small reverb, and for handling the transitions between settings.

Because small reverb is typically a lot less diffuse than the longer reverbs and will be present when the player is very close to geometry, we can have situations where a sound that is relatively distant to the player originating from a space on one side of the player will be distinctly audible in the small reverb from a wall on the other side of the player. This doesn't sound right and can be confusing. If the sound is close to the player, the effect is actually quite nice. For the medium and large reverbs, the sound is diffuse and coming from spaces in the environment, so they don't suffer from the same issue. The answer that we came up with was to set a max distance with a fade for sounds to contribute to the small reverb.

For transitions, we found that the issue only really manifested in medium and large reverbs; small reverbs don't manifest any transitioning issues due to their short duration and the fact that they are only used at close distances. For the medium and large reverbs, then, we apply a fade out over time. We don't want to fade in the new settings; they should be fully applied as soon as we enter the new space. We could track which sounds were playing in the old space and not apply the transition reverb to new sounds, but we're not doing anything so involved. Our aim here is to finesse away any audible discontinuity. If it sounds good, that's okay even if it doesn't make perfect logical sense.

Taking those things into account, we will set 5 aux send values per object: 3 for the current reverb settings and 2 for the transitions. It looks something like this:

```
void SetDynamicReverb( const SoundObject* soundObject )
{
  float distanceFromListener =
    soundObject->GetDistanceFromListener();
  float smallReverbMaxDistance =
    reverbSettings->smallRevMaxDist;
  float smallReverbFade = reverbSettings->smallReverbFade;

  float transitionValue =
    transitionTime > 0.0 ?
      currentTransitionDuration / transitionTime : 1.0;

  float smallReverbSendValue = 1.0;
  if( distanceFromListener > smallReverbMaxDistance )
  {
    smallReverbSendValue = 0.0;
  }
  else if( distanceFromListener >= smallReverbFadeThreshold )
  {
    smallReverbSendValue =
      ( ( smallReverbMaxDistance - distanceFromListener ) /
      smallReverbMaxDistance ) /
      ( smallReverbFade / smallReverbMaxDistance );
  }

  static const int numReverbSends = 5;
  AkAuxSendValue auxVals[numReverbSends];

  //Small reverb
```

```
auxVals[0].listenerID = AK_INVALID_GAME_OBJECT;
auxVals[0].auxBusID = GetBusID( settings->smallReverb);
auxVals[0].fControlValue = smallReverbSendValue;

//Medium Reverb
auxVals[1].listenerID = AK_INVALID_GAME_OBJECT;
auxVals[1].auxBusID = GetBusID( settings->mediumReverb);
auxVals[1].fControlValue = 1.0;

//Large Reverb
auxVals[2].listenerID = AK_INVALID_GAME_OBJECT;
auxVals[2].auxBusID = GetBusID( settings->largeReverb);
auxVals[2].fControlValue = 1.0;

//Transitions
if ( transitionSettings && transitionValue < 1.f )
{
  //Medium Reverb
  auxVals[ 3 ].listenerID = AK_INVALID_GAME_OBJECT;
  auxVals[ 3 ].auxBusID =
    GetBusId( transitionSettings->mediumReverb );
  auxVals[ 3 ].fControlValue = 1.f - transitionValue;

  //Large Reverb
  auxVals[ 4 ].listenerID = AK_INVALID_GAME_OBJECT;
  auxVals[ 4 ].auxBusID =
    GetBusId( transitionSettings->largeReverb );
  auxVals[ 4 ].fControlValue = 1.f - transitionValue;
}
else
{
  //Medium Reverb
  auxVals[ 3 ].listenerID = AK_INVALID_GAME_OBJECT;
  auxVals[ 3 ].auxBusID = AK_INVALID_AUX_ID;
  auxVals[ 3 ].fControlValue = 0.f;

  //Large Reverb
  auxVals[ 4 ].listenerID = AK_INVALID_GAME_OBJECT;
  auxVals[ 4 ].auxBusID = AK_INVALID_AUX_ID;
  auxVals[ 4 ].fControlValue = 0.f;
}
```

```
AK::SoundEngine::SetGameObjectAuxSendValues(
  soundObject->GetWwiseGameObjectID(),
  auxVals.numReverbSends);
}
```

The transition time, of course, needs to be updated in the tick and reset to 0.0 when it's completed.

In addition to Dynamic reverb mode, we offer alternatives that can be selected on the settings:

- StaticSingle: Use only the small reverb layer with none of the dynamic features; the classic reverb effect, and still quite useful.

- EnvironmentSmallStaticMedium: Use the small reverb layer dynamically and the medium reverb layer without any dynamic features. This setting allows the Sound Designer to have a very controlled overall reverb for a space, but still retains some of the dynamic feeling when close to a wall etc.

- VO: An additional reverb that can be specified on the settings. If the soundObject has been marked as VO and there is a VO reverb available, this will be set as a static reverb overriding the other reverb settings for this object.

- Vehicle: A reverb that comes from our current vehicle rather than the location-based reverb settings, and which can override those settings. This configuration is typically used when we are inside a car with a first-person camera.

It's worth noting that there's nothing specifically forcing any particular layer to have a given length of reverb. For example, it would be fine in StaticSingle mode to have a reverb with a long tail even though it's using the small reverb layer.

Now that our game objects are connected to the aux sends, we can set up our reverb in the Wwise Authoring Tool. The first step is to create a bus as normal with the reverb effect of your choice on it; the type of reverb (or indeed any other effect) here is purely a creative choice. To make our handling of the callback easier, we set the *Bus Configuration* to 5.1 and do the same on the direct parent bus – in our case a *Reverbs* bus which is parent to all our reverbs. Setting the configuration this way ensures that we'll have our 4 quadrant speakers available to use and we won't have to write any handling of different output formats. You don't need to worry about the final output; Wwise will handle the mixdown through the parent buses as usual. You may find it convenient to organize your buses in folders that mirror how the reverbs are defined in the settings. For example, for settings using the full Dynamic approach, a small, medium, and large reverb in one folder.

Next, we need to set our sounds in the Actor Mixer Hierarchy to use the sends that we've specified in our code by selecting *Use game-defined aux sends*. We can apply a volume adjustment here to mix the reverb levels by sound category, and even control that with an RTPC if we want to mix it dynamically for creative reasons. You can also choose to have some sounds not use the dynamic reverb by simply not checking this box, and indeed we took this selective approach in Cyberpunk 2077.

At this point we will have our sounds being sent to the appropriate reverb buses in-game, but we haven't yet applied the results from the hedgehog, so we will have all the layers in all directions. The final step in implementing our dynamic reverb is to manually control the reverb levels per channel using a bus mixer callback.

In the callback we will set the level of the 4 quadrant channels to the reverb factors that we computed earlier from the hedgehog:

```
static Uint32 s_speakerSetup[ 4 ] =
  { AK_SPEAKER_FRONT_LEFT, AK_SPEAKER_FRONT_RIGHT,
    AK_SPEAKER_BACK_LEFT, AK_SPEAKER_BACK_RIGHT };

static void ReverbBusCallback(
  AkSpeakerVolumeMatrixCallbackInfo* callbackInfo,
  ReverbSize reverbSize )
{
  //First check that our buses have been set up correctly
  if( callbackInfo->inputConfig !=
      callbackInfo->outputConfig )
  {
    return;
  }
  if( callbackInfo->inputConfig.uChannelMask !=
      AK_SPEAKER_SETUP_5_1 )
  {
    return;
  }
```

```cpp
//Clean out the speaker volumes so we don't have anything
//leak through on channels we don't want
AK::SpeakerVolumes::Matrix::Zero(
  callbackInfo->pVolumes,
  callbackInfo->inputConfig.uNumChannels,
  callbackInfo->outputConfig.uNumChannels );

//Apply the distance based reverb factors
for( uint32 chanOut : s_speakerSetup )
{
  AkUInt8 outChanIndex =
    AK::ChannelBitToIndex( chanOut, AK_SPEAKER_SETUP_5_1 );
  AK::SpeakerVolumes::VectorPtr vMixOut =
    AK::SpeakerVolumes::Matrix::GetChannel(
      callbackInfo->pVolumes, outChanIndex,
      in_pCallbackInfo->outputConfig.uNumChannels );

  if( chanOut == AK_SPEAKER_FRONT_LEFT )
  {
    vMixOut[ ConvertWwiseSpeakerFlagToChannelIndex(
      AK_SPEAKER_SETUP_5_1, AK_SPEAKER_FRONT_LEFT ) ] =
        GetReverbFactor( reverbType,
          ConvertWwiseSpeakerFlagToReverbChannel(
            AK_SPEAKER_FRONT_LEFT ) );
  }
  else if( chanOut == AK_SPEAKER_FRONT_RIGHT )
  {
    vMixOut[ ConvertWwiseSpeakerFlagToChannelIndex(
      AK_SPEAKER_SETUP_5_1, AK_SPEAKER_FRONT_RIGHT ) ] =
        GetReverbFactor( reverbType,
          ConvertWwiseSpeakerFlagToReverbChannel(
            AK_SPEAKER_FRONT_RIGHT ) );
  }
  else if( chanOut == AK_SPEAKER_BACK_LEFT )
  {
    vMixOut[ ConvertWwiseSpeakerFlagToChannelIndex(
      AK_SPEAKER_SETUP_5_1, AK_SPEAKER_BACK_LEFT ) ] =
        GetReverbFactor( reverbType,
          ConvertWwiseSpeakerFlagToReverbChannel(
            AK_SPEAKER_BACK_LEFT ) );
  }
```

```
    else if( chanOut == AK_SPEAKER_BACK_RIGHT )
    {
      vMixOut[ ConvertWwiseSpeakerFlagToChannelIndex(
        AK_SPEAKER_SETUP_5_1, AK_SPEAKER_BACK_RIGHT ) ] =
          GetReverbFactor( reverbType,
            ConvertWwiseSpeakerFlagToReverbChannel(
              AK_SPEAKER_BACK_RIGHT ) );
    }
  }
}
```

You'll notice the helper function to convert from Wwise's speaker flags to the channel index. Here it is for convenience:

```
int32 ConvertWwiseSpeakerFlagToChannelIndex(
  int32 speakerConfig, int32 speakerFlag )
{
  if( speakerConfig == AK_SPEAKER_SETUP_5_1 )
  {
    switch( speakerFlag )
    {
      case AK_SPEAKER_FRONT_LEFT:
        return 0;
      case AK_SPEAKER_FRONT_RIGHT:
        return 1;
      case AK_SPEAKER_FRONT_CENTER:
        return 2;
      case AK_SPEAKER_BACK_LEFT:
        return 3;
      case AK_SPEAKER_BACK_RIGHT:
        return 4;
      case AK_SPEAKER_LOW_FREQUENCY:
        return 5;
      default:
        break;
    }
  }

  return -1;
}
```

All we need now is to register the callbacks with Wwise:

```
void RegisterBusCallbacks_Dynamic(
  const ReverbSettings* reverbSettings )
{
  AK::SoundEngine::RegisterBusVolumeCallback(
    GetBusId( reverbSettings->largeReverb ),
    []( AkSpeakerVolumeMatrixCallbackInfo* info ) {
      ReverbBusCallback( info, ReverbSize::LargeReverb );
    } );

  AK::SoundEngine::RegisterBusVolumeCallback(
    GetBusId( reverbSettings->mediumReverb ),
    []( AkSpeakerVolumeMatrixCallbackInfo* info ) {
      ReverbBusCallback( info, ReverbSize::MediumReverb );
    } );

  AK::SoundEngine::RegisterBusVolumeCallback(
    GetBusId( reverbSettings->smallReverb ),
    []( AkSpeakerVolumeMatrixCallbackInfo* info ) {
      ReverbBusCallback( info, ReverbSize::SmallReverb );
    } );
}
```

And with that, our multilayered dynamic reverb is complete. Huzzah!

5.6 CONCLUSION

The effect provided by the multilayer dynamic reverb worked well for us in Cyberpunk 2077 given our desire to aim for a combination of grounded and interactive with artistic and cinematic style. One of the motivations was optimization of CPU load, but even as we have more power available in newer generations of consoles and PC, the combination of creative control and dynamic feel is something that still holds up. With the capabilities of newer hardware, it will be interesting to see how to take the system further while still maintaining that balance.

One approach we developed was a source reverb version of the system, but we had to drop due to it being too heavy on the CPU. In this extension multiple layers of reverb were used in a similar way, but by disabling the optimization where reverb is applied to a downmix of the source input, it was possible to mix a different amount of each source per quadrant. We calculated the contribution to the different layers of reverb based on the ambient volume that the sound source was in and even added some contributions to the reverb based on the spaces that the sound traversed through our acoustics graph. This caused a multiplication of convolution processes from 4 to 16 (i.e. one per layer, per channel), which proved too much.

I think it was an interesting idea, and on modern platforms it is probably not a prohibitive amount of reverb processing, especially where there is hardware acceleration available. That said, given the extra resources available, I'm not convinced this is the way to go for that kind of effect, but it is definitely something that requires more exploration.

One final note: the multilayered dynamic reverb is only one piece of the puzzle when it comes to acoustics. It's definitely nice to supplement it with echo style reflections, and given its nature I think it can blend nicely with a variety of other approaches in order to craft interesting and dynamic sounds.

Thanks and kudos to the CD PROJEKT RED Audio Code team and Sound Designers who worked on bringing the multichannel dynamic reverb to life and implementing it into Cyberpunk 2077.

NOTES

1. So called because hedgehogs have spines that point out in all directions.
2. Despite calling them planes, in reality they're cones. We'll keep the original naming, though, for posterity.
3. It's conic sections! A cone intersecting a plane creates a circle. Your nomenclature works, Col. Own it! –Ed
4. If you're using C++26, the standard library includes `std::function_ref`, which can be more efficient in this context. Game engines may include equivalent functionality – for example, Unreal Engine has `TFunctionRef`. –Ed

CHAPTER 6

Creating Impulse Responses for Virtual Environments

Guy Somberg

6.1 INTRODUCTION

One of the challenges with convolution reverb is finding good impulse responses. You can purchase them or record your own, but it can also be desirable to model the game's virtual world in your reverb. As discussed in Chapter 5, you may want to intentionally subvert the game environment for artistic purposes, but if you do want to capture the actual game environment, then you will have to generate an impulse response.

What this chapter will do, therefore, is go through a process of creating an impulse response from the game world that is in the correct format for use in a game. We will make certain assumptions about the capabilities of your environment and game engine – specifically around ray casts and metadata – and we'll be using FMOD Studio as the audio middleware of choice. Many of the code examples have techniques that are specific to FMOD, but most other audio middleware will have similar functionality, even if it is spelled differently.

6.2 A BRIEF INTRODUCTION TO IMPULSE RESPONSES AND CONVOLUTION

The background for this chapter will require understanding only a few components of convolution reverb implementation. You can think of a convolution reverb as a DSP that plays time-delayed volume-reduced

DOI: 10.1201/9781003519119-8

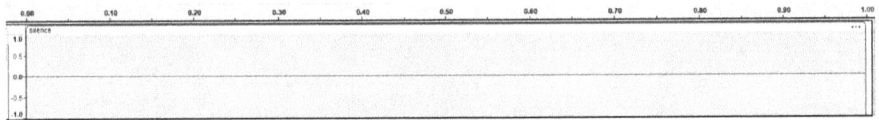

FIGURE 6.1 A silent waveform.

copies of the input signal. A naïve implementation of a convolution reverb would literally just be a collection of delay lines – it would be spectacularly inefficient, but it would be technically correct.

6.2.1 Impulse Response Files

The input signal to a convolution reverb DSP is called an Impulse Response (IR). It is typically a wav file that has been recorded in an actual environment, then deconvolved to remove the original signal. Let's look at a few examples of IR waveforms.

- **Silence** (Figure 6.1): A waveform that has no audio data will therefore generate no repeated signal. The end result of the convolution DSP will itself be silence.

- **Single Sample** (Figure 6.2): This is a file that is silent for a short period, then contains a single sample of full volume,[1] then goes back to silence. If you were to play this wav file on its own, it would sound like silence, followed by a pop, followed by more silence. However, when used as the input impulse response file for a convolution reverb, this will have the effect of repeating the input signal at full volume with a delay.

- **Recorded Impulse Response** (Figure 6.3): Finally we have a real IR file that has been recorded in a real environment. Playing this wav file would sound like the echo in a room of an initial pop. Each sample in this IR represents a time-delayed and volume-adjusted repetition of the input signal – in other words, the signal that has bounced around the environment and come back to the microphone. Using this IR file will sound as though the input were in the same environment that the IR was recorded.

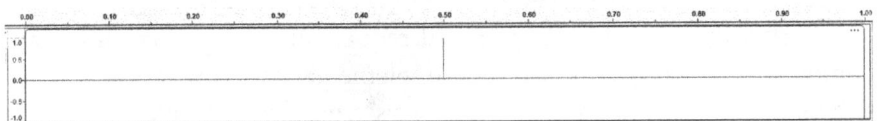

FIGURE 6.2 A waveform with a single nonzero sample.

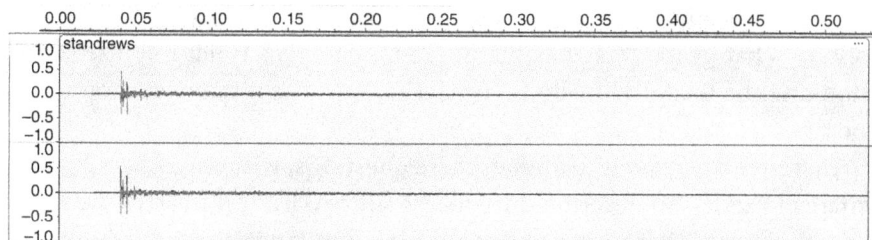

FIGURE 6.3   The waveform of a recorded impulse response.

6.2.2 How Impulse Responses Are Recorded

The general process for generating an impulse response is to bring a microphone into a space, then fire off a short impulse such as a balloon pop, hand clap, book slamming, or something along those lines. The impulse should be short, and should have as many input frequencies as possible so that the resulting impulse response can include as much aural information as possible. The resulting sound is recorded by the microphone, and then needs to be run through special software called a deconvolver. The deconvolver removes the original input signal and leaves you with just the response from the environment.

An alternative method involves playing a "sine sweep". This is a pure tone sine wave that sweeps over a short period from extremely low frequencies up through extremely high frequencies. That allows each frequency to travel through the environment independently, and guarantees that all frequencies are included in the resulting IR. Once again, special deconvolution software that understands the input signal and the way it was used can both remove the input signal and align the resulting response data into an IR that can be used as the input to a convolution reverb.

6.2.3 Virtual Environment IR Overview

In order to generate an IR for our virtual environment, we need to go through the same steps as recording an IR in real life:

- Set up a "microphone" at the attenuation position.

- Trigger a short impulse that contains aural data in as many frequencies as possible.

- Record the sound of the impulse bouncing around the room.

This list is a fine summary, but it's not really an algorithm that we can follow. What properties does the microphone have? What impulse sound should we be using? How do we track the sound as it bounces around the room?

There are many ways to answer these questions, with a number of mathematical models to describe the process. In real life, an impulse becomes a pressure wave that moves out in all directions from its source. There are mathematical models for describing how the waves travel through space, bounce off of surfaces, etc., but they are very expensive both in processing power and memory.

The alternative to wave simulation is by using raycasts: throw out a huge number of rays, bounce them around the environment, then see which ones return. In the limit, the raycasting model encodes almost all of the same information[2] as the wave modeling.[3] The paper "Computing Impulse Response of Room Acoustics Using the Ray-Tracing Method in Time Domain" by Adil Alpkocak and Malik Kemal Sis (Alpkocak and Sis 2010) walks through the actual mathematics of how this system works. In short, their system bounces rays around the environment, but presumes that each ray encodes a Dirac impulse containing every frequency. They then provide rules for how to combine Dirac impulses in both the time and frequency domains. In this chapter, we'll be modeling our code on the principles in their research paper.

6.3 ORGANIZATION OF THIS CHAPTER

It turns out that there are an inordinate number of seemingly unrelated pieces of knowledge and background that are important to the process of creating impulse responses. That makes it difficult to organize this chapter, simply because the path to getting enough put together to make it all work is so nonlinear.

I have decided to embrace the nonlinearity and present the background knowledge in a context-free manner. We'll learn about various foundational pieces of technology or mathematics or code, then move on to an unrelated piece. At some point, the pieces will start to build on each other until we're putting it all together to create an impulse response that can be used by FMOD's convolution reverb DSP.

6.4 FOUNDATIONS

This section contains the leaf nodes of our process. This is where we'll see content that does not build on anything else in the chapter.

6.4.1 Speed of Sound

Sound travels at a fast but finite speed. We have all experienced the disconnect between what we see and what we hear when we observe an event happening at a distance and then hear the sound a short time later. At short distances, the delay between seeing and hearing is short enough that we can perceive them to be instantaneous, but the further a sound has to travel, the more delay it introduces.

This delay is particularly important for impulse responses because the initial impulse travels through the environment and only comes back to the microphone after a delay. The standard value that is typically used for the speed of sound is 343 m/s, although the actual speed is affected by temperature, humidity, and other factors (Wikimedia Foundation 2024c). Whether or not you include these parameters in your speed calculations is up to you, but for this chapter we'll go ahead and stick with the standard value of 343 m/s:

```
constexpr float GetDelaySeconds(float DistanceMeters)
{
    constexpr float SpeedOfSoundMetersPerSecond = 343.0f;
    return DistanceMeters / SpeedOfSoundMetersPerSecond;
}
```

6.4.2 Attenuation over Distance

If we consider a sound as a point source, it travels outward from the origin in an expanding wave. The total energy of the sound was fixed at the moment that the sound was generated, so as it travels and occupies more and more space, it must lose energy. You can think of the sound as a sphere that grows outward. The total energy of the sphere is in effect the surface of the sphere, but as the sphere gets larger, the same amount of energy gets distributed over a larger surface area.

The surface area of a sphere is calculated by $S = 4\pi r^2$, so we expect the volume to attenuate by the square of the distance, which is exactly the Inverse Square Law. In practice, we're interested in the sound pressure level in decibels, so we can use a logarithmic formula (The Engineering ToolBox 2005) to calculate the attenuation. To apply the formula, we measure the sound pressure level at a fixed distance, and then calculate the difference in pressure level at a second distance. Ideally, we'd measure the level at zero distance, but we end up with a singularity if we do that, so we select a distance which we'll call the minimum distance and presume that the sound is at full volume within that distance. Furthermore, we can assume that the measured level at the minimum distance is 0 dB, since we are interested in the reduction in volume over the distance.

Putting all of that together, we get the following:

```
constexpr float GetDistanceAttenuationdB(
  float DistanceMeters)
{
  constexpr float MinDistance = 1.0f;
  if (DistanceMeters <= MinDistance)
    return 0.0f;
  return log2f(DistanceMeters / MinDistance) * -6.0f;
}
```

6.4.3 Atmospheric Absorption

As sound travels through the air, it doesn't just attenuate in volume. The air itself also absorbs different frequencies at varying levels, depending on the temperature, atmospheric pressure, and humidity of the air. A hot and dry climate will absorb a different set of frequencies at different levels than a cold and wet environment.

For an in-depth discussion on how this works in a game context, see Taylor (2021). For the purposes of this chapter, we will presume that we have access to the `FilterCutoffSolver` class described in that chapter.

6.4.4 Distributing Points on a Sphere

Changing gears a little bit, we now want to answer the following mathematical question: given a value N, how do we distribute N points evenly around a sphere? In practice, we will end up using these as vectors from the center of the sphere to each point, but we want the points to be as evenly distributed around the sphere as possible.

The canonical way of solving this problem is using a construct called the Fibonacci Lattice (Roberts 2020), which evenly distributes points in a square, then map that distribution to a unit sphere. The Fibonacci Lattice moves evenly up the Y axis, and uses modular arithmetic to create an even distribution of points along the X axis. Figure 6.4 shows a Fibonacci lattice at various point counts. The formula for the lattice is:

$$P_i = \left(\left(\frac{i}{\phi} \right) \bmod 1, \frac{i}{n} \right) \text{ for } 0 \le i < N$$

(a)   (b)   (c)

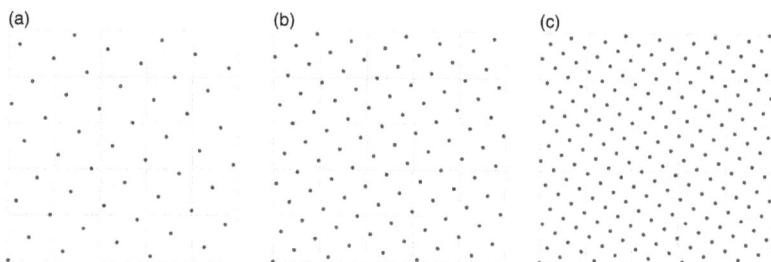

FIGURE 6.4   Fibonacci Lattices at various point counts. (a) 50 points. (b) 100 points. (c) 200 points.

Where ϕ is the "Golden Ratio", or $\frac{1+\sqrt{5}}{2}$. This value is available in C++ as std::numbers::phi if you need it as a double, or you can specify the type as in std::numbers::phi_v<float>. We can then convert this point from the unit square to the unit circle by first converting to spherical coordinates and then back to Cartesian coordinates. Figure 6.5 shows the resulting

(a)

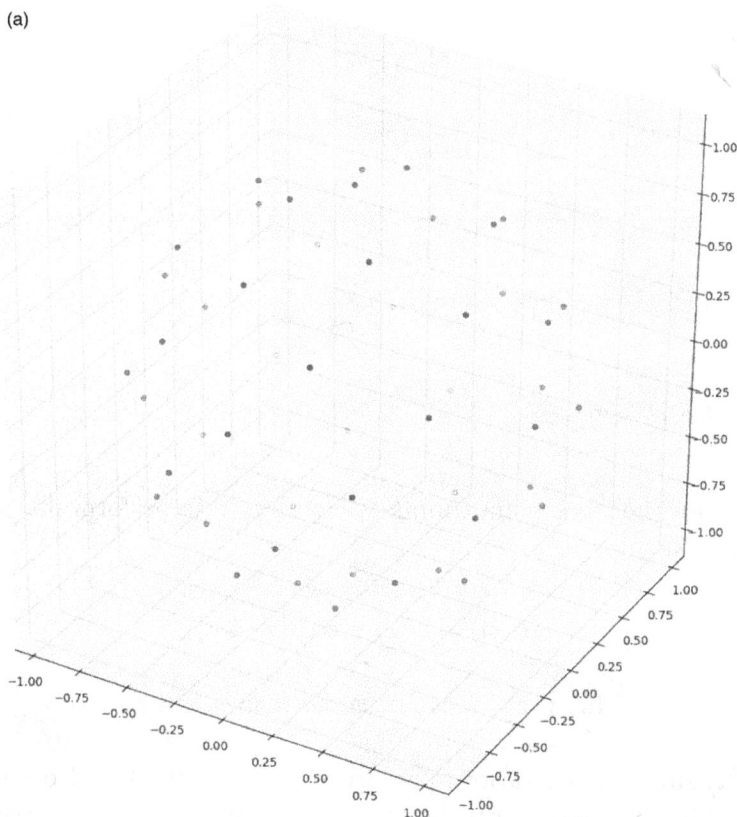

FIGURE 6.5   Fibonacci Lattices projected onto the unit sphere at various point counts. (a) 50 points. (b) 100 points. (c) 200 points. (*Continued*)

(b)

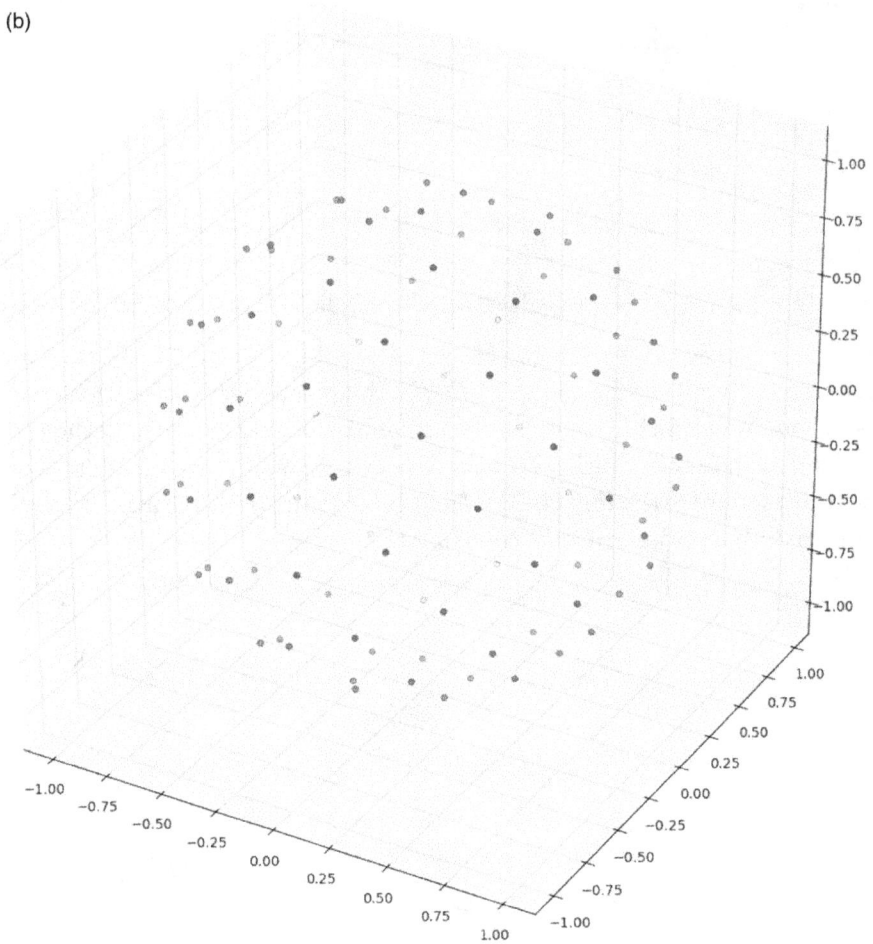

FIGURE 6.5 *(Continued)*

spheres for the same point counts as Figure 6.4. To perform the conversion, we use this math:

$$(\theta, \varphi) = \left(2\pi x, \ \arccos(1-2y)\right)$$

$$(x, y, z) = (\cos\theta \sin\varphi, \ \sin\theta \sin\varphi, \ \cos\varphi)$$

By examining the various properties of the outputs and optimizing for packing, the results can be improved for the sphere with relatively

(c)

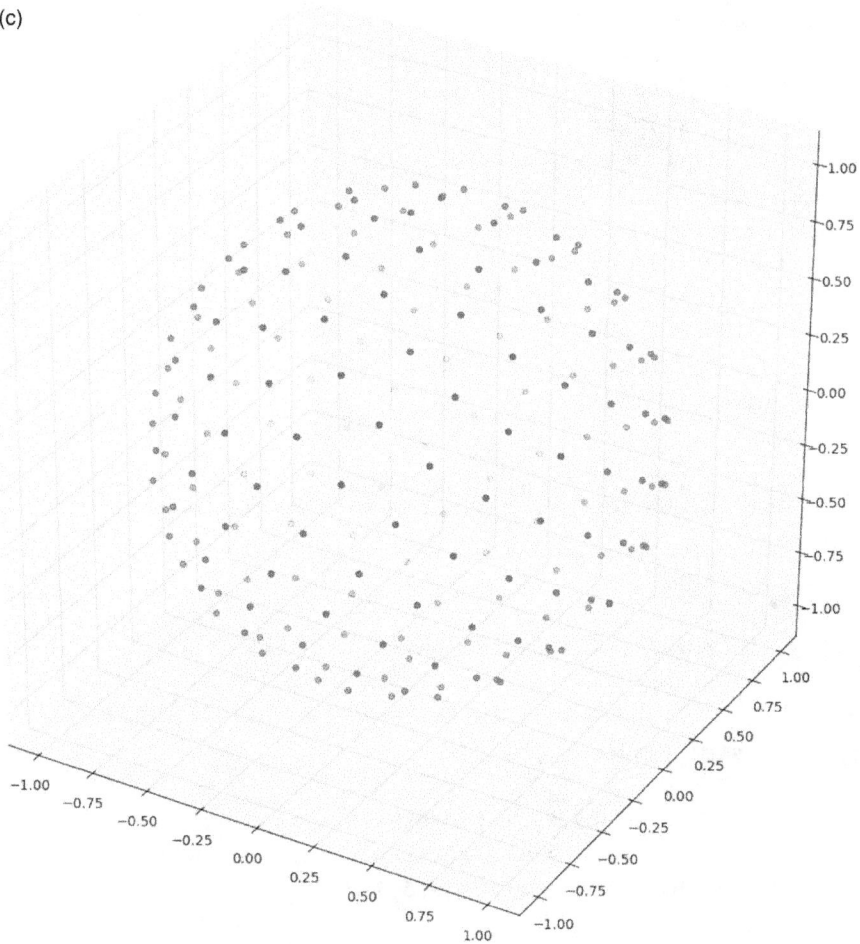

FIGURE 6.5 *(Continued)*

simple changes. The details of that are outside the scope of this chapter, but Roberts (2020) goes into much more detail on deriving it. This code is adapted to C++ from the Python code in Roberts (2020).

```
std::vector<Vector3> ArrangeVectors(unsigned int Count)
{
    std::vector<Vector3> ReturnValue;
    ReturnValue.reserve(Count);

    float Epsilon;
```

```
if (Count >= 600'000) {
  Epsilon = 214.0f;
} else if (Count >= 400'000) {
  Epsilon = 75.0f;
} else if (Count >= 11'000) {
  Epsilon = 27.0f;
} else if (Count >= 890) {
  Epsilon = 10.0f;
} else if (Count >= 177) {
  Epsilon = 3.33f;
} else if (Count >= 24) {
  Epsilon = 1.33f;
} else {
  Epsilon = 0.33f;
}

for (unsigned int i=0; i<Count; i++)
{
  auto IndexFloat = static_cast<float>(i);
  auto Theta =
    (2.0f * IndexFloat * std::numbers::pi_v<float>) /
      std::numbers::phi_v<float>;
  auto Phi =
    acosf(1.0f - 2.0f * (IndexFloat + Epsilon) /
          (Count - 1 + 2.0f * Epsilon));
  // Note here for section 6.5.7.

  auto SinPhi = sinf(Phi);
  ReturnValue.push_back(
    { cosf(Theta) * SinPhi, sinf(Theta) * SinPhi,
      cosf(Phi) });
}
return ReturnValue;
}
```

There is one improvement that we can make here, if we can guarantee that the Count is known at compile time. Instead of passing it in as a regular parameter, we can pass it in as either a non-type template parameter (template<unsigned int Count>) or as a constexpr global variable. If that is the case, then the chain of if() {} else if {} else {} at the top of the function can be converted to if constexpr() {} else if constexpr {} else {}, and do the selection of the Epsilon value at compile time.

6.4.5 Surface Material Sound Absorption

As a sound wave travels through an environment, it naturally impacts and bounces off of a number of surfaces. Each time that the wave hits a surface, a certain amount of energy gets lost, absorbed from the sound wave into the material itself. The amount of energy that is lost is different based on the properties of the material, and will also differ for various frequencies of the audio (The Engineering ToolBox 2003).

By using techniques similar to those in this chapter, the frequency absorption information can be calculated for each material type. You can find various tables of coefficients for common materials online: ASI Pro Audio Acoustics (n.d.), Acoustic Traffic (n.d.), JCW Acoustic Supplies (2024), and Yizhou the Sound Guy (2018). In general, the tables include information for absorption coefficients at 125 Hz, 250 Hz, 500 Hz, 1000 Hz, 2000 Hz, and 4000 Hz. Absorption above, below, and between these ranges is expected to be interpolated. Table 6.1 is an example of coefficient data, adapted from the above online references.

The values in Table 6.1 are reductions in volume at the given frequencies. So, for example, a plywood surface will reduce a 125 Hz signal by −6 dB, and a 250 Hz signal by approximately −10.5 dB.

6.4.6 The Master DSP Clock

There are many ways to think of time in the context of game audio, but the most precise way is using the sample clock. Every middleware describes this differently, but the idea is that it is a clock – typically of a 64-bit unsigned integer type – that increments by one for every sample that is mixed. The actual value typically increments in multiples of the mixer

TABLE 6.1 Example Absorption Coefficients

Material	125 Hz	250 Hz	500 Hz	1 kHz	2 kHz	4 kHz
Brick	0.05	0.04	0.02	0.04	0.05	0.05
Carpet	0.10	0.15	0.25	0.30	0.30	0.30
Curtains	0.05	0.25	0.40	0.50	0.60	0.50
Marble	0.01	0.01	0.01	0.01	0.02	0.02
Concrete (rough)	0.02	0.03	0.03	0.03	0.04	0.07
Concrete (smooth)	0.01	0.01	0.02	0.02	0.02	0.05
Plaster	0.04	0.05	0.06	0.08	0.04	0.06
Plywood	0.50	0.30	0.10	0.05	0.05	0.05
Wood	0.19	0.23	0.25	0.30	0.37	0.42

buffer size, but it can be used to schedule events to occur (such as starting or stopping a sound) at very precise moments in time.

In FMOD every `ChannelControl` object (which encompasses both `Channels` and `ChannelGroups`) stores its own DSP clock. In our case, we are interested in the DSP clock for the master `ChannelGroup`[4]:

```
unsigned long long GetDSPClock(const FMOD::System& System)
{
  FMOD::ChannelGroup* MasterChannelGroup = nullptr;
  System.GetMasterChannelGroup(&MasterChannelGroup);

  if (MasterChannelGroup == nullptr)
    return 0; // Replace with error handler as appropriate

  unsigned long long MasterDSPClock = 0;
  MasterChannelGroup->getDSPClock(&MasterDSPClock, nullptr);

  return MasterDSPClock;
}
```

The only other piece of information that we need in order to use the DSP clock is the system's sample rate, which we can get by calling `FMOD::System::getSoftwareFormat()`.

6.4.7 Playing Oscillator DSPs

Most audio middleware provides mechanisms for working with waveform synthesis. In FMOD, these are provided by the Oscillator DSP. The Oscillator can be configured to generate various types of waveforms: sine, square, triangle, sawtooth (up or down), and noise. See Chapter 2 for a detailed description of how to generate each of these waveforms if your middleware doesn't support it out of the box, or if you want more control over the signal. Note that each DSP can only be played on one `Channel` at a time, similar to how streams work.

```
struct PlayingDsp
{
  FMOD::Sound* Dsp = nullptr;
  FMOD::Channel* Channel = nullptr;
};
enum class OscillatorType : int
```

```
{
  Sine,
  Square,
  SawUp,
  SawDown,
  Triangle,
  Noise,
};
PlayingDSP PlayOscillator(
  FMOD::System& System,
  OscillatorType Type,
  float Rate)
{
  PlayingDsp ReturnValue;
  System.createDSPByType(FMOD_DSP_TYPE_OSCILLATOR,
    &ReturnValue.Dsp);

  ReturnValue.Dsp->setParameterInt(
    FMOD_DSP_OSCILLATOR_TYPE, static_cast<int>(Type));
  ReturnValue.Dsp->setParameterFloat(
    FMOD_DSP_OSCILLATOR_RATE, Rate);

  // We start the sound paused so that we can set its
  // properties before playing.
  constexpr bool bPaused = true;
  System.playDSP(
    ReturnValue.Dsp, nullptr, bPaused,
    &ReturnValue.Channel);

  return ReturnValue;
}
```

6.4.8 White Noise

There are a number of different so-called "colors" of noise: white, pink, brown, blue, etc. (Wikimedia Foundation 2024a). The colors themselves are only metaphorical, and don't have an actual visual analog.[5] We are particularly interested in white noise (Wikimedia Foundation 2024d) in this chapter, which is named by analogy to white light. It is a random signal that contains equal power at all frequencies, which is a particularly important property for the purposes of this chapter because that makes it suitable as an impulse for the convolution. In practice, white noise can be generated by selecting random values, and we can play white noise by selecting `OscillatorType::Noise` in the `PlayOscillator()` function above. For more detail on white noise, see Chapter 2.

6.4.9 Non-Real-Time Audio

The standard way of running an audio engine is by having it output its sound to the operating system. In that mode, the audio engine is real time – by which we mean that a real clock is driving the audio, and the system has to fill in a buffer with audio data. Audio middleware will typically create a high priority thread to service the mixer.

However, there are situations where you do not need or want to run in real time. The most common reason would be that you want to process audio for storage either into memory or on disk as fast as possible. To service those cases, most audio engines provide a way to initialize in non-real-time mode where the mixer is driven by a function call.

With FMOD, we have to do two things in order to initialize in non-real-time mode:

- Select an appropriate output mode. FMOD comes with two non-real-time modes – `FMOD_OUTPUTTYPE_NOSOUND_NRT` which just renders silence, and `FMOD_OUTPUTTYPE_WAVWRITER_NRT` which writes all output to a wav file. You can also write your own, as described in Chapter 3 of this book.

- Turn off threading features. For the low level system, there are three flags to set:

  - `FMOD_INIT_STREAM_FROM_UPDATE`: Turns off the streaming thread.

  - `FMOD_INIT_MIX_FROM_UPDATE`: Turns off the mixing thread.

  - `FMOD_INIT_THREAD_UNSAFE`: Turns off thread safety features.

- In this chapter, we'll be sticking to the Core API of FMOD, but if you're using the Studio API, then there are some flags to pass into the `Studio::System::initialize()` call:

  - `FMOD_STUDIO_INIT_SYNCHRONOUS_UPDATE`: Disables the studio thread and does all of the processing on the main thread.

  - `FMOD_STUDIO_INIT_LOAD_FROM_UPDATE`: Disables the bank and resource loading threads.

Putting it all together, we get code like the following to initialize the `System` object:

```
FMOD::System* CreateSystemObject(const char* OutputWavFile)
{
  FMOD::System* pSystem = nullptr;
  FMOD::System_Create(&pSystem);

  pSystem->setOutput(FMOD_OUTPUTTYPE_WAVWRITER_NRT);

  // The maximum number of channels that FMOD supports.
  constexpr int NumChanels = 4095;
  pSystem->init(
    NumChannels,
    FMOD_INIT_STREAM_FROM_UPDATE |
      FMOD_INIT_MIX_FROM_UPDATE | FMOD_INIT_THREAD_UNSAFE,
    OutputWavFile);

  return pSystem;
}
```

6.5 STARTING TO PUT IT TOGETHER

Section 6.4 had a lot of disparate content, much of it only vaguely connected, and some seemingly not even related to audio at all. In this section, we'll start to build on these foundational pieces to get some second-level foundations. Once again, we will present these pieces of information in a relatively context-free manner, although we will attempt to reference the appropriate previous sections in this chapter for easy lookup.

6.5.1 Playing and Stopping Sounds on a Delay

What we would like is to start playing a `Channel` at a very specific point in time based on the distance that it has traveled, and then to stop it again at a specific sample calculated by the desired length of playback, all relative to the master DSP clock. This puts together the speed of sound (Section 6.4.1) and the master DSP clock (Section 6.4.6).

First, we need to be able to convert from seconds to samples:

```
unsigned long long GetSamplesFromSeconds(float Seconds)
{
```

```
  return
    static_cast<unsigned long long>(
      Seconds * SystemSampleRate);
}
```

Now we can set up our delay:

```
void SetChannelDelay(
  FMOD::Channel& Channel,
  unsigned long long MasterDspClock,
  float DistanceMeters,
  float LengthSeconds)
{
  auto StartDelaySamples =
      GetSamplesFromSeconds(GetDelaySeconds(DistanceMeters));
  auto LengthSamples = GetSamplesFromSeconds(LengthSeconds);

  auto StartOffsetSamples =
    MasterDspClock + StartDelaySamples;

  // The first parameter is the sample to start the channel.
  // The second parameter is the sample to stop the channel.
  Channel.setDelay(
    StartOffsetSamples,
    StartOffsetSamples + LengthSamples);
}
```

6.5.2 Shaping Sounds with Fade Points

We would now like to add a quick sample-accurate volume ramp – a fade from silence up to full volume at the beginning of playback, and a fade from full volume down to silence at the end of playback. The prerequisite background here is just the master DSP clock (Section 6.4.6).

In order to implement this functionality, we will need to calculate much of the same information that we need for playing and stopping sounds on a delay that we just implemented in Section 6.5.1. Rather than implement a new function, we will rename the function, then add some new parameters and code to the bottom of the existing function:

```
void SetupChannelDelayAndFades(
  FMOD::Channel& Channel,
```

```
        unsigned long long MasterDspClock,
        float DistanceMeters,
        float LengthSeconds,
        float FadeInTimeSeconds,
        float FadeOutTimeSeconds)
{
    // Contents of SetChannelDelay() from Section 6.5.1 here...

    auto FadeInTimeSamples =
        GetSamplesFromSeconds(FadeInTimeSeconds);
    auto FadeOutTimeSamples =
        GetSamplesFromSeconds(FadeOutTimeSeconds);

    // Start with silence
    Channel.addFadePoint(StartOffsetSamples, 0.0f);
    // Fade up to full volume
    Channel.addFadePoint(
        StartOffsetSamples + FadeInTimeSamples, 1.0f);
    // Play at full volume until the fadeout starts
    Channel.addFadePoint(
        StartOffsetSamples + LengthSamples - FadeOutTimeSamples,
        1.0f);
    // Fade back down to silence
    Channel.addFadePoint(
        StartOffsetSamples + LengthSamples, 0.0f);
}
```

6.5.3 Accumulating Absorption Coefficients

As described in Section 6.4.5, when a sound wave impacts a surface, certain frequencies are absorbed according to the properties of the material. If that sound wave continues on, it will likely impact more surfaces, with each surface consuming its own set of frequencies. Conveniently enough, material absorption accumulates in a natural manner. We can either multiply our coefficients together, or convert them to decibels and add them together. Table 6.1 is in percents, so we'll show the multiplicative version here:

```
using MaterialCoefficients =
    std::array<float, NumFrequencyBands>;

MaterialCoefficients AccumulateMaterial(
```

```
  const MaterialType& Material,
  const MaterialCoefficients& Current)
{
  const auto& MaterialCoefficients =
    LookupCoefficients(Material);

  auto ReturnValue = Current;
  for (size_t i = 0; i < NumFrequencyBands; i++)
  {
    ReturnValue[i] *= MaterialCoefficients[i];
  }
  return ReturnValue;
}
```

6.5.4 Mapping Absorption Coefficients to Effect Parameters

In Section 6.4.5, we saw how materials absorb certain frequencies; how do we implement this absorption in a DSP effect? What we would like is to implement a graph like we see in The Engineering ToolBox (2003). We can certainly author our own DSP, but it would be better to use built-in functionality if we can.

FMOD includes an extremely handy effect called the Multiband EQ. With it, we can apply up to five different effects to a signal, and it will combine them together. Figure 6.6 shows an example of the UI for editing this effect in FMOD Studio with an arbitrarily-selected set of effects.

It turns out that we can represent our desired curves by starting with a combined low-shelf and high-shelf filter at 125 Hz, and then

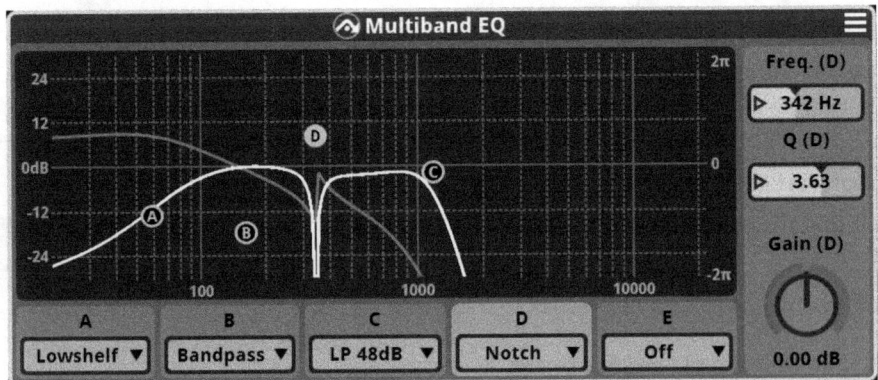

FIGURE 6.6 The editor for the FMOD Studio Multiband EQ effect, showing several different effects combined together.

assigning every other frequency band to a high-shelf filter. We can also use a low-pass filter to apply the atmospheric absorption as discussed in Section 6.4.3. There are two extra items to note:

- The multiband EQ only supports five effects, but we have six frequency bands plus a low-shelf filter and low-pass filter for a total of eight. We can work around this by chaining two multiband EQ DSPs together.

- It is nontrivial to get the filter curves to pass exactly where we want them to. Setting the frequency value for the shelf filters is simple, but in order to get the accumulated curve to pass through the desired points at the desired frequencies requires a bit more work – we cannot simply set the gain value to the desired attenuation because the accumulated attenuation from the previous effects accumulates into the current effect.

    The correct solution is not complicated, albeit a bit unintuitive. We start by setting the initial low-shelf/high-shelf pair at 125 Hz to the desired gain at 125 Hz unmodified. In order to set the remainder of the gain values, we need to accumulate all of the previous gain values up to the current frequency, then set the gain value to twice the difference between the desired gain and the accumulated gain.

Let's look at an example. We are trying to match the curve as described in Table 6.2 using two multiband EQ effects. First, we convert the percentage values to decibels, then subtract the entries from the accumulated gain

TABLE 6.2   Example Values for Multiband EQ Parameters

Frequency	Desired Value	Desired dB Value	Accumulated Gain	Effect Gain Value
125 Hz	0.82	−1.72 dB	0.0 dB	−1.72 dB
250 Hz	0.91	−0.81 dB	−1.72 dB	2(−0.81 dB − −1.72 dB) = +1.82 dB
500 Hz	0.51	−5.84 dB	−1.72 dB + 1.82 dB = +0.1 dB	2(−5.84 dB − 0.1 dB) = −11.88 dB
1000 Hz	0.33	−9.63 dB	0.1 dB + −11.88 dB = −11.78 dB	2(−9.63 dB − −11.78 dB) = +4.3 dB
2000 Hz	0.99	−0.087 dB	−11.78 dB + 4.3 dB = −7.48 dB	2(−0.087 dB − −7.48 dB) = +14.786 dB
4000 Hz	0.95	−0.44 dB	−7.48 dB + 14.786 dB = +7.306 dB	2(−0.44 dB − 7.306 dB) = −15.492 dB

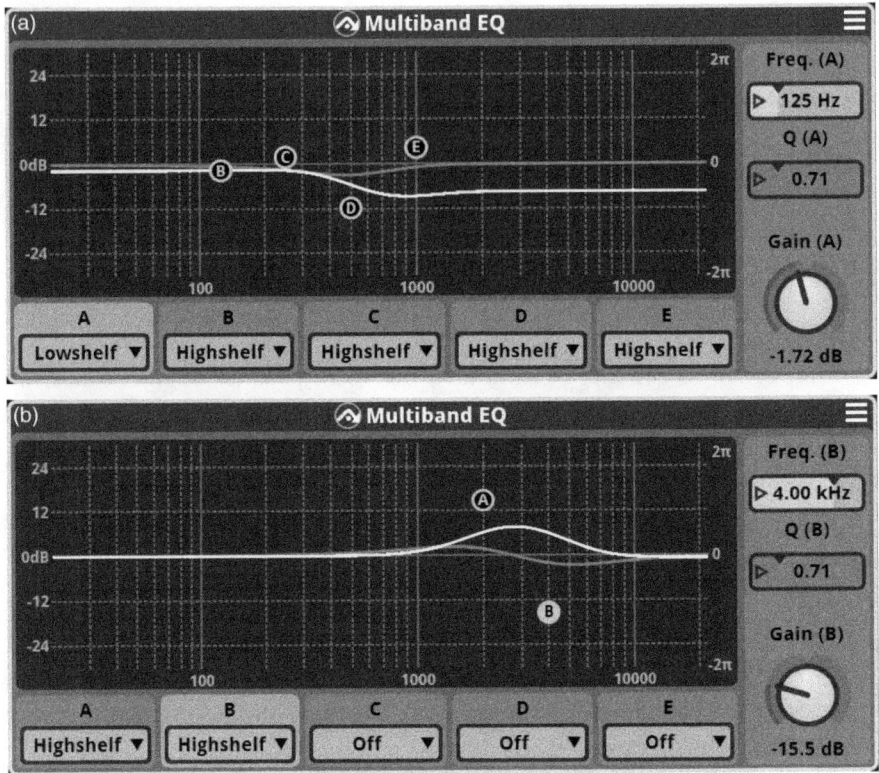

FIGURE 6.7 (a) First multiband EQ settings. (b) Second multiband EQ settings.

and double to get the actual gain values to set. The resulting effects are shown in Figure 6.7.

Note that Figure 6.7b shows a counterintuitive curve, but it is nevertheless correct. The curve comes in at 0 dB, then goes up several dB before dropping down. The reason that this is correct is that it is chained back to back with the previous effect. If you look at Figure 6.7a, the effect curve ends at a value between 0 and −12, which should be −7.48 dB, our accumulated gain to that point. This value will be the input to the second multiband EQ. A value of 0 dB on the second multiband EQ means no change from the previous, so we have to bring the value up above the zero point in order to get it to the desired value of −0.087 dB.

For the atmospheric low-pass filter, we'll use our FilterCutoffSolver to calculate the desired cutoff frequency. We can set that to the "C" effect on our second multiband EQ. Figure 6.8 shows the second multiband EQ with a low-pass filter set up to a desired low-pass filter cutoff frequency of 2.5 kHz.

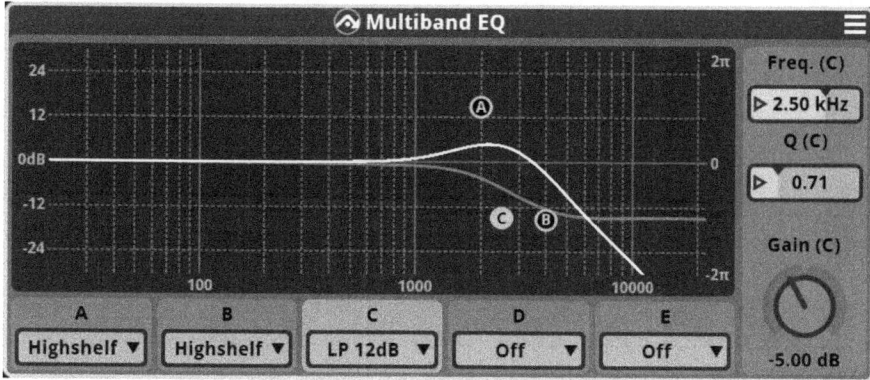

FIGURE 6.8 The second multiband EQ with a low-pass filter at 2.5 kHz added.

Let's take a look at the code to adjust the gain values first:

```
MaterialCoefficients GetAdjustedGainValues(
   const MaterialCoefficients& DesiredGainValues)
{
   MaterialCoefficients ReturnValue;
   ReturnValue[0] = VolumeTodB(DesiredGainValues[0]);
   float AccumulatedGain = ReturnValue[0];
   for (int i = 1; i < NumFrequencyBands; i++)
   {
      ReturnValue[i] =
         2.0f *
         (VolumeTodB(DesiredGainValues[i]) - AccumulatedGain);
      // FMOD's Multiband EQ limits gain values to -30..+30
      ReturnValue[i] =
         std::clamp(ReturnValue[i], -30.0f, 30.0f);
      AccumulatedGain += ReturnValue[i];
   }
   return ReturnValue;
}
```

The code to apply this is repetitive and tedious, but relatively simple for all of that:

```
struct Effects
{
   FMOD::DSP* MultibandEQs[2];
};
```

```
Effects ApplyMaterialEffects(
  FMOD::System& System,
  FMOD::Channel& Channel,
  const MaterialCoefficients& DesiredGainValues,
  float AtmosphericLowpassFrequency)
{
  Effects ReturnValue;

  // First create the two multiband EQ effects
  System.createDSPByType(
    FMOD_DSP_TYPE_MULTIBAND_EQ,
    &ReturnValue.MultibandEQs[0]);
  System.createDSPByType(
    FMOD_DSP_TYPE_MULTIBAND_EQ,
    &ReturnValue.MultibandEQs[1]);

  // Set up the filters.
  // A is a low shelf filter, B through E are high shelf.
  ReturnValue.MultibandEQs[0]->setParameterInt(
    FMOD_DSP_MULTIBAND_EQ_A_FILTER,
    FMOD_DSP_MULTIBAND_EQ_FILTER_LOWSHELF);
  ReturnValue.MultibandEQs[0]->setParameterInt(
    FMOD_DSP_MULTIBAND_EQ_B_FILTER,
    FMOD_DSP_MULTIBAND_EQ_FILTER_HIGHSHELF);
  ReturnValue.MultibandEQs[0]->setParameterInt(
    FMOD_DSP_MULTIBAND_EQ_C_FILTER,
    FMOD_DSP_MULTIBAND_EQ_FILTER_HIGHSHELF);
  ReturnValue.MultibandEQs[0]->setParameterInt(
    FMOD_DSP_MULTIBAND_EQ_D_FILTER,
    FMOD_DSP_MULTIBAND_EQ_FILTER_HIGHSHELF);
  ReturnValue.MultibandEQs[0]->setParameterInt(
    FMOD_DSP_MULTIBAND_EQ_E_FILTER,
    FMOD_DSP_MULTIBAND_EQ_FILTER_HIGHSHELF);

  // For the second multiband EQ, A and B are high shelf,
  // and C is a low pass.
  ReturnValue.MultibandEQs[1]->setParameterInt(
    FMOD_DSP_MULTIBAND_EQ_A_FILTER,
    FMOD_DSP_MULTIBAND_EQ_FILTER_HIGHSHELF);
  ReturnValue.MultibandEQs[1]->setParameterInt(
    FMOD_DSP_MULTIBAND_EQ_B_FILTER,
```

```
   FMOD_DSP_MULTIBAND_EQ_FILTER_HIGHSHELF);
ReturnValue.MultibandEQs[1]->setParameterInt(
   FMOD_DSP_MULTIBAND_EQ_C_FILTER,
   FMOD_DSP_MULTIBAND_EQ_FILTER_LOWPASS_12DB);

// Set up frequency cutoffs.
// A and B will be set to 125 Hz, and then consecutive
// values will be set to the next doubling.
ReturnValue.MultibandEQs[0]->setParameterFloat(
   FMOD_DSP_MULTIBAND_EQ_A_FREQUENCY, 125.0f);
ReturnValue.MultibandEQs[0]->setParameterFloat(
   FMOD_DSP_MULTIBAND_EQ_B_FREQUENCY, 125.0f);
ReturnValue.MultibandEQs[0]->setParameterFloat(
   FMOD_DSP_MULTIBAND_EQ_C_FREQUENCY, 250.0f);
ReturnValue.MultibandEQs[0]->setParameterFloat(
   FMOD_DSP_MULTIBAND_EQ_D_FREQUENCY, 500.0f);
ReturnValue.MultibandEQs[0]->setParameterFloat(
   FMOD_DSP_MULTIBAND_EQ_E_FREQUENCY, 1000.0f);
ReturnValue.MultibandEQs[1]->setParameterFloat(
   FMOD_DSP_MULTIBAND_EQ_A_FREQUENCY, 2000.0f);
ReturnValue.MultibandEQs[1]->setParameterFloat(
   FMOD_DSP_MULTIBAND_EQ_B_FREQUENCY, 4000.0f);

// Our lowpass filter gets set to our atmospheric
// cutoff frequency.
ReturnValue.MultibandEQs[1]->setParameterFloat(
   FMOD_DSP_MULTIBAND_EQ_C_FREQUENCY,
   AtmosphericLowpassFrequency);

// Adjust the gain values.
auto AdjustedGainValues =
   GetAdjustedGainValues(DesiredGainValues);

// Both A and B get the same initial value, and then
// every other high shelf filter after that gets set
// to the next adjusted gain value.
ReturnValue.MultibandEQs[0]->setParameterFloat(
   FMOD_DSP_MULTIBAND_EQ_A_GAIN, AdjustedGainValues[0]);
ReturnValue.MultibandEQs[0]->setParameterFloat(
   FMOD_DSP_MULTIBAND_EQ_B_GAIN, AdjustedGainValues[0]);
ReturnValue.MultibandEQs[0]->setParameterFloat(
```

```
    FMOD_DSP_MULTIBAND_EQ_C_GAIN, AdjustedGainValues[1]);
  ReturnValue.MultibandEQs[0]->setParameterFloat(
    FMOD_DSP_MULTIBAND_EQ_D_GAIN, AdjustedGainValues[2]);
  ReturnValue.MultibandEQs[0]->setParameterFloat(
    FMOD_DSP_MULTIBAND_EQ_E_GAIN, AdjustedGainValues[3]);
  ReturnValue.MultibandEQs[1]->setParameterFloat(
    FMOD_DSP_MULTIBAND_EQ_A_GAIN, AdjustedGainValues[4]);
  ReturnValue.MultibandEQs[1]->setParameterFloat(
    FMOD_DSP_MULTIBAND_EQ_B_GAIN, AdjustedGainValues[5]);

  // Add the effects to the playing channel.
  Channel.addDSP(FMOD_CHANNELCONTROL_DSP_TAIL,
    ReturnValues.MultibandEQs[0]);
  Channel.addDSP(FMOD_CHANNELCONTROL_DSP_TAIL,
    ReturnValues.MultibandEQs[1]);
}
```

6.5.5 Casting and Bouncing Rays

The general process for calculating an impulse response as described in Alpkocak and Sis (2010) is to cast a bunch of rays into the environment and reflect them around surface normals.[6] Each ray that comes back to the listener from the source will trigger an impulse in the resulting response. In this section, we'll see how to implement this ray-casting mechanism.

In Section 6.4.4, we saw how to evenly distribute points around a sphere. If we interpret those points as set of direction vectors from the attenuation position, then we can bounce the rays around the world to see which ones eventually return to the listener. Every game engine will have a different API for casting rays, but the general pattern will be something along the lines of:

```
struct RayHit
{
  Point3 Location;
  Vector3 Normal;
  MaterialType Material;
};
std::optional<RayHit> CastRay(const Ray3& Ray);
```

Every one of our input rays goes through this function. Any rays that hit the environment (that is, those which don't return std::nullopt from this function) will need to get reflected around the normal according to the law of refraction[7] (Wikimedia Foundation 2024b). Although the mathematics of this law gives us rules about materials with different refraction indices, in practice we can do a simple vector reflection around the normal. Most engines provide this as a library function, but it's also not difficult to implement:

```
Vector3 Vector3::ReflectAround(const Vector3& Normal) const
{
    return *this - (2.0f * Dot(Normal) * Normal);
}
```

The number of times that you need to bounce around the environment depends on the size and complexity of your environment. In practice, somewhere between 16 and 32 bounces will likely be enough.

At this point, we have enough to write a framework to bounce the rays around our environment. We don't have enough to actually use the rays that we're casting, but it's worthwhile to see the shape of the code for now:

```
struct Impulse
{
    float DistanceTraveled = 0.0f;
    MaterialCoefficients DesiredGainValues = {};

    auto operator<=>(const Impulse&) const = default;
};

struct Raycast
{
    Raycast() = default;
    Raycast(Point3 Center, Vector3 Direction) :
      R{ Center, Direction }
    {}

    Ray R;
    RayHit Intersection;
    Impulse CurrentImpulse;
};

std::vector<Impulse> CastRays(const Point3& Center)
{
    // Our return value
```

```cpp
std::vector<Impulse> ReturnValue;

// Our working raycasts.
std::vector<Raycast> WorkingVectors;

// Start by filling in our working vectors using the
// code that we saw earlier in Section 6.4.4 for arranging
// vectors in a sphere.
auto ArrangedVectors = ArrangeVectors(NumRaycasts);
WorkingVectors.reserve(ArrangedVectors.size());
for (auto& Vector : ArrangedVectors)
{
  WorkingVectors.emplace_back(Center, Vector);
}

// Create a sphere that we'll check against.  We are hard-
// coding the radius here, but this is something that is
// worth making data-driven, or at least adjusting for your
// game.
constexpr float HeadRadius = 0.15f;
Sphere HeadSphere{ Center, HeadRadius };

// Bounce the rays around
for (unsigned int Bounce = 0;
     Bounce < NumBounces;
     Bounce++)
{
  // Check whether the rays intersect the head sphere.
  // Since the first bounce starts at the center of the
  // head and goes outward, every ray will necessarily
  // intersect the sphere, so we ignore the first bounce.
  if (Bounce > 0)
  {
    for (auto& WorkingVector : WorkingVectors)
    {
      // Check whether the ray intersects the sphere.
      auto Intersection =
        HeadSphere.IntersectRay(WorkingVector.R);
      if (Intersection)
      {
        // We've found an intersection!  Add the current
```

```cpp
        // accumulated Impulse to the return value.
        ReturnValue.push_back(
          WorkingVector.CurrentImpulse);

        // We need to add the distance from the ray start
        // to the intersection with the sphere.  This
        // example code assumes that the intersection is
        // the point on the sphere where the intersection
        // occurs, but if that is not the case and you
        // just have a boolean indicating whether it over-
        // lapped, then you can use the sphere center.
        ReturnValue.back().DistanceTraveled +=
          (*Intersection -
          WorkingVector.R.Location).Length();
    }
  }
}

// Cast the rays and accumulate the Impulses.
for (auto& WorkingVector : WorkingVectors)
{
  // This is the function whose declaration we saw
  // earlier.
  auto Intersection = CastRay(WorkingVector.R);
  if (Intersection)
  {
    // We hit a surface!  Accumulate the distance
    // traveled from the ray's start location to the
    // intersection location to the total distance
    // traveled.
    WorkingVector.CurrentImpulse.DistanceTraveled +=
      (WorkingVector.R.Location -
      Intersection->Location).Length();

    // Accumulate the material as described in section
    // 6.5.3.
    WorkingVector.CurrentImpulse.AccumulateMaterial(
      Intersection->Material);

    // Cache the intersection for our next bounce.
    WorkingVector.Intersection = *Intersection;
```

```
    }
    else
    {
      // No impact - it probably disappeared into the sky
      // or there's nothing within the maximum raycast
      // distance.  Mark the intersection as invalid so
      // that we can remove it later.
      WorkingVector.Intersection.Invalidate();
    }
  }


  // Remove any invalid intersections from the working
  // vectors.
  std::erase_if(WorkingVectors,
    [](const Raycast& R)
    { return !R.Intersection.IsValid(); });


  // Finally, we can reflect the vectors around the impact
  // normals.
  for (auto& WorkingVector : WorkingVectors)
  {
    auto Reflection =
      WorkingVector.R.Direction.ReflectAround(
        WorkingVector.Intersection.Normal);
    WorkingVector.R = {
      WorkingVector.Intersection.GetLocation(),
      Reflection };
  }
  }


  return ReturnValue;
}
```

6.5.6 Merging Impulses

We are modeling all of the functionality in this chapter on Alpkocak and Sis (2010), which uses discrete time analysis. In other words, time under this model is not continuous, but jumps forward in steps. However, because the delay values for the impulse responses can come back at arbitrary values, the authors of that paper merge impulses together that are too close in time. This is captured in equations (4) and (5) of the paper.

The output of the code in Section 6.5.5 is an unsorted list of impulses. Sorting the list by distance is as easy as calling **std::sort()** on the result. Once we have a sorted list, we will find that in practice there are many rays that return very close in time to each other, and which we therefore need to merge together. Equation (4) of the paper (Alpkocak and Sis 2010) tells us to take the maximum value of each frequency band in order to merge impulses, and we will take the shortest distance:

```cpp
void Impulse::MergeWith(const Impulse& Other)
{
  DistanceTraveled =
    std::min(DistanceTraveled, Other.DistanceTraveled);
  for (size_t i = 0; i < NumFrequencyBands; i++)
  {
    DesiredGainValues[i] =
      std::max(DesiredGainValues[i],
        Other.DesiredGainValues[i]);
  }
}
```

In practice, we will use a hybrid discrete/continuous time model. Every new impulse can be triggered at any arbitrary point in time, but then gets merged with other incoming impulses over the desired time step.

```cpp
void MergeImpulses(
  std::vector<Impulse>& Impulses)
{
  // Sort the impulses by distance
  std::ranges::sort(Impulses);

  // We will use a 1ms time step
  constexpr float TimeStep = 0.001f;

  // Iterate over the sorted impulses
  auto NumImpulses = ReturnValue.size();

  // The index of our current impulse that we are keeping
  size_t CurrentImpulseIndex = 0;

  // Iterate from the second impulse
  for (size_t i = 1; i < NumImpulses; i++)
```

```
    {
        // Grab references to the current valid impulse and to
        // the next one that we're comparing against.
        auto& CurrentImpulse = Impulses[CurrentImpulseIndex];
        auto& NextImpulse = Impulses[i];

        // Calculate the time difference between the impulses.
        auto DeltaTime =
            NextImpulse.GetDelaySeconds() -
                CurrentImpulse.GetDelaySeconds();

        if (DeltaTime < TimeStep)
        {
            // If the next impulse is within the timestep of the
            // current impulse, then we need to merge it with the
            // current impulse and invalidate the next impulse.
            CurrentImpulse.MergeWith(NextImpulse);
            NextImpulse.Invalidate();
        }
        else
        {
            // If the time difference is more than our time step,
            // then we do not merge the impulses and the next
            // index becomes the new current impulse index.
            CurrentImpulseIndex = i;
        }
    }

    // Erase any invalidated impulses, leaving us with an
    // array containing only the merged impulses.
    std::erase_if(Impulses,
        [](const Impulse& I) { return !I.IsValid(); });
}
```

6.5.7 Adjusting the Horizon for Outdoor Environments

In Section 6.4.4, we saw how to distribute points evenly on a sphere, and we applied that in Section 6.5.5 to cast rays around. However, there may be circumstances where we don't want to distribute the points fully around the sphere.

Consider the situations in Figure 6.9. In Figure 6.9a we have an indoor environment, so we can cast rays in all directions and they will bounce

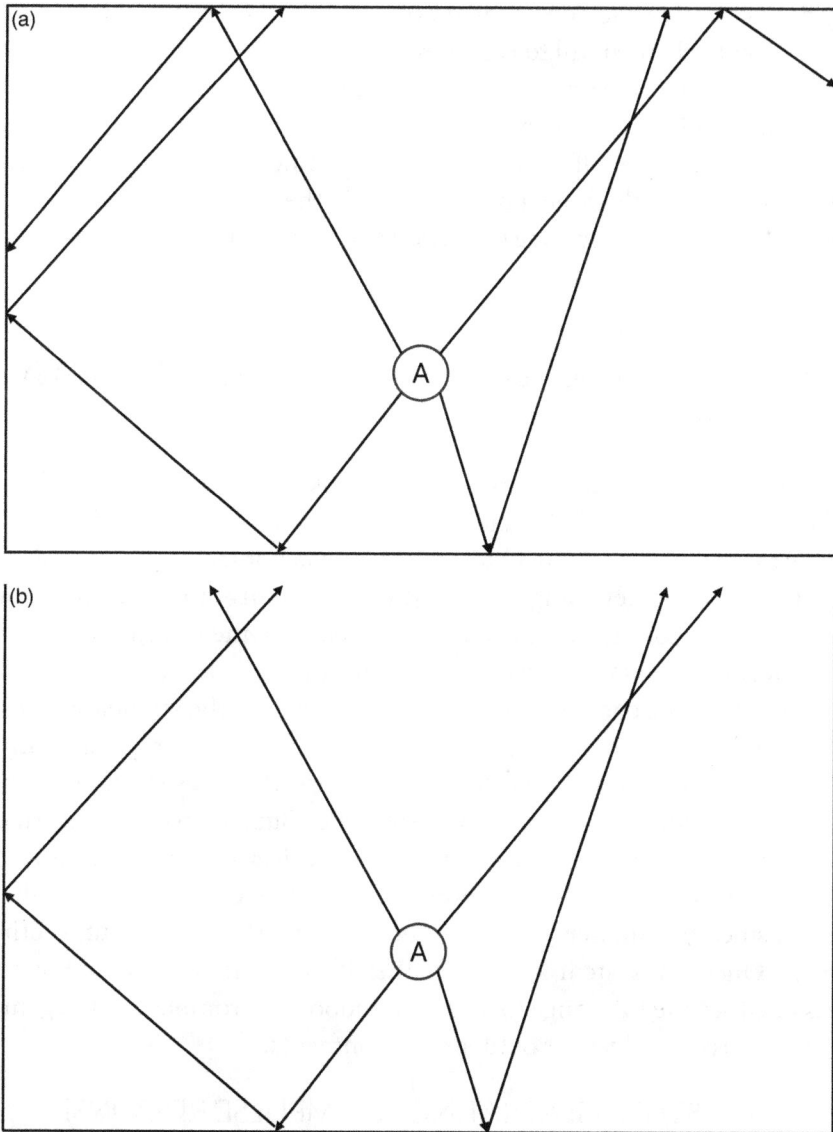

FIGURE 6.9 (a) Rays being cast in an indoor environment. (b) Rays being cast in an outdoor environment.

off of the world because the world is enclosed. However, in Figure 6.9b we have the same circumstance except that there is no ceiling – it's outdoors. In that situation, any ray that we cast upward will just disappear into the sky. Similarly, rays that we cast straight downward will bounce off of the ground and then into the sky. We can even see a situation where a ray bounces off of the floor, then off of a wall, and then into the sky. That makes it entirely wasteful to cast these rays.

What we can do in an outdoor environment is to create a "horizon" – a maximum and minimum φ value that will limit the number of rays that immediately bounce off into the sky. The specific limits on the angle will be different for each game, but we can scale the angle with the following code, to be placed at the code in Section 6.4.4 where it says `Note here for Section 6.5.7`:

```
Phi =
  (Phi / std::numbers::pi_v<float>) * (MaxAngle - MinAngle)
  + MinAngle;
```

This is the standard rescaling logic that likely exists as a math library function in middleware. It works by taking the starting value, dividing it by the range (in this case, $0..\pi$) to get a scaling factor from 0..1, multiplying that factor by the new range (`MaxAngle - MinAngle`) to get a value from zero to the size of the new range, and then adding the minimum value of the new range (`MinAngle`) to get the actual value.

To use this, the code must first determine whether the attenuation position is indoors or outdoors. A simple check for this is to raycast straight upward. If it hits something, then it is indoors; if it doesn't hit anything, then it is outdoors. However, if a system like Bubble Space as described in Bantin and Koudriavtsev (2020) already exists which can determine whether a position is indoors or outdoors, then that can be a cheaper alternative, since the answer is already known and used as an input to other events. Once the system knows whether it's indoors or outdoors, it can pass in either the full range ($0..\pi$) for an indoor environment or the game-specific horizon values for outdoor environments.

6.6 FINAL STEPS: GENERATING AN IMPULSE RESPONSE

We now have enough background and intermediate steps to put it all together. In fact, this section will largely be comprised of putting together the pieces that we've spent the chapter describing in isolation and combining them together with some glue code. Let's make some impulse responses!

```
void RecordImpulseResponseToFile(
  const Point3& Center,
  const std::filesystem::path& FilePath)
```

```
{
  // From Section 6.5.5
  auto Impulses = CastRays(Center);

  // From Section 6.5.6
  MergeImpulses(Impulses);
  RecordImpulseResponseFile(Impulses, FilePath);
}
```

We have already seen the implementations of the first two functions. All that is left is an implementation of `RecordImpulseResponseFile()`.

```
struct PlayingImpulse
{
  // From Section 6.4.7
  PlayingDsp Playing;

  // From Section 6.5.4
  Effects EQs;

  // This would be cleaner as a destructor, but that would
  // require implementing move operations and deleting
  // copy operations, which would make an already-long
  // chapter even longer.  We'll stick with the manual
  // destruction here, while acknowledging that the
  // destructor approach is superior.
  void Release()
  {
    Playing.Channel->removeDSP(EQs.MultibandEQs[0]);
    Playing.Channel->removeDSP(EQs.MultibandEQs[1]);
    EQs.MultibandEQs[0]->release();
    EQs.MultibandEQs[1]->release();
    Playing.Dsp->release();
  }
};

// Helper function to play an impulse.
PlayingImpulse PlayImpulse(
  const Impulse& I,
  FMOD::System& System,
  unsigned long long MasterDspClock,
```

```
    float LengthSeconds,
    float FadeInTimeSeconds,
    float FadeOutTimeSeconds,
    const FilterCutoffSolver& Solver)
{
    PlayingImpulse ReturnValue;

    // From Section 6.4.7
    // Play a Noise oscillator, which will play white noise
    // for our impulse.  Rate isn't used for noise oscillator,
    // so we can just pass zero.
    ReturnValue.Playing =
      PlayOscillator(System, OscillatorType::Noise, 0.0f);

    // From Section 6.4.2
    // Set the volume attenuation by distance.
    auto VolumePercent =
      dBToVolume(
        GetDistanceAttenuationdB(Impulse.DistanceTraveled));
    ReturnValue.Playing.Channel->setVolume(VolumePercent);

    // From Section 6.5.2
    // Set the channel to delay its start and stop by distance
    // and desired play length, and add fade points to shape
    // the sound.
    SetupChannelDelayAndFades(
      *ReturnValue.Playing.Channel,
      MasterDspClock,
      Impulse.DistanceTraveled,
      LengthSeconds,
      FadeInTimeSeconds,
      FadeOutTimeSeconds);

    // From Section 6.5.4
    // Apply the material effects to the Channel.
    ReturnValue.EQs =
      ApplyMaterialEffects(
        System,
        *ReturnValue.Playing.Channel,
        Impulse.DesiredGainValues,
        Solver.Solve(Impulse.DistanceTraveled));
```

```cpp
  // PlayOscillator() starts the sound paused in order to
  // avoid a pop while we're setting it up.  Technically,
  // we don't need to do this since we're in a non-realtime
  // context, but it's good form nonetheless.
  ReturnValue.Playing.Channel->setPaused(false);

  return ReturnValue;
}


void RecordImpulseResponseFile(
  const std::vector<Impulse>& Impulses,
  const std::filesystem::path& FilePath)
{
  if (Impulses.empty())
    return;

  // From Section 6.4.9
  // Create the System object in non-realtime wav writer
  // mode.
  auto* System = CreateSystemObject(FilePath.c_str());

  // From Section 6.4.6
  // Get the system sample rate
  int SampleRate = 0;
  pSystem->getSoftwareFormat(&SampleRate, nullptr, nullptr);

  // From Section 6.4.6
  // Get the current master DSP clock
  auto MasterDspClock = GetDSPClock(*System);

  // Create a vector of playing impulses.
  std::vector<PlayingImpulse> PlayingImpulses;
  PlayingImpulses.reserve(Impulses.size());

  // Note: we presume here that there is a globally-
  // accessible `Config` object that contains information
  // about the humidity, temperature, and desired impulse
  // shape.

  // From Section 6.4.3
  // Set up a filter cutoff solver for the low-pass filter.
```

```
FilterCutoffSolver Solver{
  Config.Humidity, Config.Temperature};

// Iterate over each impulse and play it
for (auto& I : Impulses)
{
  auto& PI = PlayingImpulses.emplace_back();
  PI = PlayImpulse(
    I, *System, MasterDspClock,
    Config.ImpulseLengthSeconds,
    Config.ImpulseFadeIn,
    Config.ImpulseFadeOut,
    Solver);
}


// Update the system object while the impulses are playing.
bool bAnyChannelIsPlaying = true;
while (bAnyChannelIsPlaying)
{
  // Calling this will drive the mixer.
  pSystem->update();

  // The PlayingImpulses array is sorted by start time,
  // and Channels are counted as playing even if they're
  // queued to play, so we only need to check the last
  // entry in the list. If the last one is still playing,
  // then it must be that we have not yet finished.
  PlayingImpulses.back().Playing.Channel->isPlaying(
    &bAnyChannelIsPlaying);
}


// Release all of the impulses.  See note above about a
// cleaner way to do this in production code.
for (auto& PI : PlayingImpulses)
{
  PI.Release();
}

// Release the system object.
System->release();
}
```

6.7 WHERE TO GO FROM HERE

This chapter has been a starting point for generating impulse responses. The code in this chapter will write out a wav file, which can be imported into the FMOD Studio tool, loaded by the runtime, or brought into a sound design tool to tweak. Once you have this in place, there is a lot more that needs to be done in order to be a complete system. Here are just a few of the items on the TODO list:

- Associate the resulting wav files with their appropriate locations in the game world and implement a cross-fading system to switch impulse responses.

- If loading the wav file as part of the system, then it needs to be in the appropriate format for FMOD's convolution reverb, which is signed 16-bit short, with a single extra short prepended containing the number of channels of data. (Other middleware will undoubtedly have similar constraints on their impulse responses.)

- It may be worthwhile to record the output to a memory buffer, which you can guarantee will be in the appropriate format and to which you can prepend the extra short value. See Chapter 3 for a discussion of how to do this.

- Although we use white noise in this chapter, the nature of the impulse sound used to generate the impulse response will affect the tone of the convolution reverb. You can use a recording of a real-world impulse instead of an oscillator, or apply a filter to the oscillator to have different color.

- Some environments (particularly sparse outdoor environments) may need extra work to sound good. Systems like slap backs, echoes, or even custom impulse responses or switching to classic parametric reverb are all fair game to get a good sound.

Despite all this extra work still to do, all of the context in this chapter will be a great starting point to get custom impulse responses.

NOTES

1. In digital signal processing, this is known as a Dirac Delta and is represented by the lowercase Greek letter delta (δ).

2. The raycasting method doesn't model interference, for example. For the purposes of this chapter, we're okay with that.
3. Consider an infinite number of rays being cast in all directions. These rays will naturally fill up the entirety of the sphere, and every ray will be infinitely close to its neighbors. Obviously, we can't have an infinite number of rays, but we can have a very large number, and bounce them around an arbitrary number of times. The more rays and the more bounces, the closer to our wave model we get.
4. Throughout this chapter, I have elided most error handling. Proper production code should check return codes and check for success.
5. At least, in principle they don't. Individuals with sight-sound synesthesia may experience the sounds as colors, although not necessarily the same color as the name of the noise.
6. As it turns out, this is effectively what a ray tracer is doing in graphics.
7. This is often called Snell's Law, although it was first discovered in 984 C.E. by the Persian mathematician Ibn Sahl.

REFERENCES

Acoustic Traffic. n.d. *Absorption Coefficients.* Accessed July 1, 2024. https://www.acoustic.ua/st/web_absorption_data_eng.pdf

Alpkocak, Adil, and Kemal Sis. 2010. "Computing Impulse Response of Room Acoustics Using the Ray-Tracing Method in Time Domain." *Archives of Acoustics* 35(4): 505–519. https://www.researchgate.net/publication/271383273_Computing_Impulse_Response_of_Room_Acoustics_Using_the_Ray-Tracing_Method_in_Time_Domain

ASI Pro Audio Acoustics. n.d. *Sound Absorption Coefficients.* Accessed July 1, 2024. https://www.asiproaudio.com/acoustic_IOI/101_13.htm

Bantin, Robert, and Simon Koudriavtsev. 2020. *Environmental Acoustics in Tom Clancy's The Division 2 - GDC 2020.* March 24. https://www.youtube.com/watch?v=7ME1CZyYNhg

JCW Acoustic Supplies. 2024. *Absorption Coefficients of Common Building Materials and Finishes.* Accessed July 1, 2024. https://www.acoustic-supplies.com/absorption-coefficient-chart/

Roberts, Martin. 2020. *How to Evenly Distribute Points on a Sphere More Effectively Than the Canonical Fibonacci Lattice.* June 7. Accessed June 30, 2024. https://extremelearning.com.au/how-to-evenly-distribute-points-on-a-sphere-more-effectively-than-the-canonical-fibonacci-lattice/

Taylor, Nic. 2021. "Modeling Atmospheric Absorption with a Low-Pass Filter." In *Game Audio Programming Principles and Practices 3*, edited by Guy Somberg, 51–68. Boca Raton, FL: CRC Press.

The Engineering ToolBox. 2003. *Sound - Room Absorption Coefficients.* Accessed July 1, 2024. https://www.engineeringtoolbox.com/accoustic-sound-absorption-d_68.html

The Engineering ToolBox. 2005. *Sound Propagation - The Inverse Square Law.* Accessed July 1, 2024. https://www.engineeringtoolbox.com/inverse-square-law-d_890.html

Wikimedia Foundation. 2024a. *Colors of Noise*. June 22. https://en.wikipedia.org/wiki/Colors_of_noise

Wikimedia Foundation. 2024b. *Snell's Law*. June 23. https://en.wikipedia.org/wiki/Snell%27s_law

Wikimedia Foundation. 2024c. *Speed of Sound*. June 24. https://en.wikipedia.org/wiki/Speed_of_sound

Wikimedia Foundation. 2024d. *White Noise*. June 27. https://en.wikipedia.org/wiki/White_noise

Yizhou the Sound Guy. 2018. *Table of Sound Absorption Coefficients That Can Be Found on Internet*. August 9. Accessed July 1, 2024. http://heyizhou.net/notes/absorption-coefficients

III

Game Integration

CHAPTER 7

Transient-Driven Events from Game Parameters

How to Treat Frame-Based Game Parameters as Signals and Filter Them to Post Meaningful Play Events

Robert Bantin

7.1 INTRODUCTION

A while ago I was presented with a cluster of technical challenges in the process of building some audio features for a race sim-game. The root cause of these challenges stemmed from a vehicle simulation (think "car-physics system") that could only be queried by state – via registering a callback on a car component. Because the vehicle simulation ran at 4× the game refresh rate (which was 60 fps), if you registered a callback for a collision on a car component such as the chassis, when that chassis struck something hard, your system would receive – in one game update – 4 callbacks from every triangle in the mesh that was in contact. In other words, the player could hit a barrier, and your system would get hundreds of callbacks per game frame to that effect.

There had been a prototype made for disrupting the co-driver comms whenever the car struck an object or rolled onto its roof. The gameplay

DOI: 10.1201/9781003519119-10

team had decided to pick the first callback that arrived, take the impulse data from that, and dump the rest. The issue was that this system was not reliable. Sometimes the first impulse was below the threshold required to trigger the comms-disruption, even if the player had wrapped the car around a tree. When they lowered the threshold, the comms-disruption would trigger too often, which was also undesirable. What the chief designer wanted was a system that was decisive, so that it was clear to the player that wrapping the car around a tree was more serious than rubbing past a bush.

Since I'd worked with Havok and PhysX in the past, I asked the simulation engineer if I could simply register for a coming-into-contact event, as this would at least only happen once per triangle. Unfortunately, the answer was "no, it's simply not possible". Naturally, then, I had to come up with some other way of monitoring the car simulation that was more stable.

7.2 TREATING GAME PARAMETERS LIKE DISCRETE SIGNALS

When you think about it, a simulation-type game parameter is updated synchronously just like a PCM sample. The difference is the sample rate – in this case 240 samples per second rather than 48000 – which then accumulate into each 60 fps game update. Aside from that, though, these types of game parameters are time-based signals. My thinking was that I could apply some light signal processing to some of them, inferring the event I wanted to capture. In this case, I could also query the damage to any car component, so why not monitor the components that were likely to suffer in a crash?

In Figure 7.1, the component damage increases in steps as the component takes impacts. By game update 31 it is nearly destroyed, but then at game update 37 the player performs a repair operation, and the damage falls to zero again.

So, there were my signals, all in their glorious 60 Hz PCM representation. Remembering that I was only going to build statistics from them (and not re-render them as you might with an audio-rate filter) I wasn't going to consider any listening fidelity. I just wanted to know when their trends changed in a significant way.

7.2.1 What Is Transient Detection?

In audio signals we sometimes differentiate between the features that are steady vs the features that are momentary. This is where we get

Component Damage Over Successive Game Updates

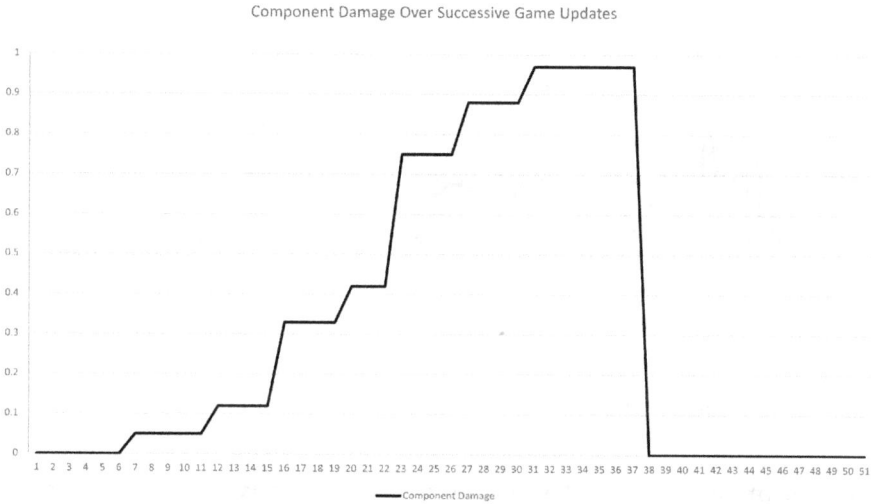

FIGURE 7.1   Graph of damage to a component over time.

nomenclature such as "steady state" vs "transient state". For example, a kick drum hit will most likely have a hard attack at the start of its recording. In a real kick drum this comes from some plosive energy emanating from the beater as it hits the skin inside the shell of the drum. Even in synthesized kick drums, this is modeled in some way, or else the listener won't recognize it as a kick drum. This is different from the overall envelope, which is more or less tonal. So, the question is, if I had a recording of a kick drum pattern and wanted to mark up the start of each hit in the timeline, how would I do that?

Figure 7.2 is a short sample of a kick drum. If you compute a short-term (or "moving") average of the squared values in this sample, you might get an envelope curve like Figure 7.3. This is a good way to estimate the change in loudness over time. The seemingly obvious answer is to trigger off of some peak loudness threshold, but that would be very content dependent, and therefore not terribly reliable. Additionally, when you are using a sample rate like 60 Hz, you aren't going to be able to collect many samples to use for a reliable short-term loudness calculation. Or worse, you acquire the right number of samples that you need, and the calculation takes several seconds to complete. That would be too late in our racing game example.

By contrast, what a simple "step-transient" (so-called for when we choose to model a transient as a step-change) type-detector does is keep a

amplitude in time

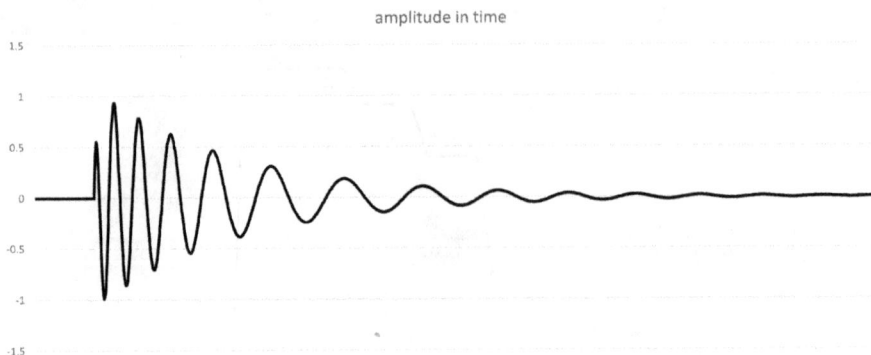

FIGURE 7.2   The waveform of a kick drum recording.

short-term history of the last few samples and compare them to the latest incoming sample. Figure 7.4 shows just such a detector using the current plus two history values.

In summary, a short-term history buffer can be used to calculate an underlying trend. In fact, a low-pass filter does exactly this – find the underlying trend – even in data that isn't audio like the lifespan of a population or bird migration patterns. So, if we want to detect a step-transient, we just need to compare the amplitude of current value with the underlying trend and pick a suitable threshold.

Probably the best aspect of doing it this way is that the algorithm is not affected by slowly varying loudness in the signal over time. In the kick drum example, the underlying trend is silence while comparing what might be the start of the attack. Even if the signal is noisy, that is part of the underlying trend when the kick isn't being hit, and so if the kick drum hits are marginally louder than the background noise, a step-transient detector will still work (see Figures 7.5 and 7.6). Note how the underlying trend

amplitude envelope in time

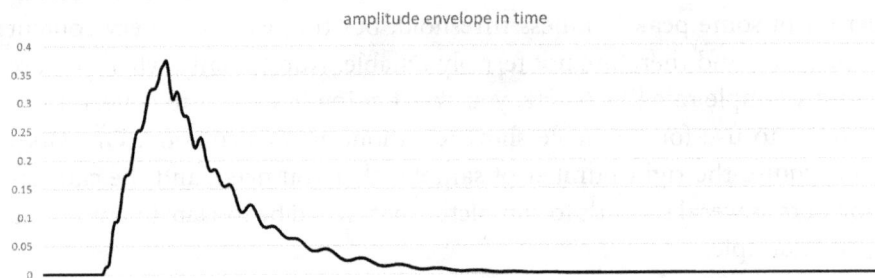

FIGURE 7.3   A kick drum loudness envelope.

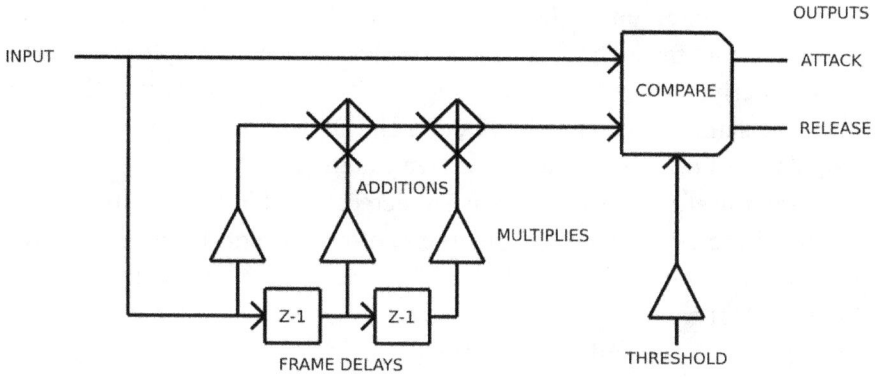

FIGURE 7.4   A simple step transient detector for 60 fps.

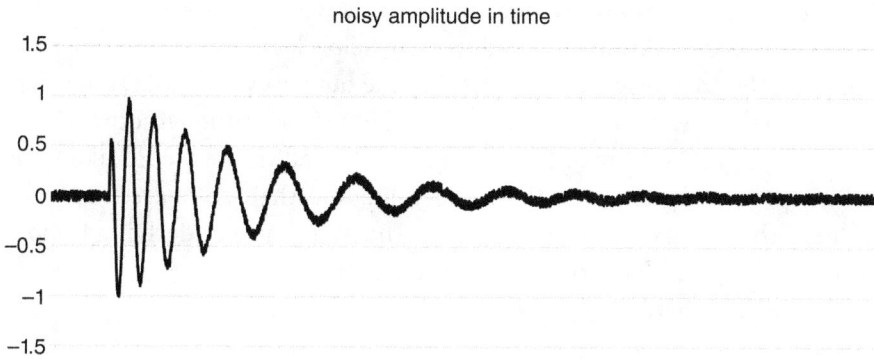

FIGURE 7.5   A kick drum recording with loud noise floor.

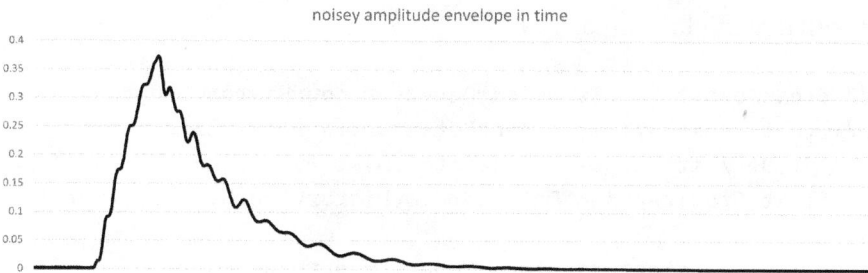

FIGURE 7.6   A kick drum loudness envelope with loud noise floor.

really does a great job of cleaning up the drum sample because of how it measures short-term changes. The noise floor in this example is uniform, so its underlying trend has no change in it. An algorithm like this also works the same irrespective of whether the signal has just positive values (unipolar) or both positive and negative values (bipolar).

Another useful aspect of a transient detector is that it also can be made to detect hard releases – the sudden end of a hit event. In our kick drum example, the underlying trend while it is ringing off is exactly that it *is* ringing off. If the kick drum was suddenly muted, you could detect the hard release by determining that the latest current value is much quieter than the underlying trend. So, in summary, a simple step transient detector can detect both attacks and releases. If you only want to detect one or the other, that is simply a matter of choosing the polarity of your comparison.

7.3 DETERMINING THE UNDERLYING TREND

To determine the trend, we need an analysis window for the current and historical values. A longer window will help clean up "noisy" data but comes at the cost of responsiveness. For the purposes of this example, let's try an analysis window of three values, giving us a time window of 3/60 of a second (that's 50 ms). For each value we read in, we would like to do a little processing to reach the trend value and then compare that trend value with the current incoming value. The most basic underlying trend is just averaging those historical values together.

Let's define that as:

$$\sigma = \frac{\left(x_k + x_{k-1} + x_{k-2}\right)}{3}$$

where σ is the current trend of x_k input values at time interval k.

You could implement it with a circular buffer (replacing the division of 3 with a multiplication of 1/3):

```
// float const StepTransientDetector::ourHistoryLength = 3;
// float const StepTransientDetector::ourNormalization =
     1.0f / static_cast<float>(ourHistoryLength);
// float StepTransientDetector::myHistory[ourHistoryLength];

void StepTransientDetector::Update(float anInput)
{
```

```
    myHistory[myStep] = anInput;

    float sum = 0.0f;

    for (int i = 0; i < ourHistoryLength ++i)
    {
        sum += myHistory[i];
    }

    myCurrentTrend = sum * ourNormalization;

    TransientCheck();

    // increment/reset myStep for next call
    ++myStep;
    myStep %= ourHistoryLength;
}
```

7.4 PERFORMING THE TRANSIENT CHECK

The comparison for detecting a step-transient is "the *magnitude* of this current value is *significantly different* from the underlying trend". If more specificity is required, an attack is detected when the "the *magnitude* of this next value is *significantly larger* than the underlying trend", while a release is detected when "the *magnitude* of this next value *is significantly smaller* than the underlying trend". Take note that I said "magnitude". This is to allow for both positive and negative values.

Before looking at **StepTransientDetector::TransientCheck()**, we can decide on three modes: only attack transients, only release transients, and both attack and release transients. By using a simple enumeration to define the mode of operation, we can pick which type of transient check to call.

```
void StepTransientDetector::TransientCheck()
{
    bool detected = false;

    switch(myMode)
    {
    case Mode::Attack:
        detected = DoAttackTransientCheck();
```

```
      break;

  case Mode::Release:
    detected = DoReleaseTransientCheck();
    break;

  case Mode::Both:
    detected = DoAnyTransientCheck();
  }

  if (detected)
    PostEvent();
}
```

From there you just need three subtle variations in the checking function. You may also want to post different events for attacks and releases. For example, a health drop sound effect vs health boost sound effect.

```
bool StepTransientDetector::DoAttackTransientCheck()
{
  return (myHistory[myStep] - myCurrentXtrend) > threshold ?
    true : false;
}

bool StepTransientDetector::DoReleaseTransientCheck()
{
  return (myCurrentXtrend - myHistory[myStep]) > threshold ?
    true : false;
}

bool StepTransientDetector::DoAnyTransientCheck()
{
  return
    fabs(myHistory[myStep] - myCurrentXtrend) > myThreshold ?
      true : false;
}
```

Figure 7.7 shows the results of applying these methods to the data in Figure 7.1 with a threshold of 0.1. On this graph, whenever a transient is detected, it outputs a 1, and is 0 everywhere else. As you can see, sometimes you get re-triggers, so implementing a cool-off counter/timer may

Component Damage With Transients Over Successive Game Updates

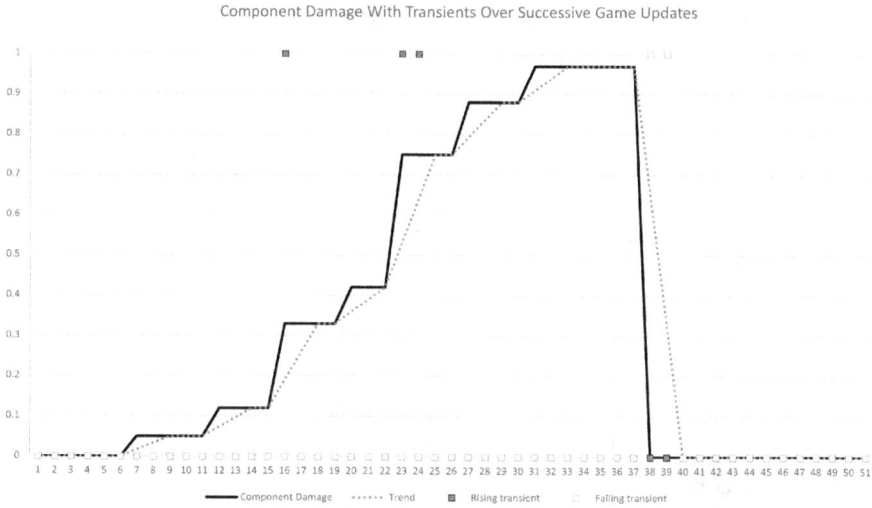

FIGURE 7.7   Graph of damage to a component over time with transients detected.

be advantageous to prevent the event of getting spammed. In my real-life example, I implemented a two-state machine that prevented further transients from posting an event until the impact noise had stopped playing. That way there was never any overlap.

7.5 WEIGHTING THE UNDERLYING TREND

So far, we've just been using a linear average, as that is the most basic underlying trend, but what if we applied some different weightings to those history values? We are using 3 history values in our example, so there is an opportunity to try some non-linear interpolation too.

Let's define our weighted underlying trend as:

$$\sigma = b_0 x_k + b_1 x_{k-1} + b_2 x_{k-2}$$

where σ is the current trend of x_k input values at time interval k. If b_0, b_1, and b_2 were all set to 1/3, you'd have the same result as before (albeit less efficiently). However, these coefficients can be anything you want so long as they sum to 1.0.

```
// float StepTransientDetector::myB0;
// float StepTransientDetector::myB1;
// float StepTransientDetector::myB2;
```

```
// float StepTransientDetector::myZ1 = 0.0f;
// float StepTransientDetector::myZ2 = 0.0f;
// float StepTransientDetector::myLastInput = 0.0f;

void StepTransientDetector::Update(float anInput)
{
  // shuffle the previous input states
  myZ2 = myZ1;
  myZ1 = myLastInput;

  myCurrentTrend =
    anInput * myB0 + myZ1 * myB1 + myZ2 * myB2;

  TransientCheck();

  myLastInput = anInput;
}
```

7.6 CHOOSING SOME COEFFICIENTS

We have just two constraints when selecting coefficients:

1. You need to choose three values.

2. Their sum must be 1.0 to not boost or attenuate the trend.

So, let's define b_0, b_1, and b_2 as shown in Table 7.1, and call it "Accelerate to target".

So, what difference would this *actually* make? As you can see with the dotted line in Figure 7.8, the filtered output has smoothed out the start of each transient but settles on the new value very quickly. Viewed in time, this is why I called it "Accelerate to target". In a sense, it's emphasized the transient components in this input data, which is why we are getting more double-triggers.

TABLE 7.1   Coefficient Values for the "Accelerate to Target" Mode

b_0	b_1	b_2
0.090909091	0.363636364	0.545454545

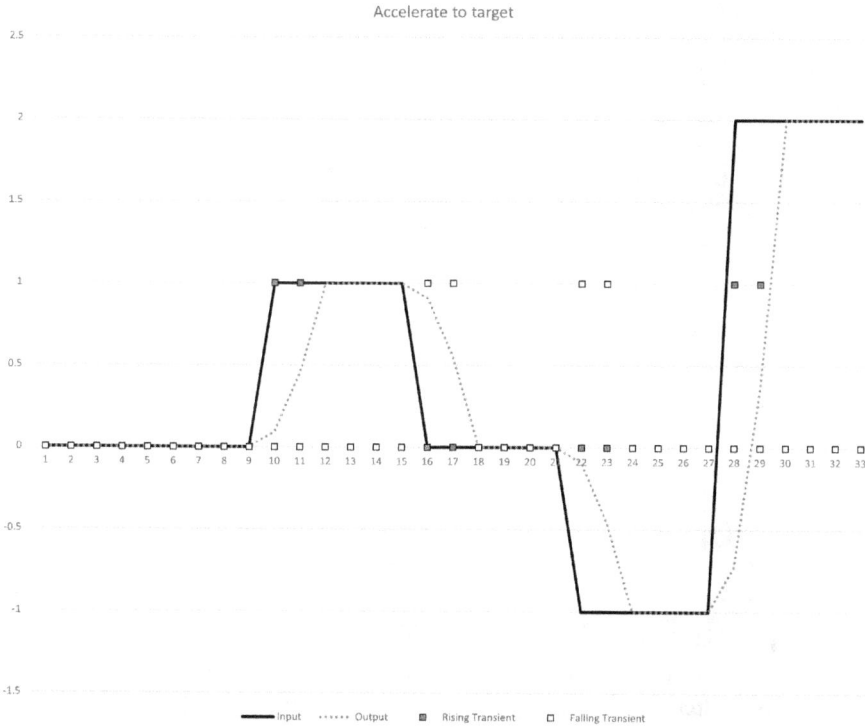

FIGURE 7.8 Filtering a bipolar input with "Accelerate to Target".

OK then. Let's instead reverse the coefficients as shown in Table 7.2 and call it "Decelerate to target".

Now in Figure 7.9 the filtered output (denoted again by the dotted line) is moving to the new value quickly, but then slows down as it settles to it – hence why I called it "Decelerate to target". When compared to the previous example, the transient components of the input signal have been deemphasized, which is why there are much fewer double-triggers.

So how does this "Decelerate to target" filter affect the damage data from the beginning of this chapter? Clearly, the transient detection in Figure 7.10 has been desensitized, which has removed the double-triggers as well as some of the transient triggers all together.

Let's lower the threshold from 0.1 to 0.09. Now in Figure 7.11 it's picking up more single-trigger transients! If you try this yourself, you might notice

TABLE 7.2   Coefficient Values for the "Decelerate to Target" Mode

b_0	b_1	b_2
0.545454545	0.363636364	0.090909091

Decelerate to target

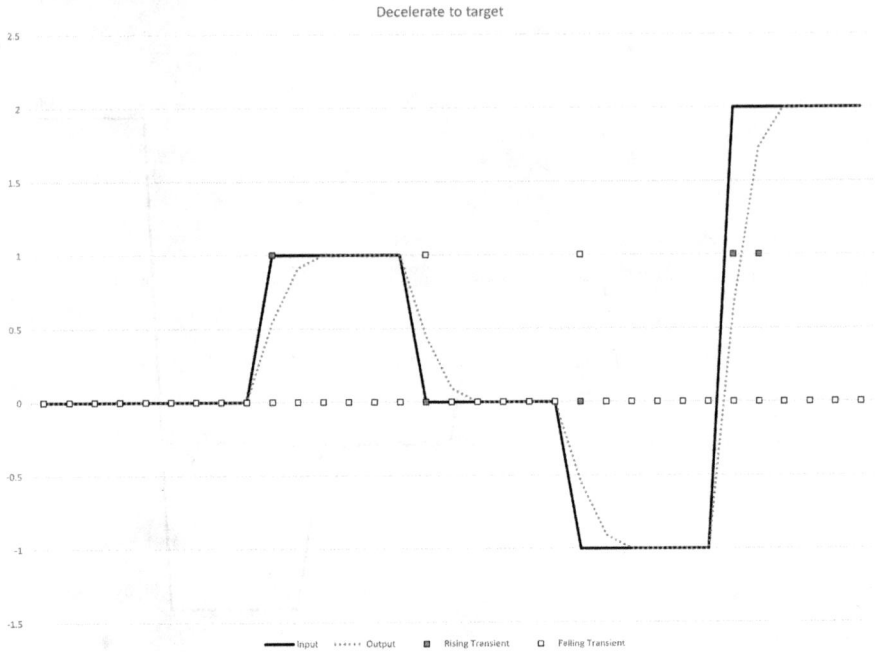

FIGURE 7.9   Filtering a bipolar input with "Decelerate to Target".

Filtered Component Damage With Transients Over Successive Game Updates

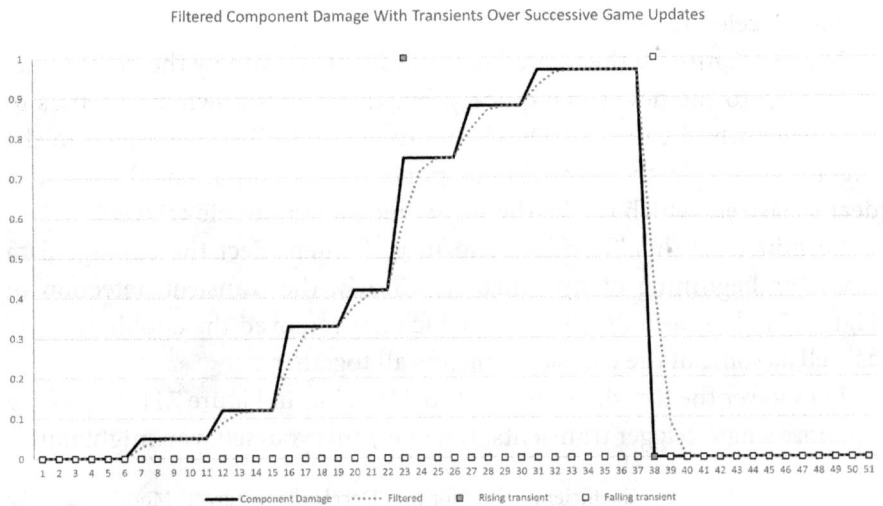

FIGURE 7.10   Graph of filtered damage to a component over time with transients detected at threshold (0.1).

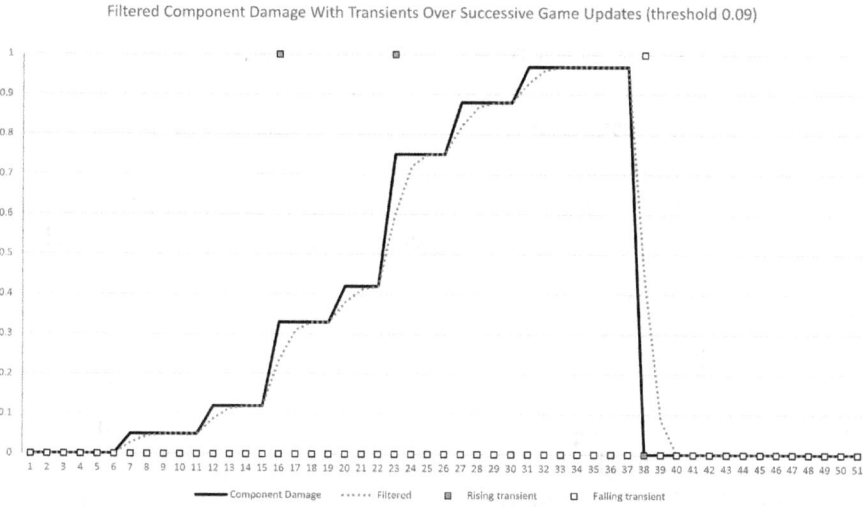

FIGURE 7.11 Graph of filtered damage to a component over time with transients detected at threshold (0.09).

that reducing the threshold to 0.09 without filtering doesn't change the outcome, so the "Decelerate to target" coefficients are definitely helping, and we are now less reliant on the cool-off timer/counter.

7.6.1 This Weighted Average Approach Might Look Familiar

You may have already realized this, but in case you haven't, this weighted average filtering shown in this chapter is known as a "Finite Impulse Response" (or FIR) filter in the audio world. The difference is that we've shown that it's also useful at lower sample rates, such as a parameter control rate of 60 fps. You may be interested in knowing that increasing the number of coefficients (and thus delay taps) will allow you to implement an FIR filter that is possibly more ornate in behavior than this one, but at the cost of a longer processing delay. Since responsiveness was key to this filter's utility, we kept it to three. However, if you are working at a high sampling rate you can get away with more coefficients. This process is generally known as increasing the order of the filter.

7.6.2 Why Do These Coefficients Work the Way They Do?

If, for a moment, you imagine an analog resistor-capacitor network inside a loudness-reactive disco light, you could decide to capture the impulse response of that network by giving it a delta function as input and thus record the result digitally. You could (with a little adjustment to normalize the DC gain) use that short recording as the coefficients of an FIR filter and thus get the same response that the resistor-capacitor has in the digital world. In this case, just three samples at 60 fps is not a lot to work with, but you can model your coefficients as some kind of decay as you would get from that analog circuit. This is where I came up with the "Decelerate to target" numbers, and honestly it was just experimentation in a spreadsheet.

7.7 CONCLUSION

If you have game parameters that routinely change with game-frame updates, you can cache them and process them in order to detect interesting changes. In the case of quantifying sudden changes, a simple step-transient detector might be what you are looking for, and if you use some filtering on the input to de-emphasize the transient components of these control-rate signals, it might help clean up the output so that you aren't having to block so many double triggers. Generally, though, it's good to have a simple state machine that resets when the last one-shot event is finished.

CHAPTER 8

Addressing the Neglect of Sound in Reused Animations

Roberto Bender

8.1 INTRODUCTION

In many games, animations are commonly reused across different characters, either by applying them to distinct meshes or by creating variations of the same character through modifications in color, size, or other attributes. This technique not only enhances visual diversity but also significantly reduces the workload of animators, allowing for more efficient content production. However, despite the emphasis on visual variety, sound design often remains static and neglected, leading to a repetitive and less immersive auditory experience.

One of the main reasons for this oversight is the tight coupling between animations and their associated sound events. In traditional implementations, a specific animation is often linked to a fixed set of sounds, meaning that regardless of the character's appearance or other variations, the same audio assets are triggered repeatedly. This creates a disconnect between the dynamic visual presentation and the static nature of the soundscape, ultimately diminishing the overall sense of variety and engagement.

To achieve a truly diverse and immersive experience, sound should evolve alongside visual elements. Just as developers invest in character customization and procedural variations, similar principles could be applied to audio design. By introducing adaptive sound systems that consider

DOI: 10.1201/9781003519119-11

163

character attributes such as size, material, and movement style, games can enhance realism and player engagement. A large, heavily armored character, for instance, should not produce the same movement sounds as a smaller, lighter counterpart, even if they share the same base animation.

Addressing this issue requires a shift in how sound is integrated into animations. Decoupling audio from rigid animation structures and instead implementing a more dynamic, context-aware system allows for greater flexibility and variety. This approach would not only improve the player's perception of uniqueness within the game world but also contribute to a richer, more immersive gaming experience overall.

8.2 UNDERSTANDING THE FOUNDATIONS

Before we delve into the proposed solution, it is crucial to grasp two fundamental components commonly present in game engines: animation sequencers and build tables. While these components might be referred to by different names across various platforms, their core functions remain consistent and are vital for dynamic entity creation:

8.2.1 The Animator/Animation Pane/Animation Sequencer

In many game engines, animation data is represented through a visualization tool resembling a storyboard or an animation sequencer. This sequencer is commonly used to associate various types of events – such as visual effects, gameplay triggers, and sound cues – with specific animation keyframes. These events are triggered in real time as the animation cursor progresses through the sequence. When it comes to audio, this typically means that sound events are directly linked to specific animations, ensuring that predefined sounds play at precise moments. Figure 8.1 shows a representation of what this editor might look like.

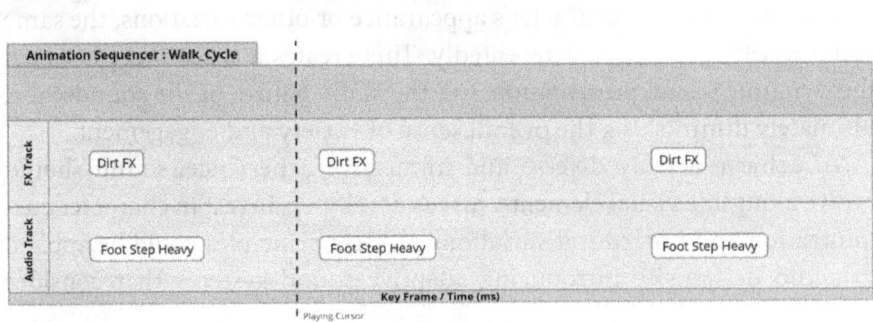

FIGURE 8.1 A representation of the animation sequencer.

However, as previously mentioned, animations are often reused across multiple models and character variations. While this enhances efficiency, it poses a challenge for audio design, as the same sound events may not always suit every character. A single animation, when applied to different characters with distinct physical attributes, materials, or sizes, may produce underwhelming or even inappropriate sound results, diminishing the overall quality of the audio experience.

8.2.1.1 Challenges with Traditional Solutions

A straightforward yet inefficient solution to this problem of animation reuse is duplicating animations and assigning different sound events to each copy. While this method technically works, it introduces several issues:

- **Data Bloat:** Duplicating animations increases memory usage and complicates asset management.

- **Reduced Productivity:** Audio designers must manually replicate their work for each character variation, leading to unnecessary redundancy.

- **Maintenance Challenges:** If an animation undergoes modifications such as timing adjustments or keyframe edits, all duplicated versions must be updated accordingly. This process is both time-consuming and error-prone, as associated audio events must be carefully remapped or shifted to match the changes.

To avoid these inefficiencies, a more flexible and scalable approach is required – one that decouples audio events from rigid animation structures while maintaining adaptability and consistency across character variations.

8.2.2 Build Tables

At their core, build tables are structured data frameworks that define how entities are assembled within a game. Think of them as recipes, where each row corresponds to an entity variation and each column specifies an attribute or parameter of that entity. These attributes can range from physical characteristics, such as size and color, to behavioral traits, equipment types, and even sound profiles.

Build tables allow for both static and dynamic attribute definitions:

- **Static Attributes** are fixed values that ensure consistency across entities. For example, a "Knight" entity might always be assigned heavy armor and a longsword.

- **Dynamic Attributes** introduce variability by incorporating randomized or conditional logic. This could include randomizing the color of a character's outfit, the type of weapon they carry, or even their behavior patterns in-game.

Let's take a look at how build tables work.

8.2.2.1 Structure and Design

Build tables are typically organized in a tabular format, whether implemented through spreadsheets, databases, or in-game data structures. Each entity type is defined in a row, while columns represent specific attributes such as:

- **Visual Characteristics:** Size, color, model variations, textures.

- **Behavioral Traits:** Aggressiveness, speed, attack patterns.

- **Equipment:** Weapons, armor, accessories.

- **Sound Profiles:** Footstep types, attack sounds, ambient noises.

- **Special Attributes:** Abilities, resistances, or weaknesses.

8.2.2.2 Entity Generation

When an entity is spawned in the game, the system references the build table to determine which attributes should be applied. The entity is then constructed based on the static attributes and any randomized selections defined by the table's rules.

8.2.2.3 Randomization and Conditional Logic

Build tables often integrate randomization logic to enhance variety. For example, an "Enemy" entity might have a 30% chance of spawning with a shield and a 70% chance without one. Conditions can also be applied, such as triggering specific equipment types based on the biome or environment where the entity spawns. Table 8.1 shows an example of what a build table might look like.

Understanding these two systems is crucial for designing a dynamic and adaptable sound framework. The animation sequencer defines when and

TABLE 8.1   An Example of a Standard Build Table

Build Table: Humanoid			
	Size	Armor Set	Animation Set
Heavy Brute	Medium	Rnd(A, B, C)	Humanoid
Infantry	Small	Infantry	Humanoid
Enemy Variation 1	Big	Rnd(A, B, C)	Humanoid
Enemy Variation 2	Rnd(Small, Medium)	D	Humanoid
Enemy Variation 3	Small	A	Humanoid

how events occur, while build tables determine what characteristics influence those events. By leveraging both, developers can create a sound system that intelligently adapts to character variations, ensuring that audio remains consistent with the visual and gameplay context. This foundational understanding sets the stage for implementing solutions that enhance sound dynamism, reduce manual workload, and enrich the overall player experience.

8.3 SOLUTIONS

Now that we understand both the animation sequencer and build tables, we can explore the proposed solution of this work, presented through two key approaches.

8.3.1 Dynamic Sound Variation Based on In-Game Elements and Character Attributes

By allowing game elements – such as a character's physical characteristics, materials, or even environmental factors – to influence sound dynamically, audio can become more organic and reactive. This approach offers greater variety with minimal manual intervention, as sound properties such as pitch, volume, and timbre can be adjusted in real time based on the entity producing them. For example, a heavier character might generate deeper footsteps, while a smaller, agile character could produce lighter, quicker sounds. While this method is less controlled, it enhances immersion by making sound feel more integrated with gameplay mechanics.

8.3.2 A Replaceable Intermediary Layer between Animation and Sound Events

Another approach involves introducing an intermediary system between the animation sequencer and the actual audible sound event. Instead of directly linking a sound to an animation, this system would act as a flexible layer that determines which sound variant should play based on the context. This allows for greater control and modularity, enabling developers to easily swap, modify, or conditionally trigger different sounds without modifying the base animation itself. By decoupling animations from rigid sound mappings, this method ensures that even repeated animations can produce a variety of auditory experiences.

8.3.3 Combined Solution

A powerful and flexible framework emerges for enhancing sound dynamism in games by combining the two proposed techniques: the replaceable intermediary layer and the dynamic influence of in-game character attributes. The intermediary layer acts as an adaptable bridge between the animation sequencer and the actual sound events. Instead of hard-linking specific sounds to animations, this layer allows for conditional logic and dynamic selection, ensuring that the most contextually appropriate sound is triggered at runtime. This decoupling not only simplifies asset management but also significantly enhances flexibility, as sounds can be easily swapped, modified, or extended without altering the core animation data.

When paired with character attributes – such as size, weight, material composition, or even environmental context – the system becomes even more dynamic. For example, a heavy, armored character could automatically trigger deeper, more resonant footstep sounds, while a nimble, lightly equipped character would produce lighter, quicker sounds, all without requiring manual intervention for each variation. Similarly, environmental factors like terrain type or weather conditions could further influence the final sound output, adding layers of realism and immersion.

This combination empowers audio designers and gameplay developers to create richer, more varied auditory experiences while reducing redundant work and simplifying maintenance. It transforms the soundscape from a static component into a living, adaptive element of the game world – one that reacts intelligently to gameplay scenarios and player interactions. Figure 8.2 shows

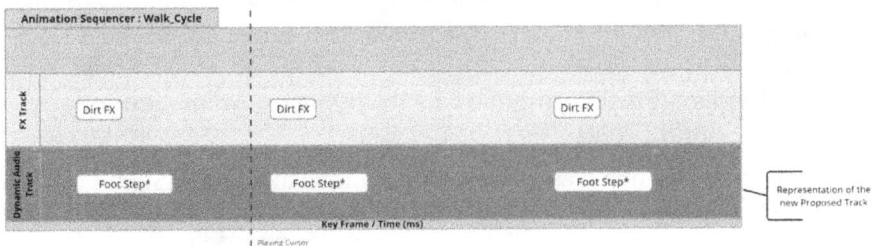

FIGURE 8.2   The animation sequencer with the new dynamic audio track.

TABLE 8.2   The Same Build Table as Table 8.1, but with the New Dynamic Sound
Set Added

Build Table: Humanoid

	Size	Armor Set	Animation Set	Dynamic Sound Set
Heavy Brute	Medium	Rnd(A, B, C)	Humanoid	Heavy Brute
Infantry	Small	Infantry	Humanoid	Infantry
Enemy Variation 1	Big	Rnd(A, B, C)	Humanoid	Boss
Enemy Variation 2	Rnd(Small, Medium)	D	Humanoid	Enemy Generic
Enemy Variation 3	Small	A	Humanoid	Enemy Generic

the animation editor with the new dynamic audio track, and Table 8.2
shows how the build table changes to include audio information.
Note how this setup allows different sounds to be hooked up to the same
animation.

Here is a simplified take in C++ of the proposed solution:

```cpp
/**
 * The tag that performs two key roles. Visualization under
 * the Animation Sequencer UI and the look up link when
 * searching actions inside the DynamicSoundSet.
 */
struct DynamicSoundTag
{
  std::string m_Name;
  bool operator == (const DynamicSoundTag& right) const
  {
    return m_Name == right.m_Name;
  }
};


/**
 * An example of specializing an
 * AnimationTag, abstracting how to connect to the Animation
 * Sequencer.
 */
class DynamicAnimationSoundTag : public AnimationTag
{
public:
  DynamicAnimationSoundTag(const DynamicSoundTag& soundTag)
```

```
      : m_SoundTag(soundTag)
  {}

  const DynamicSoundTag& GetSoundTag() const
  { return m_SoundTag; }

private:
  DynamicSoundTag m_SoundTag;
};

/**
 * The link between the tag available in the animation and
 * the sound should be played.
 */
class DynamicSoundAction
{
public:
  DynamicSoundAction(const DynamicSoundTag& soundTag,
    const AudioEvent& sound)
    : m_SoundTag(soundTag)
    , m_Sound(sound)
  {}

  virtual bool Evaluate(
    const DynamicSoundTag& soundTag) const
  {
    return m_SoundTag == soundTag;
  }

  virtual void Play(const Entity& entity) const
  {
    m_Sound.Play();
  }

private:
  DynamicSoundTag m_SoundTag;
  AudioEvent m_Sound;
};

/**
 * An exemplification of an override that reacts to runtime
```

```
 * elements.
 */
class DynamicSoundActionByStressLevel : public
DynamicSoundAction
{
public:
  DynamicSoundActionByStressLevel(
    const DynamicSoundTag& soundTag,
    const AudioEvent& sound, const AudioEvent& stressSound)
    : DynamicSoundAction(soundTag, sound)
    , m_StressSound(sound)
  {}

  void Play(const Entity& entity) const override
  {
    /* 50 is an arbitrary testing number */
    if(entity.GetStressLevel() > 50)
      m_StressSound.Play();
    else
      DynamicSoundAction::Play(entity);
  }

private:
  AudioEvent m_StressSound;
};

/**
 * The collection of actions associated with tags. These
 * actions will therefore be part of the Entity and decoupled
 * from the Animation, given the flexibility we aim for.
 */
class DynamicSoundSet :
  public std::vector<DynamicSoundAction>
{
public:
  DynamicSoundSet(
    std::initializer_list<DynamicSoundAction> il)
      : std::vector<DynamicSoundAction>(il)
  {}

  void Play(
```

```
      const DynamicSoundTag& tag, const Entity& entity) const
  {
    for(const DynamicSoundAction& action : *this)
    {
      if(action.Evaluate(tag))
        action.Play(entity);
    }
  }
};

/**
 * A simple collection for holding all the
 * DynamicSoundSet(s).
 */
class DynamicSoundSetCollection :
  public std::vector<DynamicSoundSet>
{
public:
  void Play(
    const DynamicSoundTag& tag, const Entity& entity) const
  {
    for(const DynamicSoundSet& set : *this)
      set.Play(tag, entity);
  }
};

/**
 * Example code on how different characters could be
 * configured using the same animation.
 */
void Setup()
{
  DynamicSoundTag LeftFootTag { "Left_Foot" };
  DynamicSoundTag RightFootTag { "Right_Foot"  };
  DynamicSoundTag BreathTag { "Breath" };

  DynamicSoundSet HeavyBruteSoundSet
  {
    DynamicSoundAction(LeftFootTag,
      AudioEvent("Play_FootStep_Heavy")),
    DynamicSoundAction(RightFootTag,
      AudioEvent("Play_FootStep_Heavy")),
```

```
      DynamicSoundActionByStressLevel(BreathTag,
        AudioEvent("Play_Breath_Normal"),
        AudioEvent("Play_Breath_Stress"))
  };

  DynamicSoundSet ArcherSoundSet
  {
    DynamicSoundAction(LeftFootTag,
      AudioEvent("Play_FootStep_Light")),
    DynamicSoundAction(RightFootTag,
      AudioEvent("Play_FootStep_Light")),
    DynamicSoundAction(BreathTag,
      AudioEvent("Play_Breath_Normal"))
  };

  Entity heavyBrute;
  heavyBrute.AddDynamicSoundSet(HeavyBruteSoundSet);

  Entity archer;
  archer.AddDynamicSoundSet(ArcherSoundSet);
}


/**
 * Example code on a very simplistic take on the Update of a
 * given animation. This code will fetch a list of
 * DynamicAnimationSoundTag from the current animation,
 * observing the current keyframe. If tags are found, it uses
 * the associated entity DynamicSoundSetCollection to handle
 * such tags. For the sake of simplification, we assume the
 * Animation class exists elsewhere.
 */
void Animation::OnAnimationUpdate()
{
  const DynamicSoundSetCollection&
    dynamicSoundSetCollection =
      m_Entity.GetDynamicSoundSetCollection();
  for(const DynamicAnimationSoundTag& tag :
      GetCurrentAnimationTags<DynamicAnimationSoundTag>())
    dynamicSoundSetCollection.Play(
      tag.GetSoundTag(), m_Entity);
}
```

8.4 CONCLUSION

Enhancing sound dynamism in games requires a thoughtful integration of adaptable systems that respond intelligently to gameplay context. The combination of a replaceable intermediary layer and dynamic sound variation based on character attributes forms a robust framework for achieving this goal.

The intermediary layer introduces a modular approach that decouples sound events from rigid animation timelines, allowing for flexible, context-driven sound selection. As a result, asset management is simpler, and it also enables greater creativity and responsiveness in sound design. Making use of character attributes and environmental factors also ensures that audio outputs feel authentic and immersive, adapting in real time to the nuances of each gameplay scenario. Together, these approaches empower developers to craft richer, more varied auditory experiences without the burden of manual sound assignment for every variation. The result is a soundscape that feels alive and responsive, enhancing player immersion and reinforcing the dynamic nature of the game world.

With a solid understanding of animation sequencing and character construction through build tables, developers can effectively implement these systems to maximize both flexibility and efficiency. This foundation paves the way for creating sound experiences that are not only technically robust but also emotionally resonant, elevating the overall quality and depth of the game.

CHAPTER 9

Rule Systems and Context Aware Speech in *Homeworld 3*

Jon Mitchell

9.1 INTRODUCTION

Over the last 10 years, rule systems have become a commonly used approach to implementing speech logic in games. Game worlds are growing increasingly complex, and players expect varied, dynamic, and situationally specific dialog from their characters. Rule systems offer a flexible way of handling the hookups, logic, and sequencing for context-specific dialog, helping keep the game logic and speech logic cleanly separated. Maintaining this separation can be a significant challenge in larger games with hundreds of characters, thousands of lines of dialog, and many unique gameplay situations. Rule systems are an enormous improvement over unstructured and ad-hoc approaches to dialog implementation, but they are not without their pitfalls. This chapter describes some of the characteristics of rule systems as they relate to dialog and audio, has some advice on how to best make use of them, and looks in some detail at our implementation of a rule-based dialog system for *Homeworld 3*.

9.2 WHAT IS A RULE SYSTEM?

Rule systems generally have the following components:

- **Data Base**: Stores all the information that rules can access.

DOI: 10.1201/9781003519119-12

- **Rule Base**: A set of rules on what actions to take when our data are in a specific state.

- **Rule Matcher/Resolver/Runner**:

  - **Matcher:** Identifies which rule(s) may be active for the current data context.

  - **Resolver:** Determines which of the set of matching rules will be executed.

  - **Runner:** Performs the actions specified by the chosen rule.

This is all very generic, so let's look at some simple pseudocode rules, unfortunately inspired by recent interactions with my twin toddlers.

```
// Data Base: Per-Actor data that the rules can access
Data
{
  Actor lastAttacker //the last person to attack you
  Actor lastSeen     //the last person to come into view
  int   hitCount     //number of times you've been hit
  float lastHitTime  //the last time you were hit
}


//Rule base

//Say something if Bea hits you for the first time
Rule OnHitByBea
{
event: "ActorHit"
conditions:
  last_attacker = "Bea"
action:
  say("Ow! Bea hit me!)
}

//Say something if Bea hits you within a time window
Rule OnHitByBeaAgain
{
event: "ActorHit"
conditions:
  last_attacker = "Bea",
```

```
    TimeSince(lastHitTime) < 5
action:
  say("Bea hit me again!)
}


//Say something if you see Bea and everything is fine
Rule OnSeeBea
{
event: "SeeActor"
condition:
  last_seen = "Bea"
action:
  say("Hi Bea! ")
}


//Say something if you see Bea after being hit recently a lot
Rule OnSeeBeaAfterBeingRepeatedlyHit
{
event: "SeeActor"
conditions:
  last_seen = "Bea"
  TimeSince(lastHitTime) < 10,
  hitCount > 4
action:
  say("Go away! ")
}


//Say something if you see a parent after being hit recently
//a lot
Rule OnSeeParentAfterBeingRepeatedlyHit
{
event: "SeeActor"
conditions:
  IsParent(lastSeen)
  TimeSince(lastHitTime) < 10,
  hitCount > 4
action:
  say("I need a big hug")
}
```

As this example shows, one of the more helpful features of rule systems is the ability to define ever more specific responses to the same game events, without each game event having overly complex or convoluted responses.

9.2.1 Event-Condition-Action (ECA) Pattern

The example uses the ECA pattern, which is the simplest way I've come across to implement a rule system. Each rule is broken into three steps:

- **Events**: Instigating gameplay or input events.

- **Conditions**: A set of conditions that must be true before a specific action is taken.

- **Actions**: A response appropriate for the set of conditions.

On implementing an ECA-based rule system, Martin Fowler says: "All you need is to create a bunch of objects with conditions and actions, store them in a collection, and run through them to evaluate the conditions and execute the actions" (Fowler 2009).

There are, as always, a lot of fiddly details to be thought through, but this is really the essence of it.

9.2.2 What Makes This Useful for Dialog?

I've seen the ECA pattern used for all sorts of game programming situations, like contextual input handling, granting achievements, and ability/power activations. This prevalence shouldn't be too surprising, since the pattern itself is really a thin abstraction of:

When A *happens and* Y *is true, do* Z.

which covers an enormous range of possibilities. So what makes this a good fit for dialog, specifically?

- ECA is explicitly event-based and works very well in conjunction with event-based game logic.

- It is quick to implement and easy to extend. If you don't have a good grasp on exactly what your dialog needs are for your game, this sort of system can be a good starting point to help you figure it out, even if it is only for prototyping.

- It is a simple but constrained scripting model: designers and programmers alike can contribute to speech logic implementation, but are kept "on rails".

- It can handle asynchronous responses and event chaining very simply from the user's POV, which can be challenging in more conventional scripting.

9.2.3 When Isn't This Useful for Dialog?

Despite the benefits, there are cases when this pattern is probably *not* a good fit for your dialog needs. At one end of the spectrum, your design might just be too simple to need it. If the design is purely linear, with no dynamic or conditional elements, there is no real benefit to being able to attach multiple conditional rules to the same event. At the other end, you are better off with a dedicated branching conversation system. An RPG-like design featuring deeply branching conversations and visualization of possible future conversational pathways in the UX may be *possible* with rule systems, but it would be a frustrating experience compared to a system with explicit support for those concepts. However, if the dialog is mostly "bark"-based, where characters can have many context-dependent single-line responses, or they have relatively shallow branching conversations, then this approach can be very successful. Another option is to use this pattern as a component of your dialog toolset, rather than making it responsible for all game dialog. *Homeworld 3* uses the ECA-rules approach for our systemic combat dialog, but for linear "talking heads" mission dialog, there is a simpler system for quickly triggering mission lines without requiring an associated rule.

9.3 *Homeworld 3*'s SYSTEM

Luckily for us, *Homeworld 3*'s dialog design *is* a pretty good fit for this sort of approach: the dialog is almost always a reaction to game events, sensitive to game context, and conversations are often call-response pairs. I say "luckily", but really this was a case where the dialog design and the dialog system design evolved hand-in-glove. We wrote a quick-and-dirty dialog system to handle the major features our designers knew they'd need in a few weeks. After that, the programmers and designers kept working closely together to iterate on both the system and dialog designs.

9.3.1 Three-Layer Architecture

The architecture of the system that we built for *Homeworld 3* ended up having three layers:

- **High level**: Rule system

- **Mid level**: Dialog selection

- **Low level**: Line selection and playback

Figure 9.1 has examples of how these layers fit together.

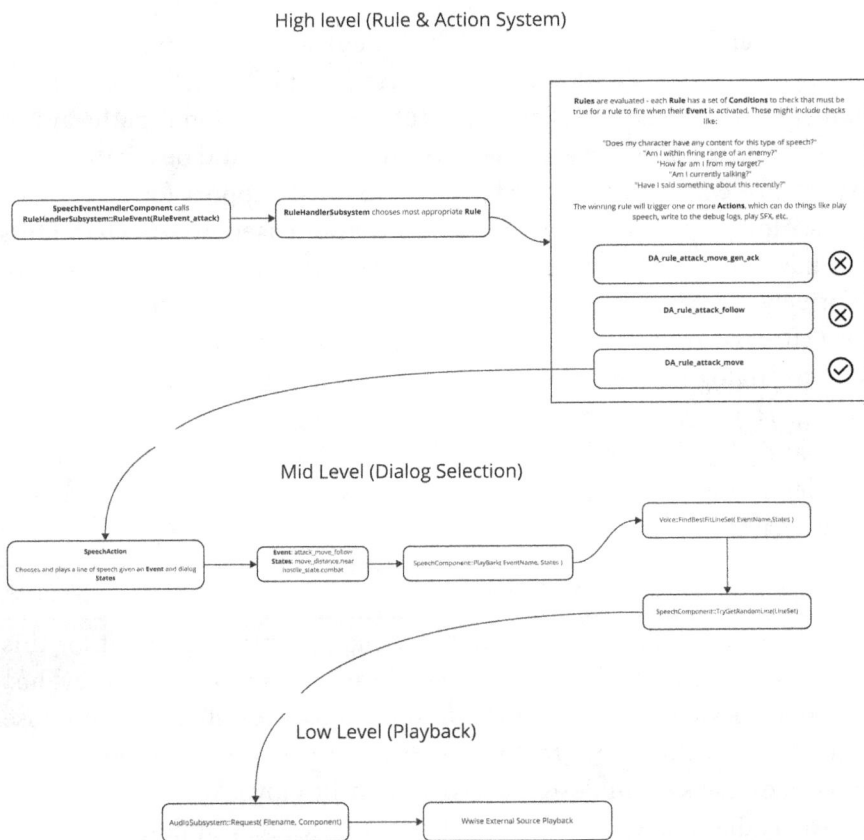

FIGURE 9.1 The three layers of *Homeworld 3*'s dialog system, showing examples of the data flow.

9.3.2 High Level: Rule System

Our `RuleHandlerSubsystem` object uses the ECA pattern explicitly: each `URule` asset contains a `URuleEvent` that will activate it, a `UCondition` to evaluate, and a `UAction` to run if it is chosen.

9.3.2.1 Conditions

Our base class for `UCondition` is simple – really all it can do is calculate a weight, where anything over zero is considered true. Returning an `int` rather than a `bool` gives us a way to resolve the priority of rules if multiple rules are active for the same event. The Unreal markup lets us create user defined Blueprint (BP) conditions, which (like BP in general) is fantastic for prototyping and quick changes, but increasingly hazardous to performance as use of the system scales up.

```
UCLASS(BlueprintType, EditInlineNew, Abstract)
class UCondition : public UObject
{
GENERATED_BODY()

public:
UFUNCTION(BlueprintCallable, BlueprintCosmetic)
virtual int CalculateWeight(
  URuleContextComponent* Context) const;
};
```

We only have 5 core C++ conditions, but they were powerful enough to implement almost all of the gameplay situations we came across. Table 9.1 lists these core conditions.

9.3.2.2 Actions

Although the actions for a generic ECA system can, in principle, do anything, this system is designed to trigger dialog lines. The actions listed in Table 9.2 show how just four audio-related actions and four procedural actions can be enough.

9.3.2.3 Group Conditions and Group Actions

It might seem restrictive to limit ourselves to a single `UCondition` and `UAction`. However, in order to work around this limitation, we implement `UGroupCondition` and `UGroupAction`, which are container objects for

TABLE 9.1   Core Conditions Used in *Homeworld 3*

Name	Description
CheckFact	True if a comparison check (>, >=, <, <=, ==, or !=) against one of the actor's Blackboard values passes.
Chance	True if a 0.0 (0% probability) to 1.0 (100% probability) random check passes.
Cooldown	True if more than *N* seconds have passed since a timestamp on the blackboard.
GroupCondition	True if Boolean logic on a set of conditions passes.
ReferenceCondition	Creates a single condition object that can be used across multiple rules, keeping complex conditions in sync across multiple rules without having to painstakingly identify repeated blocks of logic and edit them separately.

TABLE 9.2   Actions for the *Homeworld 3* Rule System

Name	Description
SetFact	CheckFact's counterpart: Assignment operations (+=, -=, or =) on Blackboard values.
SpeechAction	Selects and plays a line of speech using a set of state tags.
LineAction	Plays a specific line of speech.
SFXAction	Plays a Wwise event.
RtpcAction	Sets a Wwise control parameter.
CancelRuleAction	Stops any rules running on this Actor.
RunOnActor	Selects another Actor to run Actions on.
RuleEvent	Triggers evaluation of another Rule.

conditions and actions. **UGroupCondition** will return true if **Any**, **All**, or **None** of its child conditions are true. Similarly, **UGroupAction** runs child actions in sequence. Figure 9.2 shows an example rule with groups of two actions and conditions.

9.3.2.4 Action Sequencing

When a **UGroupAction** is run, its **UActionRunner** returns that it is either **Finished** or **WaitingToFinish**. If it finishes on that frame, then we can move onto the next action. If the runner is **WaitingToFinish**, we are reliant on the runner calling back **Finished()** to tell the parent it can move on. **UGroupActionRunner** itself doesn't wait in the sense of busy-waiting or polling – it is purely controlled by callbacks from its child objects. For example, **SpeechAction** uses Wwise's **EndOfEvent** callback to drive our callbacks. This setup is enough for us to sequence actions in time, which is the building block we need to create a basic conversation system.

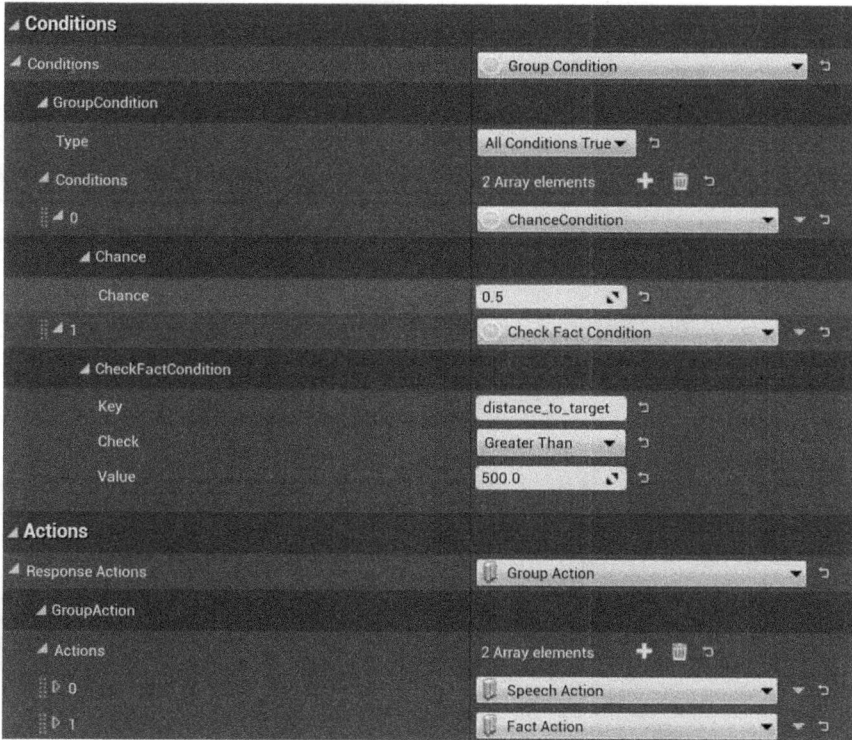

FIGURE 9.2   An example rule in Unreal featuring a Group Condition and a Group Action.

9.3.2.5 *RunOnActor and* `ActorProvider`

The other key components for making our ECA rule system usable as a dialog system are `RunOnActor` and `ActorProvider`. We want to be able to have our actors talk to each other or comment on situations they see other actors encountering. Many of the dialog lines in *Homeworld 3* are scripted as call-response pairs, but since the active actors in a 3D RTS scene are continuously in flux, we need to be able to dynamically match pairs of units which are situationally able to talk to one another:

- `RunOnActor` will run the specified Action on a different actor.

- `ActorProvider` provides a filter or set of rules for selecting which actor `RunOnActor` will target.

Figure 9.3 shows an example of how we used the system to create dynamic dialog chains by chaining `RuleEvents` via `RunOnActor` actions.

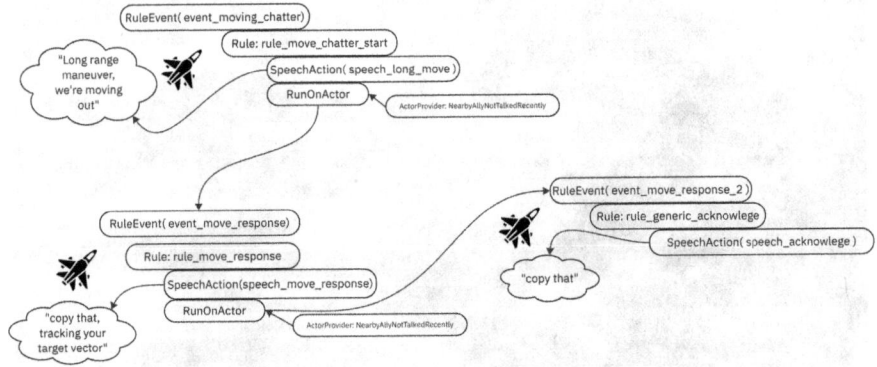

FIGURE 9.3 An example of a dialog chain triggered by `RunOnActor` actions and `ActorProviders`.

9.3.3 Avoiding the Turing Tar-pit

Beware of the Turing tar-pit, in which everything is possible but nothing of interest is easy.

(Alan Perlis 1982)

Once your rule system has these:

- **Conditions** that can perform logical tests on values,

- **Actions** that can modify values,

- **Actions** that can trigger a new **Rule** that will check **Conditions** that will run **Actions** that can...

Congratulations! Your bouncing baby rule system is now Turing Complete, or if not actually *complete*, probably more Turing than is good for it (or than is good for *you*). Unnecessary complexity should be avoided wherever possible in a Domain Specific Language (DSL). The whole point of a DSL is to give you a toolkit that makes the specific task at hand easier, not a hard-to-program virtual machine with no debugger. Thankfully, we came up with a few strategies to help keep our rule complexity manageable:

- **Identify Common Patterns and Simplify Their Use:** *Don't Repeat Yourself* (DRY) is often just as useful a maxim for DSLs and data-driven systems as it is for code. When we saw patterns used

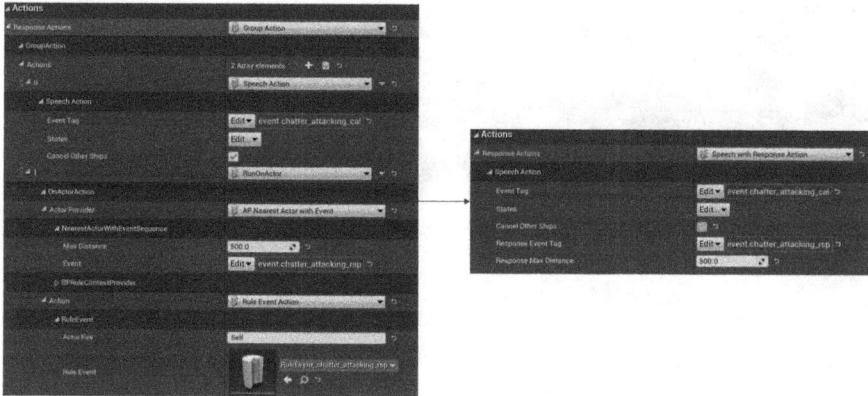

FIGURE 9.4 (Left) A call and response pair implemented as a Group Action. (Right) The same call and response pair implemented with a custom Speech with response Action.

repeatedly to implement some aspect of the dialog design, the dialog team would discuss why they were needed, and how they could be made simpler to use. Figure 9.4 shows the initial implementation of a call-and-response pair, and how we created a single action to replace it. Much nicer!

- **Be Careful What You Add:** A common pitfall when writing a system with very generic "Hey Look! It Can Do Anything!" base concepts like `Condition` and `Action` is failing to consider carefully if something *should* be added to the system. A great example of when something should *not* have been added to our system was `BranchAction`. It is really nothing more or less than an *if-else* statement. Figure 9.5 shows `BranchAction` being used to select different speech events based on the distance to a target.

  This action was a seemingly harmless addition, but it undermined the conceptual integrity of rules, which otherwise have a clear split between the phases of evaluating what is true and acting upon that information. If we preserve that constraint, more rules may be needed, but individual rules will be simpler, easier to debug, easier to reason about, and easier to apply optimization techniques to.

- **Actions as Implicit Conditions:** One pitfall we found with the earliest versions of our rules was that a rule would pass all its `Condition` checks, be selected as the highest priority `Rule`, play a `SpeechAction`,

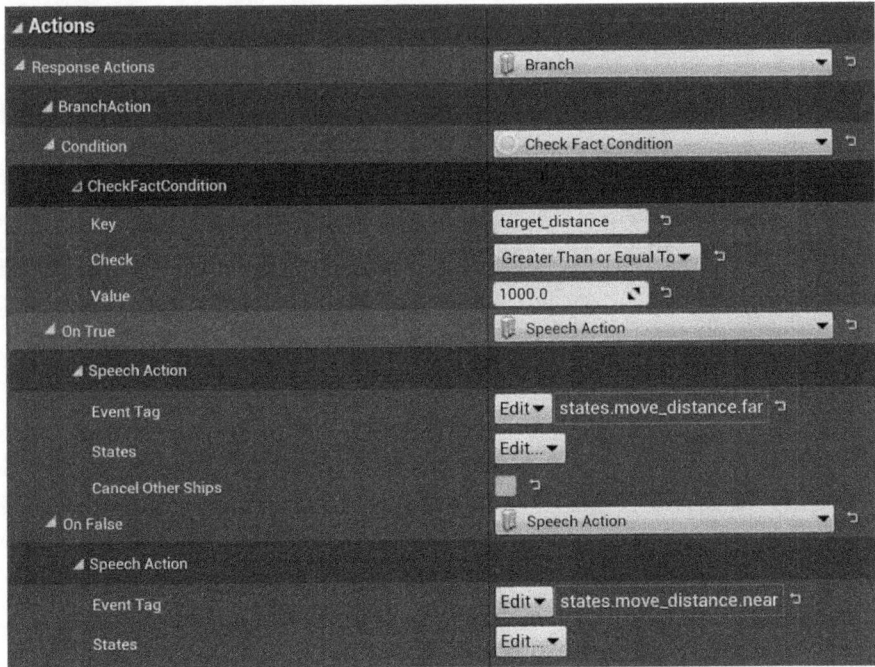

FIGURE 9.5   An example of a Branch Action, which in retrospect was a mistake to add.

then fail to actually do anything at all because the **Voice** data attached to that actor didn't even have the requested speech context. Initially we solved this by adding a **HasSpeechEvent** condition to every rule with a **SpeechAction**, ensuring at the condition-checking phase that the rule would do something. That worked, but at the cost of complicating all our rules with additional boilerplate.

We ended up finding a simple solution to this problem: we allowed our **Action** data types to implement their own **Conditions**, so a **HasSpeechEvent** check could be automatically run for every **SpeechAction** without needing to set anything else up. These checks only needed to be implemented once per **Action** type, rather than once per **Action** instance, and didn't rely on the implementers remembering that they needed to do it!

9.3.4 Mid Level: Dialog Selection

Rules are great for implementing and clarifying the game logic needed to identify a game context, but they don't scale to handling many thousands

Unit Type	Event Type	StateGroup1	State1	StateGroup2	State2	HostileStats	Text	Filename
f01_strikecraft_interceptor	chatter_moving_cal	current_action	move_move	proximity_object	terrain_close	alert	Stay tight. Watch minimums.	f01_strikecraft_interceptor_chatter_moving_cal_clear_211720
f01_strikecraft_interceptor	chatter_moving_cal	current_action	move_move	proximity_object	terrain_close	alert	Watch the corners. Call out hazards.	f01_strikecraft_interceptor_chatter_moving_cal_clear_211721
f01_strikecraft_interceptor	chatter_moving_cal	current_action	move_move	proximity_object	terrain_close	alert	Set priority tone alerts while you can. Short range.	f01_strikecraft_interceptor_chatter_moving_cal_clear_211722
f01_strikecraft_interceptor	chatter_moving_cal	current_action	move_move	proximity_object	terrain_close	alert	Pull it in. Watch the deck.	f01_strikecraft_interceptor_chatter_moving_cal_clear_211723
f01_strikecraft_interceptor	chatter_moving_cal	current_action	move_move	proximity_object	terrain_close	alert	Surface alert. Proximity avoidance to short range. Maximum resolution.	f01_strikecraft_interceptor_chatter_moving_cal_clear_211724
f01_strikecraft_interceptor	chatter_moving_cal	current_action	move_move	proximity_object	terrain_close	alert	This is lead. Redirect active array to our spec.	f01_strikecraft_interceptor_chatter_moving_cal_clear_211725
f01_strikecraft_interceptor	chatter_moving_cal	current_action	move_move	proximity_object	terrain_close	alert	Proximity caution. Set A-G for avoidance to level one.	f01_strikecraft_interceptor_chatter_moving_cal_clear_211726
f01_strikecraft_interceptor	chatter_moving_cal	current_action	move_move	proximity_object	terrain_close	alert	Flight. Correct as needed. Sensors, adjust for early warning.	f01_strikecraft_interceptor_chatter_moving_cal_clear_211731
f01_strikecraft_interceptor	chatter_moving_cal	current_action	move_move	proximity_object	terrain_close	alert	Ok. Stream buffer responding as expected. Link for update now. Signal is clear.	f01_strikecraft_interceptor_chatter_moving_cal_clear_211732
f01_strikecraft_interceptor	chatter_moving_cal	current_action	move_move	proximity_object	terrain_close	alert	Debris field alert. Flight, adjust as needed. Relay to all craft.	f01_strikecraft_interceptor_chatter_moving_cal_clear_211733
f01_strikecraft_interceptor	chatter_moving_cal	current_action	move_move	proximity_object	terrain_close	alert	Tracking particulate debris field. Local operators to avoid contact.	f01_strikecraft_interceptor_chatter_moving_cal_clear_211734
f01_strikecraft_interceptor	chatter_moving_cal	current_action	move_move	proximity_object	nebula	clear	Pushing through Nebula. Area is clear.	f01_strikecraft_interceptor_chatter_moving_cal_clear_211735
f01_strikecraft_interceptor	chatter_moving_cal	current_action	move_move	proximity_object	nebula	alert	Adjusting nav for E-O-S.	f01_strikecraft_interceptor_chatter_moving_cal_clear_211736
f01_strikecraft_interceptor	chatter_moving_cal	current_action	move_move	proximity_object	nebula	alert	Sensors compensating for nebula density.	f01_strikecraft_interceptor_chatter_moving_cal_clear_211737
f01_strikecraft_interceptor	chatter_moving_cal	current_action	move_move	proximity_object	nebula	clear	Density is fluctuating. All craft monitor your vectors.	f01_strikecraft_interceptor_chatter_moving_cal_clear_211738
f01_strikecraft_interceptor	chatter_moving_cal	current_action	move_move	proximity_object	nebula	clear	Surrounding craft. Ensure you adjust sensor offsets as needed to compensate for interference.	f01_strikecraft_interceptor_chatter_moving_cal_clear_211739
f01_strikecraft_interceptor	chatter_moving_cal	current_action	move_move	proximity_object	nebula	clear	Range detection will be affected. Maintain overlay from all locals and cross-check.	f01_strikecraft_interceptor_chatter_moving_cal_clear_211740
f01_strikecraft_interceptor	chatter_moving_cal	current_action	move_move	proximity_object	nebula	alert	Optical Sensors are now primary. Flight to adjust.	f01_strikecraft_interceptor_chatter_moving_cal_clear_211741
f01_strikecraft_interceptor	chatter_moving_cal	current_action	move_move	proximity_object	nebula	alert	Nebula is affecting range. Correct your offsets.	f01_strikecraft_interceptor_chatter_moving_cal_clear_211743
f01_strikecraft_interceptor	chatter_moving_cal	current_action	move_move	proximity_object	nebula	alert	Flight update. Confirm offsets. Monitor and report.	f01_strikecraft_interceptor_chatter_moving_cal_clear_211744
f01_strikecraft_interceptor	chatter_moving_cal	current_action	move_move	proximity_object	nebula	alert	Flight, take note. Update to embedded minimums.	f01_strikecraft_interceptor_chatter_moving_cal_clear_211745
f01_strikecraft_interceptor	chatter_moving_cal	current_action	move_move	proximity_object	nebula	alert	Sensor interference growing. Density map embedded for reference.	f01_strikecraft_interceptor_chatter_moving_cal_clear_211746
f01_strikecraft_interceptor	chatter_moving_cal	current_action	move_move	proximity_object	nebula	alert	Sensor data errors keep creepin in. Switching to manual control.	f01_strikecraft_interceptor_chatter_moving_cal_clear_211747
f01_strikecraft_interceptor	chatter_moving_cal	current_action	move_move	proximity_object	nebula	alert	Reading density changes. Sensor faults. Adjusting.	f01_strikecraft_interceptor_chatter_moving_cal_clear_211748
f01_strikecraft_interceptor	chatter_moving_cal	current_action	move_move	proximity_object	nebula	alert	This density is throwing everything off.	f01_strikecraft_interceptor_chatter_moving_cal_clear_211749

FIGURE 9.6   A screenshot of the source CSV file for the interceptor pilot character.

of lines without additional help. A medium-size game like *Homeworld 3* has about 40000 lines of dialog, and using hand-created rule assets to select those lines is not a practical solution. In the end, we had maybe 40 or so actual rules that handled the higher-level logic and sequencing, and used our USpeechVoice objects to handle lower-level line selection. Our speech designer is most comfortable working in spreadsheets, so we have a small conversion pipeline which takes a single speech CSV as input and creates a separate USpeechVoice data asset for each character. Figure 9.6 shows a portion of our source CSV file for our interceptor pilot character. Figure 9.7 shows a USpeechVoice asset for the same character.

9.3.4.1 Gameplay Tags

Selection of dialog at this layer is entirely driven by Unreal's FGameplayTag. FGameplayTags are a way of representing a set of all possible values of a state, but go one step further, as they can also represent a hierarchical set of values. Figure 9.8 is an example of how we might use gameplay tags to organize a hierarchy of object types for a set of vehicles.

With our object tags organized hierarchically, we can write dialog for each object type to handle less specific to more specific contexts. Table 9.3 shows example dialog we might use for when one of our Jeeps spots an incoming enemy.

This type of approach can work especially well for games like RPGs, RTSs, and open world games, where writing specific dialog for all possible interactions isn't particularly practical. It also helps handle situations like user created and downloadable content, where we may still need

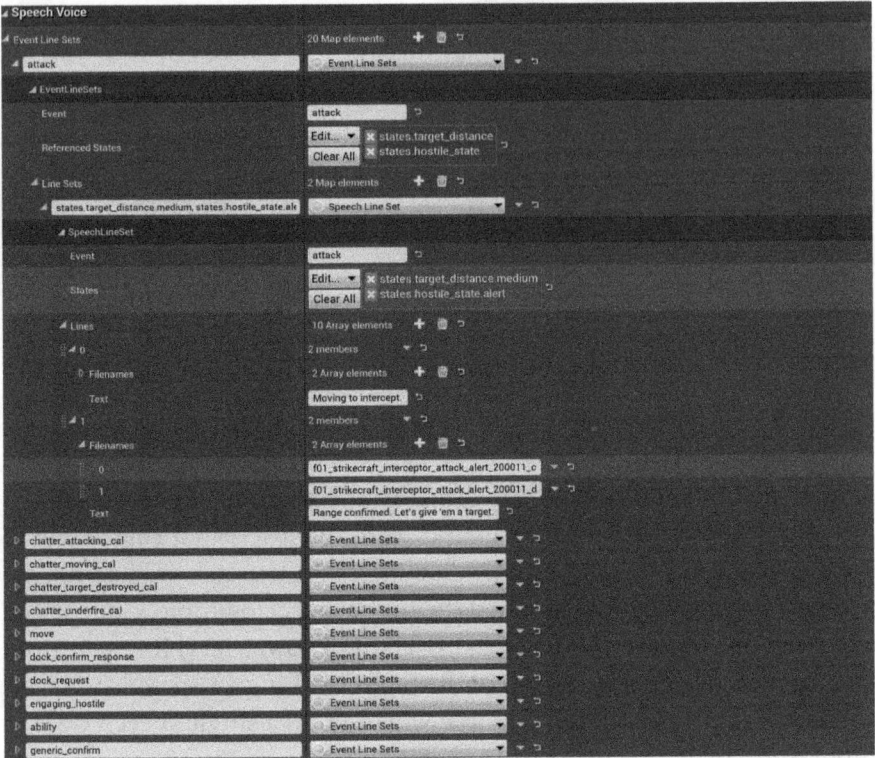

FIGURE 9.7 A screenshot of the USpeechVoice asset for the interceptor pilot character.

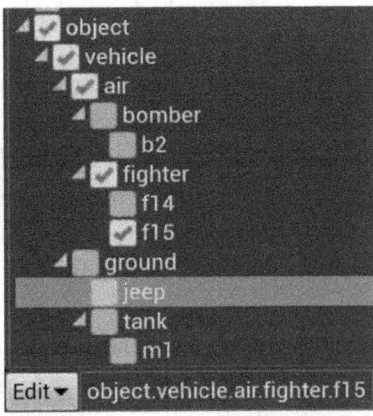

FIGURE 9.8 An example of a GameplayTag hierarchy.

TABLE 9.3   Example Dialog for a Jeep when It Sees Actors with Particular Gameplay Tags Set

ObjectType	Sees Object w/ Gameplay Tag	Dialog
Jeep	`object.vehicle`	Enemy incoming!
Jeep	`object.vehicle.air`	Eyes on the sky, we've got incoming!
Jeep	`object.vehicle.air.fighter`	Aircraft inbound, moving fast!
Jeep	`object.vehicle.air.fighter.F14`	Tomcats incoming!

some broad coverage for gameplay interactions, but don't have the time or budget to record new specific dialog. Of course, this is just one approach to handling fallback or missing dialog – we could also quite easily use the high-level rule system to play an entirely different dialog context altogether if no matching content is found.

9.3.4.2 Building the Gameplay Tag Query Data

Unreal has an interface class `IGameplayTagAssetInterface`, which allows any object that implements it to provide an `FGameplayTagContainer`. Complex objects like ships may aggregate many tags from a wide range of sources, where something like a simple static environmental mesh may have only a single static tag for its object type. This allows all our tag queries to work identically, regardless of what underlying logic or data structures are used to populate the containers. Figure 9.9 shows two very different objects supporting `IGameplayTagAssetInterface`.

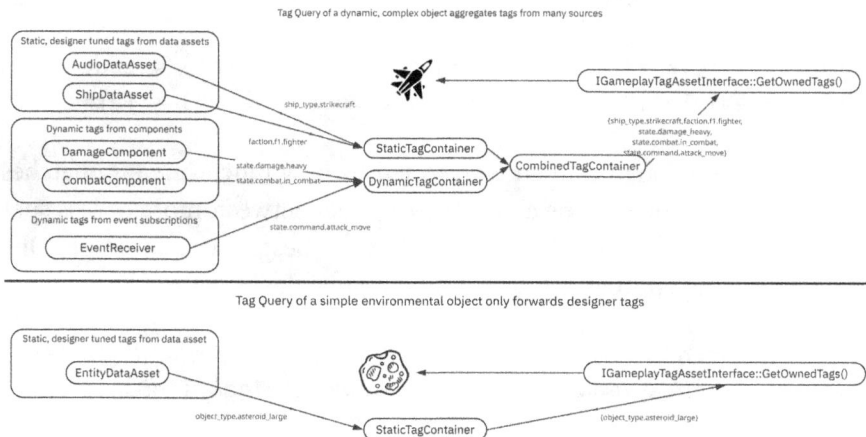

FIGURE 9.9 Example of two objects that both implement an `IGameplayTagAsetInterface`. (Top) A complex object that has tags from multiple sources. (Bottom) A simple object that has a single static gameplay tag.

9.3.4.3 Lazy Tag Updating

One nice aspect of having our `LineSet` selection driven entirely by tag matching is we can know ahead of time exactly what context is required to select from our possible responses – it is the union of the root nodes of all tags referenced by all possible `LineSets` for an event. This set is built during data export time, and directly used as part of building the `FGameplayTagContainer` used for our `FindBestFitLine` query. Rather than push-updating all of the possible tags on an Actor every frame – which can be horribly slow when dealing with hundreds of objects – we can use our container of only the tags we *might* need to pull-update an Actor's tags just before speech is selected.

9.3.4.4 Finding a Matching `LineSet`

Helpfully, `FGameplayTag` contains all the methods we need to quickly write a little `LineSet` matcher. If you aren't using Unreal, there are extremely similar hierarchical tag packages available for both Unity and Godot. If you are one of the brave souls still working in a custom engine, it's also not too difficult to roll your own equivalent functionality. The ability to match hierarchically comes from:

```
bool FGameplayTag::MatchesTag(const FGameplayTag& TagToCheck)
```

This function will match *less or equally* specific tags, but not *more* specific ones, for example:

```
"object.vehicle.air".MatchesTag("object.vehicle") = true
"object.vehicle".MatchesTag("object.vehicle.air") = false
```

This function isn't quite enough to tell us how much one tag matches another. We still need to be able to distinguish between more or less specific matches to know which `LineSet` will work best for our situation. One effective scoring approach we can use is the matched depth:

```
int32 TagMatchScore(
  const FGameplayTag& TagA, const FGameplayTag& TagB)
{
  if (!TagA.MatchesTag(TagB)){return 0;}
    return
      UGameplayTagsManager::Get().GetNumberOfTagNodes(TagA);
}
```

```
// Examples:
TagMatchScore(
  "object.vehicle.ground","object.vehicle") = 2
TagMatchScore(
  "object.vehicle.ground","object.vehicle.ground") = 3
TagMatchScore(
  "object.vehicle","object.vehicle.ground") = 0
```

Figuring out how much a `GameplayTagContainer` containing the tags coming from the game matches the ones stored with our `LineSet` is now as simple as adding up the tag match scores. Just like with individual tags, we allow more generic matches, but not more specific ones. If any of the tags required by our `LineSet` don't have a match found in the game data, we reject them entirely.

```
int32 ContainerMatchScore(
  const FGameplayTagContainer& InContainerA,
  const FGameplayTagContainer& InContainerB)
{
  int32 totalScore = 0;
  TArray<FGameplayTag> gameplayTags;

  InContainerB.GetGameplayTagArray(gameplayTags);
  for (const FGameplayTag curTag : gameplayTags)
  {
    FGameplayTag matchedTag;
    int32 curScore =
    FindBestMatchInContainer(
      curTag, InContainerA, matchedTag);

    //No match! Container as a whole cannot match.
    if (curScore == 0){return 0;}

    totalScore += curScore;
  }

  return totalScore;
}
```

Now that we can numerically rank how much a container matches another container, finding the `LineSet` with the best match is just calculating the rank for our candidates and then picking the highest one.

9.3.4.5 Tag Mirroring

Well – it's almost just that. Using a single `FGameplayTagContainer` to contain all the state we need to select a `LineSet` works well – until we need to deal with multiple values of the same type. Imagine we have an event `see_attack`, where an offscreen radio voice tells you who is attacking whom:

```
//You see an M1 tank attacking an F15 Fighter
{ object.vehicle.ground.tank.M1,
  object.vehicle.air.Fighter.F15}
```

```
//You see an F15 fighter attacking an M1 tank
{ object.vehicle.air.Fighter.F15,
  object.vehicle.ground.tank.M1}
```

Oh dear. Our `ContainerMatchScore` code will return the exact same score for both, but one of those dialog lines would be completely wrong. What we ended up doing for cases like this is creating mirrors of portions of the tag hierarchy, so we could disambiguate between use cases. Figure 9.10 shows an object tag hierarchy containing `object.vehicle.air` and `object.vehicle.ground`, which is mirrored in its entirety under a separate `attacker` tag. Separating the tags out like this allowed us to distinguish the context that a tag is being used in.

The above example now becomes:

```
//You see an M1 tank attacking an F15 Fighter
{ attacker.object.vehicle.ground.tank.M1,
  object.vehicle.air.Fighter.F15}
```

```
//You see an F15 fighter attacking an M1 tank
{ attacker.object.vehicle.air.Fighter.F15,
  object.vehicle.ground.tank.M1}
```

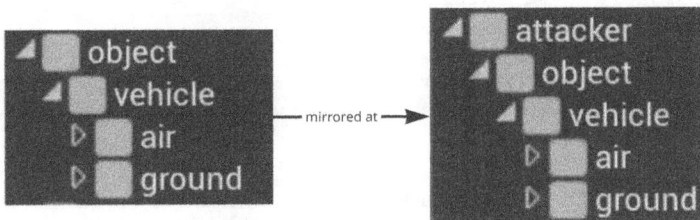

FIGURE 9.10 The same GameplayTag hierarchy mirrored in two different places.

Hurray! Our scoring code is kept nice and simple, and it also makes things easier when it comes to gathering our dialog context. If one of the tags required by our `LineSet` is a child of the attacker tag, we now know exactly which game object to pull tags from when responding to game events.

This solution is not without its drawbacks. Creating the mirrored branches is annoying, and without an automatic method to create those mirrors, you're all but guaranteed to have bugs in development as people add new object types without updating the mirrors. We didn't have too many issues with this mirroring in *Homeworld 3*, largely because we had enough validation of the input spreadsheets that non-existent tags being referenced would at least log some helpful errors.

9.3.5 Low Level: Line Selection and Playback

Once we've decided which `LineSet` to play, we need to select an actual line. All the lines in a `LineSet` are scripted to be interchangeable from a gameplay point of view, so our main concern at this point is making sure we have an appropriate amount of variation in the content. After trying several different line selection algorithms over our last couple of projects, we came up with something we called `WeightedRandomShuffle`. This is arguably a terrible name, since the weighting makes it more of a probability distribution than actually *random*, and `Shuffle` suggests that we play all the lines before there are any repeats, which is not what it does, even if the output can sound like it. The `Weighted` part, at least, is accurate. Misleading name aside, the algorithm *does* let us set up a good range of different choice behaviors with just two controls:

- **Weight:** A per-line value controls the probability that a line will play relative to other lines. A line with a weight of 2.0 is twice as likely to play as one with a weight of 1.0.

- **WaitUntilRepeat:** A line is guaranteed not to be chosen again until this many other lines have played. Scales from 0 to 1, where 0 allows lines to repeat freely, and 1 prevents the last `numLines/2` from being repeated. This system allowed us to get good shuffle-esque behavior with minimal computational effort.

9.4 TESTING AND DEBUGGING

Dialog implementation can be time consuming and fiddly! I am a huge proponent of spending a significant proportion of development time on utilities and tools to help you debug and test your work. This becomes even more important when your team gets larger. If you are working on bigger budget games, you will likely be working with a dedicated QA team, who will find issues that then need to be triaged, assigned to the correct discipline, then to the correct person, then investigated, and finally (hopefully) fixed. Good debugging and testing tools built into development versions of the game can be used by and benefit QA, technical audio designers, and programmers alike.

9.4.1 Testing GUI

One of the challenges with implementing context-specific dialog in a game is getting the game into that context in the first place. Making a sandbox level can be a good solution to this, but one of the big advantages of implementing a dialog system where the hookup and implementation logic are mostly self-contained and runnable independently of the game, is being able to test it independently. The GUI lets us select or spawn in-game units, then run `RuleEvents` and `SpeechEvents` on them directly. These two options map neatly to the high- and mid-levels of the system. Being able to test the two levels independently can make it much easier to figure out exactly where things are misbehaving. Figure 9.11 shows our in-game GUI for Rule and Speech event testing.

9.4.2 Debug Actions

Since our `URule` assets are live-tunable while the game is running, new `Actions` can be added at runtime to help us figure out what is going wrong. `DebugPrintAction` lets us insert an on-screen message into the rule responses, write to the game log, and draw a sphere at a given actor position. Figure 9.12 shows an example `DebugPrintAction`.

9.4.3 Logging

As with almost any moderately flexible system, sometimes the resulting behavior is going to be complex enough that offline inspection of the output is the most tractable solution. We added options to log as many things as we could, including:

- Calls to `RuleEvent`
- All `Condition` evaluations
- Rule resolution

FIGURE 9.11   A screenshot of the in-game testing GUI for Rule and Speech event testing.

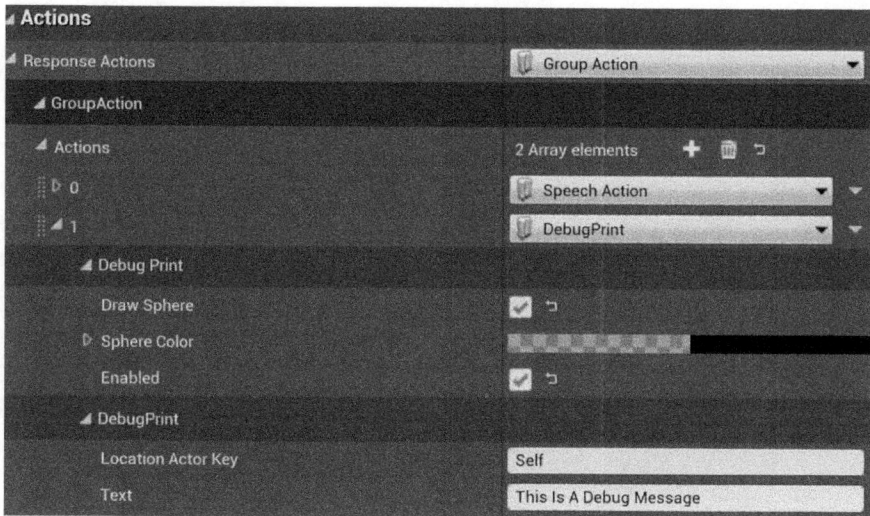

FIGURE 9.12   A screenshot of an example Debug Print Action.

- All `FGameplayTagContainer` objects passed to `SpeechAction`

- All `FGameplayTagContainer` and match scores from `FindBestFitLineSet`

We still had some challenges debugging things as the game and dialog grew bigger, but these tools at least made things manageable.

9.5 CONCLUSION/WRAP UP

Despite being a well-worn approach at this point, I think the ECA/rule-based approach is still well worth spending some time with and being aware of the pros and cons of – even if you never use it directly for dialog or audio – the pattern and its components are broadly applicable enough that there's a good chance you'll encounter them in the wild. If you want to poke around further in our dialog implementation for more details, you can check it out on the Epic store at the name *Homeworld 3 – Mod Tools & Editor*. The C++ code isn't available, but the debugging tools and Blueprint portions of the system are all there.

REFERENCES

Fowler, Martin. 2009. "Rules Engine." *martinfowler.com*. January 7. Accessed April 11, 2025. https://martinfowler.com/bliki/RulesEngine.html

Perlis, Alan J. 1982. "Epigrams on Programming." *ACM SIGPLAN Notices* 17 (9): 7–13. https://doi.org/10.1145/947955.1083808

IV

Audio Engine Architecture
and Features

CHAPTER 10

Updates to the Sound Engine State Machine

Guy Somberg

10.1 INTRODUCTION

The architecture of an audio engine is in many ways driven by the way in which the lifetimes of the playing sounds are managed. In Somberg (2016), I built up and presented a state machine to describe the life cycle of a playing sound, which is presented in Figure 10.1. I still use a variant of this state machine as a starting point when working on a new audio engine, but in the nearly ten years since that chapter was written, it has undergone a few minor revisions. In this chapter, we'll examine these revisions and how they affect the state machine.

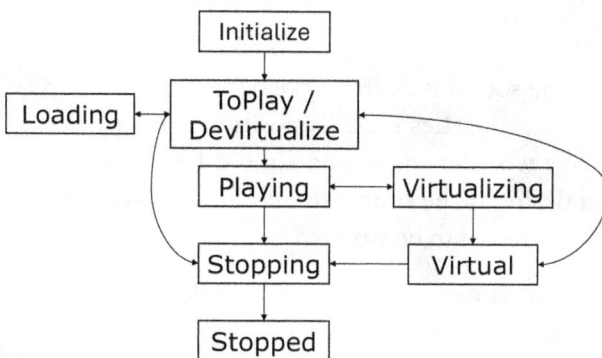

FIGURE 10.1 The state machine presented in Somberg (2016) that describes the life cycle of a playing sound.

DOI: 10.1201/9781003519119-14

10.2 THE STATE MACHINE

Before we get into the updates to the state machine, let's take a look at our starting point. This section will just be a summary overview of the state machine. For a detailed explanation of how we arrived at this specific machine and the reasoning behind the various states, see Somberg (2016). There are nine states in the machine:

- **Initialize**: This state is used only very briefly. It is used to initialize data that should remain the same throughout the lifetime of the sound, such as volume and pitch variation. Sounds in this state immediately transition to the **ToPlay** state without waiting for the next update.

- **ToPlay**: The sound is queued to play, but hasn't started yet. This state plays the sound from the beginning and then sets up all of its properties. It can transition to **Loading** if the sound hasn't loaded yet, to **Virtual** if the sound should be virtualized before being played, to **Stopping** if the sound has already been stopped, or to **Playing** if everything is started as normal.

- **Devirtualize**: This state is identical to the **ToPlay** state, except that we may execute some devirtualization logic, such as starting the sound from the middle or doing a quick fade in.

- **Loading**: Waits for the sound to be loaded asynchronously. Transitions back to the **ToPlay** state once the sound has finished loading.

- **Playing**: The sound is currently playing. This state updates the playing sound's properties such as position and any event parameters, and checks whether the sound should be virtual. It can transition to **Virtualizing** if the sound should be virtual or to **Stopping** if the sound is requested to be stopped.

- **Virtualizing**: The sound does a quick fade-out. When the fade-out is complete, this state transitions to **Virtual**, or it can transition back to **Playing** if the sound should not be virtual anymore.

- **Stopping**: For consistency, all sounds go through this state when they are fading out, completing their final tails, or even just completely stopped. This state transitions to **Stopped** when the sound has completed playing.

- **Virtual**: The sound is not playing, but its life cycle is still being tracked. This state checks whether the sound should continue to be virtual or whether it is stopped. It transitions to **Devirtualize** if it should no longer be virtual or to **Stopping** if the sound is stopped.

- **Stopped**: The sound has completed its life cycle and is ready to be cleaned up.

10.3 UPDATING THE STATE MACHINE

Although this state machine is still the foundation of all of my audio engines, it has evolved over the years. Changes in middleware and the patterns that I use have simplified the state machine by removing two of the states.

10.3.1 Eliminating the Initialize State

At one point, I looked at all of the audio engines that I had written recently, and I observed that the **Initialize** state was always a no-op. The code inevitably looked something like this:

```
void PlayingEvent::Tick()
{
  ...
  switch(CurrentState)
  {
    case State::Initialize:
      [[fallthrough]];
    case State::ToPlay:
      ...
  }
  ...
}
```

In the `switch` statement, it always fell through straight into the **ToPlay** state with no code in between. The state existed in *code* purely because it existed on *paper*. Its intended use – to perform one-time initialization of data that should be maintained across virtualization – either became a part of the constructor of the class or was initialized as part of the creation of the data.

It turns out that we can trivially delete the **Initialize** state without any loss of generality or functionality. This simplifies our state machine to look like Figure 10.2.

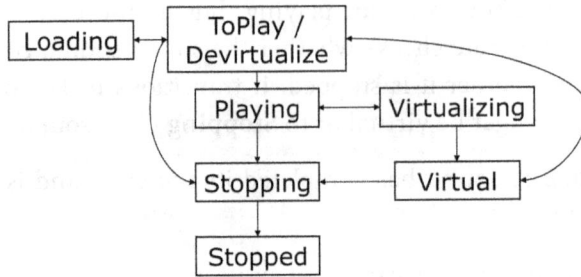

FIGURE 10.2   The state machine with the Initialize state removed.

10.3.2 Eliminating the Loading State

The **Loading** state is important. If a sound is triggered, but the audio data hasn't been loaded into memory yet, then we can't play the sound immediately. The **ToPlay** state can start the asynchronous loading of the required assets, then transition to the **Loading** state to wait until they're ready before trying again. At least, this is the idea.

And for lower-level APIs such as FMOD Core or SDL_Mixer, this idea works: the **Loading** state is the way that we can ensure that audio data is loaded before a sound is played. When using a higher-level API such as FMOD Studio or WWise (and likely others as well), an Event whose audio data is not yet loaded can be treated exactly the same as an Event with loaded assets. The assets themselves are asynchronously loaded under the hood on-demand and the Event will play when they are ready. Also, any commands you execute – volume or pitch adjustments, parameter changes, etc. – will be correctly handled and addressed by the middleware whether the audio data is loaded or not.

This last point is the crucial one: *an Event with fully loaded assets can be treated identically to an Event that is currently loading assets or which has not yet loaded any of its assets.* We can explicitly preload the assets for a single Event or for an entire Bank in order to guarantee that the assets are in memory (or at least shorten the waiting time), but that is an optimization rather than a requirement.

As a result, we can eliminate the **Loading** state entirely and just start the Events whenever we're ready. Figure 10.3 shows our final state machine with the **Initialize** and **Loading** states removed.

To reiterate, we can only do this if we are building our audio engine on top of a higher-level abstraction such as the FMOD Studio API or Wwise. If we are using a lower-level API such as the FMOD Core API, SDL_Mixer, or some other engine, then we will need to retain our **Loading** state.

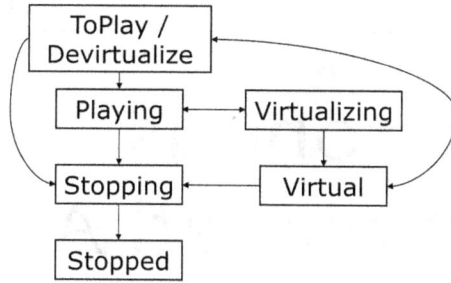

FIGURE 10.3 The state machine with the Initialize and Loading states removed.

10.4 CONCLUSION

It can be valuable to revisit fundamental assumptions about design and architecture. The audio engine state machine has been a foundational part of every audio engine that I have built for most of my career, but I'm always looking for small ways to improve it. The updates in this chapter are relatively small, but they simplify the resulting code, and they're a good reminder of the value of reevaluating the design choices that we've made.

REFERENCE

Somberg, Guy. 2016. "Sound Engine State Machine." In *Game Audio Programming Principles and Practices*, edited by Guy Somberg, 13–30. Boca Raton, FL: CRC Press.

CHAPTER 11

Asynchronous Multithreaded Audio Engine Architecture

Guy Somberg

11.1 INTRODUCTION

In Chapter 10, we started with the state machine described in Somberg (2016) and simplified it by removing a couple of states. The idea was to re-examine the fundamental assumptions that went into the architecture and see whether they matched reality. By doing some analysis of the usage patterns and the middleware APIs, we were able to make some small changes to the state machine that ended up informing the layout of the audio code.

In this chapter, we're going to re-examine the assumptions about the way that we architect audio engines. By making two important observations about the audio engine's relationship to the rest of the game, we'll end up turning the code on its head and splitting the state machine up and moving it around – all while keeping its intention intact.

11.1.1 A Strawman "Standard Audio Engine"

Audio engines are complex beasts, but their primary purpose at their core is to play audio data and track the lifetime of the playing sounds. The standard way to approach this problem is to store an array of playing events (or, more likely, a map from playing event ID to playing event context) and iterate over it, updating each event. We can boil down this idea into

DOI: 10.1201/9781003519119-15

this strawman[1] audio engine update function, which we will be updating throughout this chapter.

```cpp
void AudioEngine::Tick()
{
  // Other stuff...
  for (auto& [Id, Event] : PlayingEvents)
  {
    Event.UpdateStateMachine();
  }
  // Other stuff...
}
```

The state machine that this code updates is exactly what is described in Chapter 10 and shown visually in Figure 10.3. In order to update our audio engine, we will make two fundamental observations about audio code in general, which I will call steady state and one-way pipeline. We'll examine what these observations are and their ramifications in the next section.

11.2 THE STEADY STATE

Most objects in our game world are in a steady state. That is, if I ask a question about a playing sound, such as its position, whether it should currently be virtual, or – more generally – any property of the sound itself or of the game entity that it is attached to, the extreme likelihood is that the answer will not change from frame to frame. There will be moments where the answer to any question that you might ask does change, but they are just that: moments. It is wasteful to be constantly asking a question if the answer isn't going to change.[2]

The steady state tells us that the answer to any question that we might ask is likely to be the same from one update to the next, and that it is only at certain moments that the answer can change. To take advantage of this observation, we must figure out when those moments are and find a hook that we can get a callback to trigger any changes that will happen. Let's take a look at some examples:

- **Should this sound be virtual?** The answer to this question will always remain unchanged so long as the sound's position and the attenuation position remain unchanged. If we've implemented a Max Within Radius scheme (see Chapter 14), then playback of a new sound can also update the answer to this question. While it is true that position updates, attenuation position updates, and sound playback are all fairly common operations, they are not changed every frame. The most common of these will be the attenuation position update, and we will address that later in the chapter.

- **Has the sound stopped playing?** The answer to this question will only change when the sound has actually stopped playing, which happens exactly once. The middleware will provide a callback when the playback has finished, so we can use that to trigger anything that occurs when the sound stops.

- **Has the fade completed?** If we know how long the fade was supposed to take, then we can just wait until that timer has completed. Either the middleware already has a timing mechanism for this, or we can make one without too much trouble.

- **Has the game property associated with this Event property changed?** A player's health or mana, or a boss's charge counter, or an enemy's minion count won't change from frame to frame. The details of how to get notifications when these properties change will be game-specific, so we won't dive into the details other than to note that it is worthwhile to figure it out. Creating these callback mechanisms may require working in a number of different game systems.

What this observation does in practice is that it changes the underlying model from a synchronous polling-based mechanism to an asynchronous callback-based mechanism. From the perspective of the state machine, it changes the important parts from the *boxes* to the *lines*. Table 11.1 shows this perspective of the state machine as a disconnected collection of state transitions.

Importantly, when developing this sort of state machine, both the interpretation of Figure 10.3 from Chapter 10 and Table 11.1 are important to understand. The holistic view from the figure helps us to understand the life cycle of the sound and the relationships between the various states. The independent view from Table 11.1 helps us to understand when the state can possibly change, and how to organize the code to capture that.

11.2.1 A Pervasive Change

When making this change to the audio engine, it is important to note that it can be all-encompassing. In the extreme, we forbid looping over

TABLE 11.1   The Same State Machine as Figure 10.3 in Chapter 10, Showing the State Transitions and What Triggers Them

Input State	Event	Output State
To Play/Devirtualize	Played	Playing
To Play/Devirtualize	Stop requested	Stopping
To Play/Devirtualize	Should be virtual	Virtual
Playing	Should be virtual	Virtualizing
Playing	Stop requested	Stopping
Virtualizing	Should not be virtual	Playing
Virtualizing	Fade complete	Virtual
Virtual	Stop requested	Stopping
Virtual	Should not be virtual	Devirtualize
Stopping	Done playing	Stopped

all events, as well as any polling-based mechanism. Some event-based setup is already built into the system; we won't query the 3D position of a sound every frame, for example, but rather just update when the game entity it is attached to updates. What this observation does for us is it makes every system work that same way, sometimes incurring added complexity, either in the audio engine itself or in the related game code.

One example of this added complexity is character health. In previous games, we have implemented character health as a special value (called an "active trait" in our game engine) that stores a combined value and time-stamp, along with other metadata like min value, max value, and regen rate. We can then get the updated value without ever ticking by returning `value + (current_time - timestamp) * regen`. Doing this calculation on the fly can save a ton of CPU time, particularly on game servers,[3] but it causes problems for audio code that is interested in passing the character health to an Event parameter because there is no event to hook into that will tell us when the value is changing.

To solve this problem, we ended up adding a client-only mechanism that detected when a character had a playing sound interested in the value. The system had to be aware of the minimum value and maximum value, as well as the regen and a number of other features in order to ensure that there was always a value being provided to the audio engine when the value was changing (as well as a final callback when the value stopped changing), and – equally important – there was no callback when the value wasn't changing.

11.2.2 Updates to the Strawman Audio Engine

With our update to make the whole engine asynchronous, our strawman audio engine changes to look something like this:

```
void AudioEngine::Tick()
{
  // Other stuff...
  for (auto& Change : Changes)
  {
    Change.DoIt();
  }
  // Other stuff...
}
```

Now instead of iterating over every event and updating it, we iterate over every requested change to an event and trigger just that change.

11.3 ONE-WAY PIPELINE

Playing sounds is at the very end of the pipeline for a game engine, in terms of both workflow and technology. When it comes to workflow, the general pattern is that the audio department will work on any given feature or piece of content last – after it has been concepted, modeled, animated, hooked up to the game, and had VFX created.[4] This flow extends into the game engine as well.

In most games, most sounds are either "fire and forget" – that is, played at a constant world location (or in 2D) and then left to finish their lifetime, or they are tracked and updated whenever something about their attached game object changes, such as 3D position or a game property like character health. In other words, the communication stream is almost entirely one way: from the game to the audio engine. Occasionally, the game will be interested in some property of a playing sound, but most sounds that are playing won't be interested.

The most common information that the game will need from the audio engine is a callback when the sound stops, which can be used for situations like triggering UI updates for dialog subtitles or toggling VFX. Less commonly, the game will be interested in other information such as amplitude, frequency spectrum information, or music beat data, but those are rare. In general, no sound other than the music will contain beat data that the game needs to respond to, and most sounds will not be using their amplitude or frequency data to drive anything in the game.

All of these statements are, of course, to within experimental error, and they should all be qualified with "for most games". One can imagine a game or circumstance where the above assertions are false (such as music beat information coming from multiple sources or majority of sounds needing amplitude/frequency information), but those games are going to be edge cases and will need to handle their special circumstances anyway. With those caveats out of the way, we can assert that in *most* games, *most* of the sounds will follow the above truisms.

So, the one-way pipeline observation means that – to within experimental error – the entire operation of the audio engine is *unimportant* to the main game thread. Consequently, any time spent doing work on the game thread on behalf of the audio engine is not contributing meaningfully to the game's simulation frame rate.

Another way to think about it is with an example. Let's say that we profile a game frame, and we find that the audio engine update takes up 1100 µs, which is a bit high, but not unreasonable. But at 60 fps we only get a grand total of 16666 µs, which means that our 1100 µs is approximately 6.6% of our total frame time. And that time isn't spent updating unit positions, calculating combat results, or doing animation work. It's not even spent rendering audio – that already happens in another thread. It's purely bookkeeping. Important bookkeeping, but bookkeeping nonetheless.

The solution here is to do as little work as possible in the main thread and move as much as we can to another thread. We still need to do some work on the main thread, such as accessing game object data or doing raycasts, but our goal should be to move a majority of the work to a separate thread.

It is important to note that this change does not come for free, or even cheap. Overall, we are doing *more* work than if we had just kept the updates on the main thread. The main thread has to collect the changes and send them to the audio thread, and then the audio thread still has to actually do the work. Similarly, moving some of the work to a separate thread will take up more memory, since both the main thread and the audio thread will require copies of at least some of the information about each playing sound.

Before embarking on this change, it is worth acknowledging that moving work onto a separate thread adds a significant amount of complexity to an audio engine. Many patterns that were fine and simple before now require some mechanism to prevent access across thread boundaries. There will be an ongoing non-zero cost to the design of every new feature to split its functionality out into the part that runs on the game thread and the part that runs on the audio thread.

11.3.1 Which Thread?

Before we get to the code, we need to figure out where it is going to live. Audio middleware naturally runs a number of threads: a mixer thread, a streaming thread, async loading threads, file reading threads, and more. When using FMOD Studio, there is also a Studio API thread that executes commands to the Studio System object; Wwise has a similar thread called `AK::EventManager`.

When moving functionality off of the game thread, we have a couple of options of where to run our audio engine code: we can spin up a new bespoke thread, or we can use one of the middleware's existing threads. It is tempting to spin up a new thread because the code remains logically identical to running off of the main game thread, except for the associated message passing. The problem with spinning up a new thread is that it introduces extra latency into a system that is already sensitive to latency. Every command must travel from the main thread to the intermediate thread and then from the intermediate thread to the middleware thread.

A better option is to hook into the middleware thread directly. FMOD provides callbacks that allow us to hook our own code into the Studio System thread. Using one of these callbacks avoids the latency penalty because the intermediate thread *is* the Studio thread. It can also simplify some of the code because we no longer need to be concerned about inter-thread communication due to Event callbacks occurring on different threads – the callbacks occur on the Studio thread, and the Studio thread is already where all of our code is executing. There can be no contention in that case.[5]

11.3.2 Thread Communication

As soon as you have multiple threads, the question arises how those threads will communicate. In this chapter, we will use the `ThreadSafeCommandBuffer` class described in Somberg (2024), which uses a triple buffer and lock-free semantics under the hood. This class has a number of advantages: it's efficient, lock-free, and – in some ways most importantly – already exists.[6] However, it is not the only possible solution for this problem. Lock-free circular buffers are commonly used for thread communication, but even something as relatively simple as a class that wraps a `std::vector` and a `std::mutex` would work.

Ultimately, you should pick a thread communication mechanism that works for you. The problem that we are solving features low contention across only two threads, and only has to solve one-way communication with no hard real time requirements. If such a thing as "easy mode" for threading exists, this is it.

11.3.3 State Machine Split

The audio engine state machine described in Chapter 10 represents the life cycle of a playing sound, and we will be using that in the audio thread. But from the main game thread, much of the functionality of the state machine is unimportant. Let's take a look at the states and see which ones are relevant to the main thread:

- **ToPlay:** *Relevant* to the main thread. Anything in the **ToPlay** state hasn't yet been sent to the audio thread, so we know that we can send it all as one "play event" message instead of individual property change messages.

- **Playing:** *Relevant* to the main thread. Sounds that are in the **Playing** state are being tracked as alive by the audio thread. That doesn't necessarily mean that they're causing audio to be played, but they exist and will be interested in any changes to properties.

- **Stopping:** *Relevant* to the main thread. Sounds in the **Stopping** state have been requested to be stopped by the main thread, and we're just waiting for them to be cleaned up by the audio thread and a message to be sent indicating that they're fully cleaned up.

- **Stopped:** *Not relevant* to the main thread. As soon as a sound has stopped playing, the audio thread will send a message to the main thread, which can release the memory for the event immediately.

- **Virtualizing, Virtual, and Devirtualize:** *Not relevant* to the main thread. The main thread does not care if a sound is virtual. From the main thread's perspective, there is no difference between a virtual sound and a non-virtual one. This is similar to how we can ignore whether or not a sound has had its audio assets loaded, as discussed in Chapter 10.

Putting all of this together, our main thread state machine now only has three states: **ToPlay**, **Playing**, and **Stopping**. This is a new state machine,

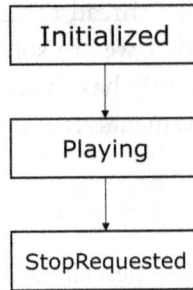

FIGURE 11.1   The state machine used by the main thread.

however, and we are not obligated to keep the names, so let us rename the states to better reflect their actual functionality. We'll rename **ToPlay** to **Initialized** and **Stopping** to **StopRequested**, both of which better reflect the status of the playing sound on the game thread. With all of these changes, it looks like Figure 11.1. Much simpler!

11.3.4 Updates to the Strawman Audio Engine

Moving large parts of our audio engine to another thread has changed our strawman audio engine, but not drastically. In particular, the game thread update still follows the same pattern as before, with only a few minor changes:

```
void AudioEngine::Tick()
{
  // Other stuff...
  for (auto& Change : Changes)
  {
    SentChanges.Enqueue(Change);
  }
  SentChanges.Send();
  // Other stuff...
}
```

We now have to add a new update for the audio thread, which does the actual work:

```
void AudioEngine::AudioThreadUpdate()
{
  // Other stuff...
```

```
if (auto& ReceivedChanges = SentChanges.Receive())
{
  for (auto& Change : ReceivedChanges)
  {
    Change.DoIt();
  }
}
// Other stuff...
}
```

11.4 DATA FLOW OVERVIEW

We have created a flow of data and events that can be relatively complicated to keep track of. Let's follow the operation of the respective threads,
as shown in Figure 11.2.

We start with the game's tick function (a), which gets executed once per
game simulation frame. This function is often called Tick() or Update()
or something along those lines. During the game tick (a), new events get
played (b), positions and other properties get updated (c), and various callbacks get called (d) that update properties of the audio engine. These operations all get queued up in a New Events list and an Event Changes list.

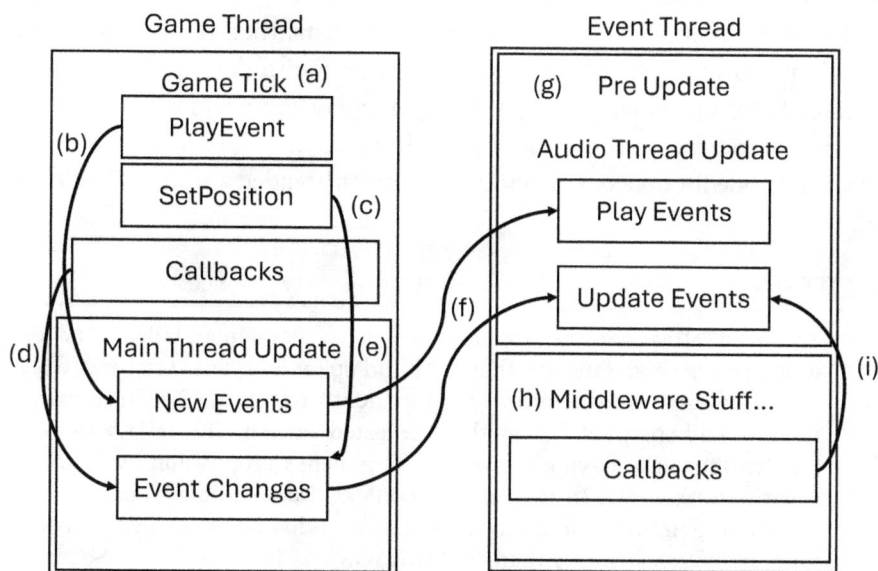

FIGURE 11.2   A representation of the flow of data and messages between the
game thread and the audio thread.

When the game tick reaches the part where the audio engine ticks (e), the audio engine sends the queued data off to the audio thread (f). When the audio thread runs (g), we hook into the pre-update call so that our changes happen with the lowest latency. The audio thread plays the new events and triggers the requested changes in the events. After the pre-update, the regular middleware event loop runs (h), which can trigger its own set of callbacks. Sometimes those callbacks will change things immediately, but other times it will enqueue changes to happen on the next update (i).

11.5 NEXT STEPS

Adding asynchrony and multiple threads to an audio engine creates a system with high performance and low latency. The cost of making these changes is in the complexity of the resulting code. Asynchrony splits the code out into multiple locations, and because it is pervasive, it also increases the cost of building new features by requiring them to be asynchronous as well. Multithreading, by its nature, increases complexity and creates opportunities for all of the sorts of threading issues that you learn about in school: deadlocks, lifetime issues, race conditions, and more. It also increases the cost of building new features by requiring them to be split up into a main thread component, a communication component, and an audio thread component.

However, if you are willing to pay these costs, then the benefits are a highly performant, low-latency system. Your sound designers will thank you for the reduced latency, and your gameplay engineers will thank you for the extra time on the game thread. In Chapter 12, we'll do a dive into what the code for an asynchronous and multithreaded audio engine looks like.

NOTES

1. The word "strawman" here refers obliquely to a strawman fallacy. The idea with the strawman fallacy is that you build up (or otherwise interpret) a perverted or simplified version of your opponent's argument (the "straw man"), then expend energy defeating that perverted version. This fallacy can create the illusion of having refuted the opponent's proposition by replacing it with another one. In this specific context, I am calling it out explicitly as such to point out that it is a strawman, and that we are using it only as a point of reference, rather than anything real.
2. Parents of young children will be familiar with the constant refrain of re-asked questions, as exemplified by the stereotypical question "are we there yet?"

3. It may seem counter-intuitive at first that performing this calculation every time we read the value is actually a CPU savings. The thing to recall is that it is being compared against iterating over every single character's active traits on every frame, regardless of whether that active trait is being read. Doing a little bit of extra math here and there for the cases where we truly need the value is a lot cheaper than updating every single active trait all the time.

4. Of course, the audio department should be involved with the design of the game and its various features from the beginning, but that is a topic for a different chapter.

5. Note that there can still be contention between the Studio thread and the mixer thread, since some callbacks must occur on the mixer thread.

6. Or, at least, it exists in my codebase!

REFERENCES

Somberg, Guy. 2016. "Sound Engine State Machine." *Game Audio Programming Principles and Practices*, edited by Guy Somberg, 13–30. Boca Raton, FL: CRC Press.

Somberg, Guy. 2024. "Thread-Safe Command Buffer." *Game Audio Programming Principles and Practices 4*, edited by Guy Somberg, 238–261. Boca Raton, FL: CRC Press.

CHAPTER 12

Asynchronous Multithreaded Audio Engine Code

Guy Somberg

12.1 INTRODUCTION

In Chapter 11, we introduced the idea of an asynchronous multithreaded audio engine, along with a strawman version of what the code might look like. In this chapter, we will take a look at what the real code for one of these engines could look like. In order to save space in what is already a very long chapter, we will not be presenting code for a number of functions and data structures such as timing callbacks, event accessors, and others. These omitted items are all fairly straightforward to implement, and spending too much ink on them will distract from the purpose of the chapter.

The ultimate goal is to transition a standard synchronous single-threaded audio engine to take advantage of both the steady state and one-way pipeline observations. To get there, we could first take our audio engine and make it asynchronous and then move it to another thread – or vice versa (that is, move to another thread and then make asynchronous). However, we will skip the intermediate step and go directly to doing both at once in this chapter.

12.1.1 Code Architecture

We will split our engine up into three primary classes:

- **AudioEngine:** The core object owning the FMOD System object and driving the whole system.

DOI: 10.1201/9781003519119-16

- **MainThreadEvent**: An object representing the state of a playing sound on the main thread.

- **AudioThreadEvent**: An object representing the state of a play sound on the audio thread.

Every change that is requested to be made to a `MainThreadEvent` will be coalesced into a message that gets sent to the audio thread, which can then make the appropriate change to the matching `AudioThreadEvent`. As discussed in Section 12.3.2, we will send these messages using a `ThreadSafeCommandBuffer`, as described in Somberg (2024). One of the nice things about this mechanism is that it addresses both observations: we've moved code to a separate thread, and the messages provide great hooks for some of the event-driven changes.

12.2 THE AudioEngine CLASS

The `AudioEngine` class is driven by calling its `MainThreadUpdate()` function on the main thread, and it sets itself up to call the `AudioThreadUpdate()` function on the FMOD Studio thread. New events are started by calling `PlayEvent()`, and the listener can be updated using the `UpdateListenerPostion()` and `UpdateAttenuationPosition()` functions. This architecture ends up being fairly similar to a single-threaded audio engine, which is good because it means that the external API for interacting with this new engine is basically the same.

We won't show the entire class declaration here, since it is quite long, but all of the functionality in this section will be a part of this class:

```
class AudioEngine
{
    // Functionality in this section goes here...
};
```

12.2.1 AudioEngine Setup

Let's start by taking a look at how the engine gets set up:

```
AudioEngine::AudioEngine()
{
    // Create and initialize the FMOD System object.  Real code
    // will doubtless need a lot more detail here and have
```

```
    // more initialization to do, but these are the
    // fundamentals.
    FMOD::Studio::System::create(&pStudioSystem);
    pStudioSystem->initialize(
      128, FMOD_STUDIO_INIT_NORMAL, FMOD_INIT_NORMAL, nullptr);

    // Set the UserData for the System object so that we can
    // access the AudioEngine from the callback.
    pStudioSystem->setUserData(this);

    // Schedule the callback to be run on the Studio thread
    // before any other updates are done.
    pStudioSystem->setCallback(
      &AudioEngine::AudioThreadCallback,
      FMOD_STUDIO_SYSTEM_CALLBACK_PREUPDATE);

    // We need the system sample rate in order to be able to
    // interpret the DSP clocks.
    pStudioSystem->getCoreSystem(&pCoreSystem);
    pCoreSystem->getSoftwareFormat(
      &SystemSampleRate, nullptr, nullptr);
}

AudioEngine::~AudioEngine()
{
    // Shut down and clean up.  Here we just do a release(),
    // but again real code will doubtless have more components
    // to shut down.
    pStudioSystem->release();
}

// Our callback function.  This is static, so it does not
// have access to the AudioEngine instance by default.
FMOD_RESULT F_CALL AudioEngine::AudioThreadCallback(
    [[maybe_unused]] FMOD_STUDIO_SYSTEM* System,
    FMOD_STUDIO_SYSTEM_CALLBACK_TYPE CallbackType,
    [[maybe_unused]] void* Commanddata,
    void* UserData)
{
    // UserData is set up with the contents of whatever was
    // passed into pStudioSystem->setUserData(), so we just
    // need to cast it to AudioEngine* in order to get our
```

```
// AudioEngine instance.
auto* Engine = static_cast<AudioEngine*>(UserData);

// Double-check the callback type.  Production code may be
// interested in other callbacks here as well, so this
// could become either a switch or a sequence of ifs.
if (CallbackType == FMOD_STUDIO_SYSTEM_CALLBACK_PREUPDATE)
{
    // Forward to our member function for the audio thread
    // update.
    Engine->AudioThreadUpdate();
}
return FMOD_OK;
}
```

With this initialization sequence, our audio engine is now set up to run correctly with the `MainThreadUpdate()` function being driven as normal by the main game thread, and the `AudioThreadUpdate()` function being driven by the FMOD Studio thread. The single-threaded code presented in Somberg (2016) already followed a pattern where external code would set data, which would then be applied in the `Update()` function. The difference in implementation details (other than renaming `Update()` to `MainThreadUpdate()`) is that now the `MainThreadUpdate()` function forwards those changes on to the Studio thread, rather than updating immediately. We will show the code for the `MainThreadUpdate()` and `AudioThreadUpdate()` functions in Sections 12.4 and 12.5, but before that we will dive into how the listener update functions and playing event classes work.

12.2.2 Listener Update

The listener update functions are called from the main thread whenever the listener transform changes or the attenuation position changes. This functionality is the same as for a single-threaded audio engine, and the basic structure of these update multithreaded functions is more or less the same. The actual difference is in the backing store of the listener data and how the listener gets updated in the audio thread.

The backing store is comprised of a few new entries:

```
// Our cached Listener data
ListenerSettings Listener;
```

```
// Inter-thread communication
ThreadSafeCommandValue<ListenerSettings> ListenerTransfer;

// Whether the listener is currently dirty and needs to be
// sent to the audio thread
bool bListenerIsDirty = false;
```

With these data members in place in our audio engine, we can see how the listener functions have been updated to send data across to the audio thread.

```
void AudioEngine::UpdateListener(
  const Transform& NewTransform)
{
  // Grab the listener value from the backing store, which is
  // the send value for the ThreadSafeCommandValue storing
  // the listener data.
  auto& SendValue = ListenerTransfer.GetSendValue();

  // Check to see if the transform is different and update
  // the listener if so.
  if (!SendValue.ListenerTransform.IsNearlyEqual(
      NewTransform))
  {
    // We update the send value to deliver to the audio
    // thread, and also the cached backing store.  After
    // the value gets sent to the other thread it will have a
    // stale value, so we need the correct cached value to
    // overwrite the stale value.
    SendValue.ListenerTransform = NewTransform;
    Listener.ListenerTransform = NewTransform;
    bListenerIsDirty = true;
  }

  // If you need to support listener velocity, then set it
  // up here in a similar manner to the above.
}

void AudioEngine::UpdateAttenuationPosition(
  const Point3& NewAttenuationPosition)
{
```

```
// Again, the backing store for the listener data is the
// send value of the ThreadSafeCommandValue.
auto& SendValue = ListenerTransfer.GetSendValue();
if (SendValue.AttenuationPosition.IsNearlyEqual(
        NewAttenuationPosition))
    return;

SendValue.AttenuationPosition = NewAttenuationPosition;
Listener.AttenuationPosition = NewAttenuationPosition;
bListenerIsDirty = true;
}
```

12.3 THE `MainThreadEvent` CLASS

The purpose of the `MainThreadEvent` class is to store data and track when it changes so that the `AudioEngine` can send it to the audio thread. Its interface and implementation are therefore relatively simple. As discussed in Section 12.3.3, the main thread has a much coarser view of the life cycle of a playing sound than the audio thread. This coarser view translates into a simpler state variable than the audio thread events: just **Initialized**, **Playing**, and **StopRequested** states that we can use to make sure that the correct functionality gets executed. As before, we'll leave off the details of the class declaration, and just note that all of the code in this section belongs in this class:

```
class MainThreadEvent
{
    // Functionality in this section goes here...
};
```

12.3.1 `MainThreadEvent` Implementation

The `MainThreadEvent` class has a very small and simple implementation on purpose. There are a few interesting details, but we will skip over the implementation of several of the functions where they are sufficiently similar to their brethren in order to save space in the chapter.

```
// This function is used to update the internal state after
// the event has been sent to the audio thread to be played.
void MainThreadEvent::SetPlaying()
{
```

```
  // Prevent the state from going backwards - that is, it is
  // disallowed to go from StopRequested to Playing.  We must
  // be in the Initialized state to go to the Playing state.
  if (CurrentState != State::Initialized)
    return;
  CurrentState = State::Playing;
}


// This is the model of all of the other Set functions.
void MainThreadEvent::SetLocation(const Point3& NewLocation)
{
  // Don't bother doing the update if the value hasn't
  // changed.
  if (Parameters.Location.IsNearlyEqual(NewLocation))
    return;

  // Update the internal value, then set the DirtyFlag.
  Parameters.Location = NewLocation;
  SetDirtyFlag(DirtyFlagType::Location);
}
```

These two functions set up a pattern that the remainder of the external API follows. SetVolume(), SetPitch(), and SetEventParameter() all follow the same pattern as SetLocation(), so we have omitted the implementation here in order to save space. Stop() is similar to the Set family of functions, but we check for CurrentState == State::StopRequested instead of whether the new value matches the parameters.

12.3.2 Dirty Flags and MainThreadEvent Creation

With these basics out of the way, we can now look at how the dirty flags are set and managed by the main thread event. These dirty flags are the primary interaction between the AudioEngine and the MainThreadEvent. First, the dirty flags are declared thus in our class:

```
// A set of flags indicating which parameters are dirty.
// This implementation supports just four event parameters
// as a demo, but it can be extended to support arbitrary
// numbers without too much trouble.
enum class DirtyFlagType
{
  Location,
```

```
    Volume,
    Pitch,
    Stopped,
    Parameter1, Parameter2, Parameter3, Parameter4,
    Count,
};

// Bit field indicating which flags are currently dirty.
static constexpr auto FlagCount =
  static_cast<size_t>(DirtyFlagType::Count);
std::bitset<FlagCount> DirtyFlags;
```

From here, we can see the implementation of `SetDirtyFlag()`. Other than setting the flag itself, the code has to inform the audio engine that the event has changed.

```
void MainThreadEvent::SetDirtyFlag(DirtyFlagType Flag)
{
    // We don't bother adding newly-created events to the
    // dirty list.  Their entire state needs to be sent to the
    // audio thread anyway.
    if (CurrentState == State::Initialized)
      return;

    // Set the appropriate dirty flag
    DirtyFlags.set(static_cast<size_t>(Flag));

    // Add the event as dirty so that the next update will
    // send it to the audio thread.
    AudioEngine::Get().AddMainThreadDirtyEvent(EventId, Flag);
}
```

That last piece, the `AddMainThreadDirtyEvent()` function, is adding to the following list:

```
// Dirty events for the main thread.
std::vector<std::pair<int, MainThreadEvent::DirtyFlagType>>
  MainThreadDirtyEvents;
```

In other words, it's a vector of pairs of playing event IDs and the property that is dirty on those events. Using this data structure will require us to do a linear search through the vector, which should be okay given our use case. Our expectation is that the number of properties of events that are changed on any given frame is relatively small, so the search will be fast (and the vector will ensure cache locality). If these assumptions end up being different for your use case, then it is a relatively simple transformation to change this into an `unordered_map` or similar data structure.

It's worth noting that although this code is set up to work asynchronously, it is nearly identical to the classic code. The primary difference is when and where we actually do the update, which is managed by the aforementioned `MainThreadDirtyEvents` structure, and the `AddMainThreadDirtyEvent()` function:

```
// Adds an EventId/DirtyFlag pair to the list if it's not
// already in it.
void AudioEngine::AddMainThreadDirtyEvent(
  int EventId, MainThreadEvent::DirtyFlagType Flag)
{
  auto FoundIt = std::ranges::find(
    MainThreadDirtyEvents, std::pair{ EventId, Flag });
  if (FoundIt == std::ranges::end(MainThreadDirtyEvents))
  {
    MainThreadDirtyEvents.emplace_back(EventId, Flag);
  }
}
```

With the dirty flags in place, we are almost ready to see the `AudioEngine::MainThreadUpdate()` function. The only thing missing is creating the events. First, the backing store in the `AudioEngine` class:

```
// Our main thread events
std::unordered_map<int, MainThreadEvent> MainThreadEvents;

// Newly-played events on the main thread
std::vector<int> MainThreadNewlyPlayedEvents;
```

And now we can see how `PlayEvent()` is implemented:

```
MainThreadEvent& AudioEngine::PlayEvent(
  PlaybackParameters&& Parameters)
{
  // Select the new EventId.  We will be both storing it in
```

```
// the MainThreadEvent itself and storing it in the list
// of newly-played events.
auto EventId = NextEventId++;

// try_emplace() allows us to use emplacement to construct
// the value of the map, rather than just the key. The key
// is just an integer in this case, but the value is a
// MainThreadEvent, which is more complex and we'd rather
// not make a copy.  Emplacing allows us to construct the
// value in-place.
// The return value is an iterator to the entry and a flag
// indicating whether it a newly-added entry or a
// pre-existing entry.  (In our case, it will always be
// newly-added, since we generate a unique Id for every
// playing sound.)
auto [NewIt, bAdded] = MainThreadEvents.try_emplace(
  EventId, EventId, std::move(Parameters));

// Add the EventId to the list of newly-played events.
MainThreadNewlyPlayedEvents.push_back(EventId);

// Finally, we can dereference the returned iterator to
// return a reference to the new entry.
return NewIt->second;
}
```

12.4 THE `MainThreadUpdate()` FUNCTION

With all of this infrastructure in place, we can finally see how the main thread updates. For all that there are a lot of lines of code here, there is actually very little going on: we send changes to the audio thread if there are changes, and we receive stop messages from the audio thread. The new parts of the backing store are just the transfer buffers for the various messages:

```
ThreadSafeCommandBuffer<PlaySoundCommand> PlayCommands;
ThreadSafeCommandBuffer<SoundStoppedCommand> StopCommands;
ThreadSafeCommandBuffer<AdjustPlayingSoundCommand>
  Commands;
```

And with those in place, we can take a look at the `MainThreadUpdate()` function.

```
void AudioEngine::MainThreadUpdate()
{
  // Send messages to the audio thread if the listener has
  // changed.
  SendListenerChanges();

  // Send newly-played events to the audio thread. The return
  // value is a list of Event Ids that have stopped and need
  // to be cleaned up.
  auto StoppedEventIds = SendNewlyPlayedEvents();

  // Send changes to currently-playing events to the audio
  // thread.
  SendDirtyEvents();

  // When an audio thread event finishes, the audio thread
  // sends a "sound stopped" message, which we receive here.
  auto ReceivedStoppedEvents = ReceiveStoppedEventMessages();
  StoppedEventIds.append_range(std::move(StoppedEventIds));

  // Clear out the memory for the stopped events.
  ClearStoppedEvents(StoppedEventIds);

  // Update the FMOD system. This will trigger listener
  // updates, callbacks, etc.
  pStudioSystem->update();
}
```

The functionality is split into a few utility functions. None of them are particularly complicated, but there are a few subtle details that are worth diving into.

12.4.1 Sending Listener Changes

We'll start with the SendListenerChanges() function. The interesting bit about this function is that we need to overwrite the ListenerTransfer with our cached value after sending it. The ThreadSafeCommandValue class works by transitioning among three copies of the data. After a successful send operation, the value will contain an old stale value that was previously sent to the audio thread. We overwrite it immediately with the correct value in order to maintain consistency.

```
void AudioEngine::SendListenerChanges()
{
  // Send the listener update if it is dirty
  if (!bListenerIsDirty)
    return;

  if (ListenerTransfer.Send())
  {
    // Overwrite the stale listener data with our cached
    // version.
    ListenerTransfer.GetSendValue() = Listener;
    bListenerIsDirty = false;
  }
}
```

12.4.2 Sending Newly-Played Events

Next is the `SendNewlyPlayedEvents()` function. Here the function actually does three things: it finds events that have stopped before they had a chance to start, sends play event messages to the audio thread, and updates the state of the newly-played `MainThreadEvents`.

```
std::vector<int> AudioThread::SendNewlyPlayedEvents()
{
  // A list of Event Ids that have stopped and need to be
  // cleaned up.
  std::vector<int> StoppedEventIds;

  // Early out if there are no events to send
  if (MainThreadNewlyPlayedEvents.empty())
    return;

  // Send the newly-played events
  // Grab the send buffer for the play commands
  auto& SendBuffer = PlayCommands.GetSendBuffer();

  // We'll store a cache of the pointers so that we don't
  // have to look them up later.
  std::vector<MainThreadEvent*> CachedPlayedEvents;
  CachedPlayedEvents.reserve(
    MainThreadNewlyPlayedEvents.size());
```

```cpp
  // Iterate over each newly-played event.
  for (auto NewlyPlayedEventId : MainThreadNewlyPlayedEvents)
  {
    // Find the event
    auto* Event = GetMainThreadEvent(NewlyPlayedEventId);
    if (Event == nullptr)
      continue;

    // Early exit if the event is stopped before it's even
    // started.
    if (Event->IsStopped())
    {
      StoppedEventIds.push_back(NewlyPlayedEventId);
      continue;
    }

    // Add the pointer to the cache, and the information
    // for the newly-played event to the command queue.
    CachedPlayedEvents.push_back(Event);
    SendBuffer.emplace_back(
      NewlyPlayedEventId, Event->GetPlaybackParameters());
  }

  // Clear out the list of newly-played events.
  MainThreadNewlyPlayedEvents.clear();

  // Mark all of the newly-played events as played.
  for (auto* Event : CachedPlayedEvents)
  {
    Event->SetPlayed();
  }

  // Send the message
  PlayCommands.Send();

  return StoppedEventIds;
}
```

12.4.3 Sending Changes to Dirty Events

Now that we've sent the listener and newly-played events, we can update the changed events with **SendDirtyEvents()**. This function is straightforward, but the one thing that we do is an optimization to prevent having to look up the same event multiple times if there are multiple properties that have changed for an event. We do this by sorting the list of changes and then keeping a cache of the last used `MainThreadEvent` pointer so that it can be reused if the Event ID hasn't changed.

```cpp
void AudioThread::SendDirtyEvents()
{
  // Early out if nothing has changed.
  if (MainThreadDirtyEvents.empty())
    return;

  // Send changes to any dirty events.

  // Sort the dirty events first.  This will help to avoid
  // multiple lookups by guaranteeing that all dirty flags
  // for the same event will be in sequence.
  std::ranges::sort(MainThreadDirtyEvents);

  // Grab the send buffer for the commands.
  auto& SendBuffer = Commands.GetSendBuffer();

  // Cached data to save on lookups
  int PreviousEventId = -1;
  MainThreadEvent* PreviousEvent = nullptr;

  // Iterate over the list of dirty events
  for (auto& DirtyEvent : MainThreadDirtyEvents)
  {
    // Find the Event.
    MainThreadEvent* Event;
    if (DirtyEvent.first == PreviousEventId)
    {
      // If the Id is the same as the previous one, then
      // we can save the lookup.
      Event = PreviousEvent;
    }
    else
    {
      // Id is different, so we have to look it up.
      Event = GetMainThreadEvent(DirtyEvent.first);
```

```
    PreviousEventId = DirtyEvent.first;
  }
  if (Event == nullptr)
    continue;

  // Add the dirty event to the send buffer
  SendBuffer.emplace_back(DirtyEvent.second, *Event);
}

// Clear out the dirty events list and send the commands
MainThreadDirtyEvents.clear();
Commands.Send();
}
```

12.4.4 Stopped Sounds

Our last two functions are related to stopping sounds. First, we receive messages for any stopped events coming from the audio thread and accumulate them all into a vector, which is added to the vector of IDs for events that were stopped before they were started as returned by SendNewlyPlayedEvents(). The last step is to take the combined list of events and remove them entirely, since their lifetime is over.

```
std::vector<int> AudioEngine::ReceiveStoppedEventMessages()
{
  std::vector<int> StoppedEventIds;

  // We know that an Event has stopped when the audio thread
  // informs us through this StopCommands buffer.
  if (!StopCommands.Receive())
    return StoppedEventIds;

  // Get the receive buffer.
  auto& StoppedSoundCommands =
    StopCommands.GetReceiveBuffer();

  // Reserve space for all of the stopped event IDs in
  // order to avoid extra allocations.
  StoppedEventIds.reserve(StoppedSoundCommands.size());

  // Add each stopped sound to the list.
  for (auto& StoppedSoundCommand : StoppedSoundCommands)
```

```
  {
    StoppedEventIds.push_back(StoppedSoundCommand.EventId);
  }
  return StoppedEventIds;
}

void AudioEngine:: ClearStoppedEvents(
  const std::vector<int>& StoppedEventIds)
{
  for (auto StoppedEventId : StoppedEventIds)
  {
    // If there is a callback to communicate to the game
    // that a sound has stopped, this is where that will be
    // triggered from.
    MainThreadEvents.erase(StoppedEventId);
  }
}
```

12.5 THE `AudioThreadUpdate()` FUNCTION

For all that there's a lot of code, the `MainThreadUpdate()` function does very little. It iterates over the list of things that have changed and sends them to the audio thread to do the actual work. But this is exactly what we want! A bare minimum of time spent in the game thread means that we're handling the Fire and Forget observation by forwarding the actual work to another thread. As our exploration of the audio engine architecture travels to the audio thread, we are going to start seeing how we handle the steady state observation.

The backing store for the audio thread consists of a few pieces of data:

```
std::unordered_map<int, AudioThreadEvent> AudioThreadEvents;
std::vector<int> AudioThreadNewlyPlayedEvents;
std::vector<int> AudioThreadStoppedEvents;
unsigned long long CurrentDspClock = 0;
```

With that in place, we'll start with the `AudioThreadUpdate()` function, which follows a similar pattern to the `MainThreadUpdate()` function. Although it is somewhat longer than the `MainThreadUpdate()` function, the pattern is still to detect changes and respond to them – it just does it in the opposite direction of the main thread.

Here we begin to see how the multithreaded functionality ties into the event-driven nature of the audio engine. If there are no changes, then we do nothing. The goal as we add functionality should be to maintain this pattern: detect when a thing has changed, and only then respond to it.

```
void AudioEngine::AudioThreadUpdate()
{
  // Get the DSP Clock so that we can use it to schedule
  // events later. First get the Master ChannelGroup...
  FMOD::ChannelGroup* MasterChannelGroup = nullptr;
  CoreSystem->getMasterChannelGroup(&MasterChannelGroup);

  // ...from which we can get the current DSP Clock.
  MasterChannelGroup->getDSPClock(&CurrentDspClock, nullptr);

  // Update any changed events. We return a list of moved
  // events for to handle virtualization.
  auto MovedEvents = ReceiveChangeCommands();

  // Update if the listener has changed.
  bool bListenerChanged = ReceiveListenerUpdate();

  // Update the virtualization.
  UpdateVirtualization(MovedEvents, bListenerChanged);

  // Allocate memory for newly-played events.
  ReceiveNewlyPlayedEvents();

  // Timing callbacks are called at this point in the update.
  // Implementation details have been omitted here.
  UpdateTimingCallbacks();

  // Trigger playback of all newly-played events. The reason
  // we do this separately is so that we can make sure that
  // all of the Events exist in the map before we do
  // certain virtualization checks, such as Max Within
  // Radius (see Chapter 14). Also, if a callback triggers
  // that stops a sound, it may remove it from the list of
  // newly-played events.
  StartPlayingNewlyPlayedEvents();
```

```
// Send any events that have stopped this update to the
// main thread.
SendStopEventMessages();
}
```

As before, the `AudioThreadUpdate()` function is split up into a number of steps. Most of these functions follow the same pattern: receive messages from the main thread and then act on those messages. The audio thread is where the actual work of the audio engine happens, so there are also some steps that are unique to the audio engine.

12.5.1 Event Changes

We'll start with `ReceiveEventChanges()`, which largely follows the same pattern that we saw in `ReceiveStoppedEventMessages()` in Section 12.4.4. The only extra bit that we get here is that we cache off the list of Events that have received `Move` messages as an optimization on the virtualization checks.

```
std::vector<AudioThreadEvent*>
AudioEngine::ReceiveChangeCommands()
{
  // A cache of events that have moved this update.  We
  // use this to handle virtualization.
  std::vector<AudioThreadEvent*> MovedEvents;

  // See whether we have received any changes this update.
  if (!Commands.Receive())
    return MovedEvents;

  // Get the receive buffer
  auto& ReceivedCommands = Commands.GetReceiveBuffer();

  // Reserve memory for the moved events cache.  We don't
  // know which messages will involve moved events, so we
  // reserve enough memory for all of them.
  MovedEvents.reserve(ReceivedCommands.size());
  for (auto& Command : ReceivedCommands)
  {
    // Get the audio thread event for this message.
    // We can use a similar caching mechanism to the
    // MainThreadUpdate() in order to save lookups, which
```

```
    // we have omitted here to save space.
    auto* Event = GetAudioThreadEvent(Command.EventId);
    if (Event == nullptr)
      continue;

    // Make the desired change to the Event.
    switch (Command.CommandToExecute)
    {
      case AdjustPlayingSoundCommand::Command::Location:
        Event->UpdateLocation(Command.PointValue);
        MovedEvents.push_back(Event);
        break;
      case AdjustPlayingSoundCommand::Command::Volume:
        Event->UpdateVolume(Command.FloatValue);
        break;
      case AdjustPlayingSoundCommand::Command::Pitch:
        Event->UpdatePitch(Command.FloatValue);
        break;
      case AdjustPlayingSoundCommand::Command::Parameter:
        Event->UpdateEventParameter(
          Command.Key, Command.FloatValue);
        break;
      case AdjustPlayingSoundCommand::Command::RequestStop:
        Event->RequestStop();
        break;
    }
  }
  return MovedEvents;
}
```

12.5.2 Listener Updates

Listener updates follow the same pattern as Event changes: try to receive, then apply the changes. The primary difference here is that we're receiving a single value instead of a command buffer. To save space in this chapter, I have omitted code that detects whether the listener has actually changed position or orientation. These extra checks can be useful to determine what sorts of updates to perform later. I have left in the attenuation position check, since we want to do the more expensive virtualization check only if the attenuation position has moved, but not if the listener position or orientation has moved.

```cpp
bool AudioEngine::ReceiveListenerUpdate()
{
  // Cache the previous attenuation position
  auto PreviousAttenuationPosition =
    ListenerTransfer.GetReceiveValue().AttenuationPosition;

  // Update the listener if it has changed.  The return value
  // is used in the virtualization check later on.
  if (!ListenerTransfer.Receive())
    return false;

  // Get the updated value that the main thread sent.
  auto& NewListenerSettings =
    ListenerTransfer.GetReceiveValue();

  // Convert to FMOD structure and update the actual
  // listener.
  FMOD_3D_ATTRIBUTES ListenerAttributes =
    ToFMOD3dAttributes(NewListenerSettings);
  auto FMODAttenuationPosition =
    ToFMODVector(
      NewListenerSettings.AttenuationPosition);
  pStudioSystem->setListenerAttributes(
    0, &ListenerAttributes, &FMODAttenuationPosition);

  // Return whether the attenuation position has changed.
  return
    PreviousAttenuationPosition !=
      NewListenerSettings.AttenuationPosition;
}
```

12.5.3 Updating Virtualization

Our previous two functions have returned useful pieces of information. ReceiveChangeCommands() told us which Events have moved this update, and ReceiveListenerUpdate() told us whether the attenuation position has moved. We can use this information to update the virtualization of all events efficiently. If the attenuation position has changed, then we'll need to do a more expensive update, but if it hasn't, then only Events that have moved could possibly change their virtualization state.

Note that the code in this chapter commits the cardinal sin of iterating over all of the Events when the attenuation position changes.[1] I have left that in for brevity, but a proper implementation will use a spatial partitioning scheme to minimize the set of Events that are examined in that case.

```
void AudioEngine::UpdateVirtualization(
  const std::vector<AudioThreadEvent*>& MovedEvents,
  bool bListenerChanged)
{
  // Update the virtualization
  if (bListenerChanged)
  {
    // If the listener has moved, then potentially every
    // Event could update its virtualization.  Here we are
    // iterating over every Event, but a better system
    // would be to use a spatial partitioning system to
    // minimize the number of Events whose virtualization
    // needs to be updated.
    for (auto& [EventId, Event] : AudioThreadEvents)
    {
      Event.UpdateVirtualization(*this);
    }
  }
  else
  {
    // If the listener hasn't moved, then we only need to
    // update the virtualization for Events that have moved.
    for (auto* Event : MovedEvents)
    {
      Event->UpdateVirtualization(*this);
    }
  }
}
```

12.5.4 Handling Newly-Played Events

The penultimate step of the audio thread update is to handle newly-played events. The comment in `AudioThreadUpdate()` explains why we split this out into two functions. The short version is that we want to trigger the timing callbacks during the update, which might also play events. I've fully omitted timing callbacks from this chapter (other than a couple of nods to their existence) in order to save space. Nevertheless, we continue to see the same pattern as before: receive messages, then handle them.

```cpp
void AudioEngine::ReceiveNewlyPlayedEvents()
{
  // Start up the newly-played sounds.
  if (!PlayCommands.Receive())
    return;

  // Get the receive buffer of all newly-played sounds this
  // update.
  auto& ReceivedCommands = PlayCommands.GetReceiveBuffer();
  for (auto& Command : ReceivedCommands)
  {
    // Add the newly-played Event to the map.
    auto [NewEventIt, bAdded] =
      AudioThreadEvents.try_emplace(
        Command.EventId,
        Command.EventId, std::move(Command.Parameters));

    // Add the newly-played event to a list.
    AudioThreadNewlyPlayedEvents.push_back(
      Command.EventId);
  }
}

void AudioEngine::StartPlayingNewlyPlayedEvents()
{
  // Start playback on the newly-played events.
  for (auto EventId : AudioThreadNewlyPlayedEvents)
  {
    // Grab the event
    auto* Event = GetAudioThreadEvent(EventId);
    if (Event == nullptr)
      continue;

    // And start playback!
    Event->StartPlayback(*this);
  }
  AudioThreadNewlyPlayedEvents.clear();
}
```

12.5.5 Informing the Main Thread about Stopped Events

Finally, we have done all of the work of the audio thread, and we just need to tell the main thread which sounds have stopped so that it can clean up its memory. This function loops over the stopped events and does double duty by both removing the Events from the audio thread and informing the main thread.

```cpp
void AudioEngine::SendStopEventMessages()
{
  // Send any stopped Events to the main thread and clean
  // them up from the map.
  if (AudioThreadStoppedEvents.empty())
    return;

  // Grab the send buffer
  auto& SendStopCommands = StopCommands.GetSendBuffer();

  // Iterate over newly-stopped Events
  for (auto EventId : AudioThreadStoppedEvents)
  {
    // Erase from the map and send to the main thread.
    AudioThreadEvents.erase(EventId);
    SendStopCommands.emplace_back(EventId);
  }
  AudioThreadStoppedEvents.clear();
  StopCommands.Send();
}
```

12.6 THE `AudioThreadEvent` CLASS

The last piece of the puzzle is the `AudioThreadEvent` class, which tracks the playback and life cycle of a sound. As a result, we see the fully-featured state machine being handled in this code, rather than the trimmed down version that the main thread uses. It is also where we will begin to see more of the event-driven nature coming through.

As with the rest of this chapter, we'll leave off the details of the class declaration:

```cpp
class AudioThreadEvent
{
  // Functionality in this section goes here...
};
```

12.6.1 `AudioThreadEvent` Implementation Basics

Like the `MainThreadEvent` class, the actual implementation of most of the `AudioThreadEvent` is relatively simple. We'll take a look first at the basics of the implementation, then move on to the more interesting bits. The one bit of subtlety is that the functionality of setting variables is split out into two functions per entry: one to request to set the value, and the other to trigger when the value gets set. We do this in order to be able to either set the value externally or apply a previously-set value internally (such as when an event devirtualizes).

```
// Update the position of the playing Event
void AudioThreadEvent::UpdateLocation(
  const Point3& NewLocation)
{
  Parameters.Location = NewLocation;
  OnLocationUpdated();
}

// Update 3D Attributes when the location updates.
void AudioThreadEvent::OnLocationUpdated()
{
  FMOD_3D_ATTRIBUTES Attributes =
    ToFMOD3dAttributes(Parameters.Location);
  EventInstance->set3DAttributes(&Attributes);
}

// Update volume when the volume updates
void AudioThreadEvent::OnVolumeUpdated()
{
  EventInstance->setVolume(Parameters.Volume);
}

// Update pitch when the pitch updates
void AudioThreadEvent::OnPitchUpdated()
{
  EventInstance->setPitch(Parameters.Pitch);
}

// Update the Event parameter when the value updates
void AudioThreadEvent::OnParameterUpdated(
  const std::string& ParameterName, float Value)
```

```
{
  EventInstance->setParameterByName(
    ParameterName.c_str(), Value);
}

// Stop the Event when a stop has been requested.
void AudioThreadEvent::OnStopRequested()
{
  EventInstance->stop(FMOD_STUDIO_STOP_ALLOWFADEOUT);
}
```

Similar to the `MainThreadEvent` class, the `UpdateVolume()`, `UpdatePitch()`, and `UpdateEventParameter()` functions all follow the same pattern as `SetLocation()`, so we have omitted the implementations here in order to save space. Also, `RequestStop()` is similar to the `Set` family of functions, but we set `bStopRequested = true` instead of modifying a value on the parameters.

These functions are event-driven "for free". That is, we won't update the volume or an event parameter unless something else in the game explicitly triggers that change. But that was already true in the classic single-threaded system. We'll see more event-driven functionality in the next section.

12.6.2 Starting and Stopping Playback

So far this has all been fairly pedestrian, but we start to see some event-driven functionality crop up in Event playback. Let's take a look and see how that is accomplished:

```
void AudioThreadEvent::StartPlayback(AudioEngine& Engine)
{
  // Sanity check that we're in the correct state.
  assert(CurrentState == State::ToPlay ||
         CurrentState == State::Devirtualize);

  // Has the sound stopped before it ever played?
  if (bStopRequested)
  {
    OnSoundStopped(Engine);
    return;
  }
```

```cpp
// Grab the EventDescription so that we can ask questions
// about the Event
Engine.pSystem->getEventByID(
  &Parameters.EventId, &EventDescription);
if (EventDescription == nullptr)
{
  OnSoundStopped(Engine);
  return;
}

// Update any virtualization checks that need to happen
UpdateVirtualization(Engine);

// If we decide that we should be virtual, then handle
// that here
if (ShouldBeVirtual())
{
  bool bIsOneShot = false;
  EventDescription->isOneshot(&bIsOneShot);
  if (bIsOneShot)
  {
    // Oneshot Events don't virtualize, so we just stop
    // them.
    OnSoundStopped(Engine);
  }
  else
  {
    // Looped Events virtualize, so we can jump straight
    // to the virtual state.
    CurrentState = State::Virtual;
  }

  // Either way, we can early exit from this function.
  return;
}

// Create the EventInstance from the EventDescription.
EventDescription->createInstance(&EventInstance);
if (EventInstance == nullptr)
{
  OnSoundStopped(Engine);
```

```
    return;
  }

  // Update the EventInstance with the values from the
  // Parameters.  This is the reason that we split out the
  // Update functions from the OnUpdated functions: so that
  // we don't have to waste cycles overwriting values with
  // unchanged data.
  OnLocationUpdated();
  OnVolumeUpdated();
  OnPitchUpdated();
  for (const auto& [Name, Value] : Parameters.Parameters)
  {
    OnParameterUpdated(Name, Value);
  }

  // Add a callback to determine when the Event has stopped.
  EventInstance->setUserData(
    reinterpret_cast<void*>(static_cast<intptr_t>(EventId)));
  EventInstance->setCallback(
    &AudioThreadEvent::Callback,
    FMOD_STUDIO_EVENT_CALLBACK_STOPPED);

  // Start the Event and update the state.
  EventInstance->start();
  CurrentState = State::Playing;
}
```

Here is our first instance of the explicit event-driven nature of the system. Rather than asking every update for the current playback state, we add a callback that triggers when the Event has stopped, which we can then use to change states.

```
FMOD_RESULT F_CALL AudioThreadEvent::Callback(
  FMOD_STUDIO_EVENT_CALLBACK_TYPE Type,
  FMOD_STUDIO_EVENTINSTANCE* FmodEvent,
  [[maybe_unused]] void* Parameters)
{
  // Convert from the C type to the C++ type.
  auto* EventInstance =
    reinterpret_cast<FMOD::Studio::EventInstance*>(
```

```
    FmodEvent);

  // Grab the System object from the EventInstance
  FMOD::Studio::System* System = nullptr;
  EventInstance->getSystem(&System);

  // Get the System's UserData...
  void* SystemUserData = nullptr;
  System->getUserData(&SystemUserData);

  // ...which we will cast to the AudioEngine type.
  auto* Engine = static_cast<AudioEngine*>(SystemUserData);

  // Grab the EventInstance's UserData...
  void* EventUserData = nullptr;
  EventInstance->getUserData(&EventUserData);

  // ...which we will cast to an integer ID...
  auto EventId = static_cast<int>(reinterpret_cast<intptr_t>(
    EventUserData));

  // ...and get at the underlying AudioThreadEvent.
  auto* Event = Engine->GetAudioThreadEvent(EventId);

  // Sanity check callback type.  Production code will likely
  // be interested in other callback types as well.
  if (Type == FMOD_STUDIO_EVENT_CALLBACK_STOPPED)
  {
    // Forward to the member function.
    Event->OnSoundStopped(*Engine);
  }

  return FMOD_OK;
}

void AudioThreadEvent::OnSoundStopped(AudioEngine& Engine)
{
  // A virtual sound stopping is an unremarkable occurrence.
  // It just means that we've officially stopped our Event
  // after the Virtualizing state fadeout is complete.
  if (CurrentState == State::Virtual)
```

```
    return;

    // Update the current state.
    CurrentState = State::Stopped;

    // Add to the list of stopped Events.
    Engine.AudioThreadStoppedEvents.push_back(EventId);

    // Remove from the list of newly-played Events so that we
    // don't try to play it.
    std::erase(Engine.AudioThreadNewlyPlayedEvents, EventId);
}
```

12.6.3 Virtualization Basics

The last piece of the puzzle that we have not yet seen is virtualization, which is a bit more complex. We already saw calls to `UpdateVirtualization()` in the `AudioThreadUpdate()` function when the attenuation position or Event location moved. Let's take a look at that function first. Its ultimate goal is to ask whether the sound should be virtual – or, more precisely, to determine whether the virtualization has changed:

```
void AudioThreadEvent::UpdateVirtualization(
  AudioEngine& Engine)
{
    // Cache the previous value so we can tell if it changed.
    bool bPreviouslyVirtual = bShouldBeVirtual;

    // Check whether we should be virtual by distance.
    // Production code will likely have more kinds of
    // virtualization checks in addition.

    // Get the Event's max distance. (The first parameter is
    // min distance, which we don't care about here.)
    float MaxDistance = 0.0f;
    EventDescription->getMinMaxDistance(nullptr, &MaxDistance);

    // Calculate the squared distance to the attenuation
    // position and check if it's within the max distance.
    auto DistanceToAttenuationPosition =
      Parameters.Location.DistanceSquared(
        Engine.Listener.AttenuationPosition);
```

```
bShouldBeVirtual =
  (DistanceToAttenuationPosition > Square(MaxDistance));

// If the virtualization has changed, then update the
// virtualization status.
if (bShouldBeVirtual != bPreviouslyVirtual)
{
  OnVirtualizationUpdated(Engine);
}
}
```

12.6.4 Virtualization Details

Now that we've determined that the virtualization has changed, we can act on that. Our first layer of functionality here is a simple check to wrap the more complex behaviors:

```
// Desired virtualization has changed.  Either we were
// virtual and are no longer virtual, or we were not virtual
// and now need to be.
void AudioThreadEvent::OnVirtualizationUpdated(
  AudioEngine& Engine)
{
  if (bShouldBeVirtual)
  {
    // We want to be virtual, so virtualize the Event
    Virtualize(Engine);
  }
  else
  {
    // We want to no longer be virtual, so devirtualize
    // the Event
    Devirtualize(Engine);
  }
}
```

Virtualizing an Event is only meaningful in the Playing state. In every other state, the act of virtualizing is a no-op. If we are in the Playing state, then we add a fade down to silence. FMOD does not currently have a mechanism to provide us with a callback when a fade point is hit, so we use our own timing mechanism to set a callback to execute when the fade has completed. This callback does not need to be sample-accurate: if the fade completes and then a few milliseconds later we get the callback, it will not be perceptible to the player.

```cpp
void AudioThreadEvent::Virtualize(AudioEngine& Engine)
{
  // Check whether we're in a state where we need to do
  // anything at all.
  if (CurrentState != State::Playing)
    return;

  // Grab the EventInstance's ChannelGroup
  FMOD::ChannelGroup* ChannelGroup = nullptr;
  EventInstance->getChannelGroup(&ChannelGroup);

  // Add a fade point to automate a fade down to silence
  ChannelGroup->addFadePoint(
    Engine.CurrentDspClock + VirtualizeFadeSamples, 0.0f);

  // There is no way to register a callback for when
  // the fade point completes, so we'll have a side-
  // channel timing callback.
  VirtualizeCallbackEventId =
    Engine.RegisterTimingCallback(
      VirtualizeFadeDuration,
      [EventId = EventId](AudioEngine& Engine)
      {
        // The callback needs to re-get the Event, in
        // case it got removed in the meantime.
        auto* CallbackEvent =
          Engine.GetAudioThreadEvent(EventId);
        if (CallbackEvent == nullptr)
          return;

        // The virtualize fade has completed, so let
        // the Event know.
        CallbackEvent->OnVirtualizeFadeFinished();
      });

  // Mark this Event as virtualizing.
  CurrentState = State::Virtualizing;
}
```

Opposite of virtualization is devirtualization. Here we have two cases: if we are currently in the middle of virtualizing, then we need to clear any fadeouts and callbacks, fade back up to full volume, and switch back to the Playing state. The only other state that we care about is the Virtual state, where we can just switch to the Devirtualize state, which will handle the details of starting up the sound again.

```cpp
void AudioThreadEvent::Devirtualize(AudioEngine& Engine)
{
  // We would like to no longer be virtual.  If we are
  // currently virtualizing, then we need to fade back up
  // to full volume.  If we are virtual, then we need to
  // enter the Devirtualize state and queue the Event to
  // start.
  switch (CurrentState)
  {
  case State::Virtualizing:
  {
    // Grab the Event's ChannelGroup
    FMOD::ChannelGroup* ChannelGroup = nullptr;
    EventInstance->getChannelGroup(&ChannelGroup);

    // Remove any fade points between now and the end of
    // the fade.
    ChannelGroup->removeFadePoints(
      Engine.CurrentDspClock + 1,
      Engine.CurrentDspClock + VirtualizeFadeSamples);

    // Fade up to full volume.
    ChannelGroup->addFadePoint(
      Engine.CurrentDspClock + VirtualizeFadeSamples,
      1.0f);

    // Clear out the callback so that it won't trigger
    Engine.UnregisterTimingCallback(
      VirtualizeCallbackEventId);
    VirtualizeCallbackEventId = -1;

    // Update back to the Playing state.
    CurrentState = State::Playing;
  }
```

```
    break;
  case State::Virtual:
    // We're virtual, so we just need to switch the state
    CurrentState = State::Devirtualize;

    // And enqueue the sound to play.
    Engine.AudioThreadNewlyPlayedEvents.push_back(EventId);
    break;
  }
}

void AudioThreadEvent::OnVirtualizeFadeFinished()
{
  // Just update the state when the virtualize fade has
  // completed.
  CurrentState = State::Virtual;
}
```

12.7 WHERE TO GO FROM HERE

The framework described in Chapter 11 and implemented in this chapter is just a starting point. The next steps are to continue implementing features using the steady state and one-way pipeline observations.

One of the big challenges in using this engine is maintaining the event-driven nature for every feature that we add. In particular, Event parameters that are driven by game updates may require some work to make them event-driven. The character health system described in Chapter 11 is a good example of this challenge. It is usually easier to poll a value than to detect when that value changes, so the event-driven nature of this engine may end up becoming viral to parts of the rest of the codebase. The nature of these changes will vary from one game engine to another, and from one game system to another.

For all of the complexity that we have added here, this audio engine does more or less the same work as the one introduced in Somberg (2016). However, the new architecture does less work on the main thread, and minimal work on the audio thread. It is overall significantly more efficient, which is a win!

NOTE

1. Sorry.

REFERENCES

Somberg, Guy. 2016. "Sound Engine State Machine." *Game Audio Programming Principles and Practices*, edited by Guy Somberg, 13–30. Boca Raton, FL: CRC Press.

Somberg, Guy. 2024. "Thread-Safe Command Buffer." *Game Audio Programming Principles and Practices 4*, edited by Guy Somberg, 238–261. Boca Raton, FL: CRC Press.

CHAPTER 13

Automated Testing for Game Audio Systems

Charlie Huguenard

13.1 SAVING TIME (MONEY) AND REDUCING STRESS

It's the run-up to shipping, everyone is exhausted, and QA encounters a crash. It doesn't happen 100% of the time, the repro steps are complicated, and it has only been seen on two of the six shipping platforms. The crash dump shows the call stack ends in an audio system, but there's nothing obviously wrong with that code and the logs don't provide any useful information. None of the typical strategies to narrow it down have helped, and it doesn't occur in debug builds. So, you spend the next few days adding extra-verbose logging, changing the code to make the breakage more obvious, waiting for builds, and banging your head against your desk while your producer breathes down your neck and you question your choice of career.

We've all been there. It's not fun. It costs hours or days of your time, which translates into a lot of money for your project and company. But thankfully, nightmare scenarios like the one above can usually be avoided with a well-placed automated test. For large, long-term projects with many developers on the team, incorporating automated testing into the development process can make the difference between a smooth launch and an extended crunch – or worse, a failed launch and another shuttered game studio.

DOI: 10.1201/9781003519119-17

At the end of this chapter, you should:

1. Understand the benefits of automated testing in game audio development.

2. Know which kinds of tests you can create and how to create them.

3. Understand how to effectively and efficiently test your game audio systems.

4. Know where to look to learn how to integrate popular test automation frameworks into your workflow.

13.2 WRITING AUTOMATED TESTS

Automated testing of computer software has been around since the 1950s (Benington 1956), and its adoption in game development has grown in recent years. The goal of automated testing is, simply put, to enable sustainable growth of a software project.[1] When we first begin a project, our game systems are small enough that we can easily see if they're working. But as the project matures, those systems and their interactions often become too complex to reason about.

There's nothing clever or magical about automated testing. In fact, you have probably written an automated test without knowing. If you have set up a test level where non-player characters run around and interact with the world, and then you listen and make sure it sounds right, that's a kind of automated test.

1. You set up an environment where some actions are automatically performed.

2. You verified that the behavior (in this case, sound output) was as you expected.

You can take that one step further and automate the **verification** of the behavior. This is all test automation frameworks do.

1. You set up an environment where some actions are automatically performed.

2. You tell the test framework what you expect to happen (or hear), and the results are automatically verified.

The real power of automated testing comes from a computer's ability to quickly test large amounts of inputs and their corresponding outputs on as many target platforms and environments as you want. Consider a game that targets three consoles, two desktop platforms, and two mobile platforms. If you want to verify one test case with a human QA tester, and it takes 5 minutes for the tester to perform the test, that's (3 + 2 + 2) * 5 = 35 minutes of testing. A half an hour of testing is probably no big deal, but what if you want to test ten variations of input to your system? Then we're talking about 35 * 10/60 = ~6 hours of testing. Accounting for the human needs like food, water, and bathroom breaks, that's a QA tester's entire day! If you instead write an automated test for your system that isolates only the functionality you want to test, you can test hundreds of inputs to your system on all platforms in a matter of minutes, if not seconds.[2] That leaves plenty of time for the QA tester to handle subjective testing and other things that humans are better at.

13.2.1 Kinds of Tests

There are many kinds of automated tests, each targeting a different level of the software stack, with some specialized for the kind of software being developed. Let's focus on a few of the most common and useful kinds of tests:

- **Unit tests:** Test one component of a system.

- **Integration tests:** Test the interaction of multiple components in a system.

- **End-to-end tests:** Test the entire system or application.

13.2.1.1 Unit Tests

Unit tests verify the correctness of individual components of a system by isolating that component from the rest of the system. A unit test typically validates a single function or method, but it can also validate behavior of an object over its lifecycle. These are the simplest – but often most important – tests in a test suite[3] because misbehavior of a low-level component can manifest in subtle and bewildering ways in the context of an entire game. They also come with a handy side effect: making a component of a system testable often means decoupling it from other components, which usually leads to a more maintainable design (Fowler 2018).

For example, consider a gain function with the following signature:

```
void applyGain(
  float gain,
  const float* inputBuffer,
  float* outputBuffer,
  size_t size);
```

A test for this function, using Google Test[4] for demonstration purposes, might look like this:

```
TEST(GainTest, ApplyGain)
{
  std::vector<float> testGains{0.0f, 0.1f, 0.5f, 0.987f};
  std::vector<float> inputBuffer{/*some audio*/};
  std::vector<float> outputBuffer;
  outputBuffer.resize(inputBuffer.size());

  for (const float gain : testGains)
  {
    applyGain(
      gain,
      inputBuffer.data(),
      outputBuffer.data(),
      inputBuffer.size());

    for (size_t i = 0; i < inputBuffer.size(); ++i)
    {
      float expectedValue = inputBuffer[i] * gain;
      float outputValue = outputBuffer[i];
      EXPECT_FLOAT_EQ(expectedValue, outputValue);
    }
  }
}
```

When this test passes, we will have verified that the applyGain() function does the following:

- It applies a linear gain to the input buffer.

- It assigns the result to the output buffer.

- It behaves appropriately with subsequent calls using the same input and output buffers.

On any platform that can run games, this test will probably take nanoseconds to run. If we want to be more thorough, we could give it more gain values to test (e.g., negative or very large gains), and we could give it a variety of input buffers to test. Extend the test input data to hundreds or thousands of permutations, and you can see how we're far outpacing what a human tester could do.

13.2.1.2 Integration Tests

Integration tests verify interactions between multiple components in a system. They do this by isolating two or more components from the rest of the system and performing a series of actions on them. Similar to unit tests, integration tests often test a single piece of functionality. But integration tests take this a step further and validate that the components behave as expected when used in conjunction with other components.

Let's add a simple mix function to our system:

```
void mix(
    const float* inputBuffer1,
    const float* inputBuffer2,
    float* outputBuffer,
    size_t size);
```

Then, let's make another test which applies gain to two input buffers, then mixes them together:

```
TEST(MixerIntegrationTest, ApplyGainThenMix)
{
  std::vector<float> testGains{0.0f, 0.1f, 0.5f, 0.987f};
  std::vector<float> inputBuffer1{/*some audio*/};
  std::vector<float> inputBuffer2{/*some more audio*/};
  const size_t numSamples = inputBuffer1.size();
  std::vector<float> gainOutput1(numSamples);
  std::vector<float> gainOutput2(numSamples);
  std::vector<float> mixOutput(numSamples);

  for (const float gain : testGains)
```

```
{
  applyGain(
    gain,
    inputBuffer1.data(),
    gainOutput1.data(),
    numSamples);
  applyGain(
    gain,
    inputBuffer2.data(),
    gainOutput2.data(),
    numSamples);
  mix(
    gainOutput1.data(),
    gainOutput2.data(),
    mixOutput.data(),
    numSamples);

  for (size_t i = 0; i < numSamples; ++i)
  {
    const float expectedValue =
      inputBuffer1[i] * gain + inputBuffer2[i] * gain;
    float outputValue = mixOutput[i];
    EXPECT_FLOAT_EQ(outputValue, expectedValue);
  }
}
}
```

With this test, we have verified that the result of applying gain to two buffers and then mixing them together works as we expect. Note that we don't need to test the output of the two individual functions in this test. That will be covered by the functions' corresponding unit tests. As with the unit tests, this integration test can be scaled to hundreds or thousands of permutations without taking up much time.

13.2.1.3 End-to-End Tests

End-to-end tests validate the entire flow of a system or application from a user's perspective. These are most often the kind of playtests human QA testers do. While humans do excel at validating complex interactions and can give subjective feedback about the look and feel of a game, there are still many things we can automatically test. For example, we could write end-to-end tests to validate:

- Sound effects playing when the player character collides with an object.

- Music transitions based on game state.

- Dynamic sound mixing based on priority and ducking rules.

End-to-end tests require all of the game systems in order to do their validation, so the test itself will be game- and game-engine-specific (more on this later). But some common concepts apply for testing audio systems within games:

- Use verbose logging to report sound event triggers. This could satisfy the first and second examples if you know the name of the event(s) and the time at which they should be triggered.

- Hook into an audio bus or final mix to detect that there is *any* sound. This could be useful if you just want to make sure the game is making sound when it should be. In fact, it's advisable to make one "game is not silent" test at the beginning of a project to catch someone accidentally disabling the entire audio engine.[5]

- Use ground truth data to ensure that the sound output from the game is what you expect it to be. This can be useful for testing your mixing systems and any case where you expect the sound output to be deterministic.

13.2.2 Using Ground Truth Audio Data

Sometimes you know ahead of time what you expect the output of your test (or entire game mix) to be. In these cases, you can create audio files or hard-coded audio buffers to compare against your test's output. For simple tests, you can just compare the buffers sample by sample. If you expect some minor variations, you can add some error tolerance to this. But in some cases, you'll want to allow the test output to shift temporally or spectrally by some amount as development progresses and catch it when the actual output has diverged too much from its original state. That's when techniques like peak signal-to-noise ratio (PSNR) comparison can come in handy. This topic could be its own chapter, so this will be left as a research project for you.[6]

13.3 MAXIMIZING THE IMPACT OF AUTOMATED TESTING

Now that we know how to write tests, how do we ensure our project benefits from them? After all, tests are code, and all code has a maintenance cost.[7] This has been the topic of numerous entire books. Instead of regurgitating them here, let's visit some of the highlights:

- **Write good tests:** Make sure the test is worth the lines of code.

- **Write enough tests (but not too many):** Be aware of the conditions which make a test valuable and only write those tests.

- **Run your tests often (but not too often):** Utilize your build system to automatically run the tests but avoid slowing down the development process too much.

13.3.1 Write Good Tests

As mentioned above, tests are code and all code has a maintenance cost. When you are deciding whether to write a test, it's helpful to ask the following questions[8]:

- Will it catch breakages from future changes (AKA regressions)?
- Will the test have to change if the tested code is refactored?
- Is automating the test faster than having a human do the same thing?

13.3.1.1 Will the Test Catch Regressions?

The first question may appear obvious, but it's helpful to determine whether your test will ever actually catch a regression by asking yourself these questions:

- Is this code likely to change?
- If the tested code changes, is it likely to break when integrated with other parts of the system?
- If the tested code changes and breaks while integrated with the rest of the system, will it be hard to tell if this code is the cause of the breakage?

If you answer "no" to all these questions, you probably don't need to write that test.

13.3.1.2 Will the Test Have to Change if the Tested Code Is Refactored?

The second question is a little trickier. If you decide to refactor[9] the code being tested, does that mean your test should expect different output or require different input? As mentioned above, writing tests can have the pleasant side effect of improving the design of a piece of code. Part of the reason that the design improves is due to the shift in thinking that takes place when you decide how to test that code. Instead of thinking about an implementation, you begin thinking about input and output relationships, and your user-facing API tends to become more abstract. A well-written test assumes no knowledge of the underlying implementation and instead concerns itself with the expected output given a set of inputs.

13.3.1.3 Is Automating the Test Faster Than Having a Human Do the Same Thing?

Finally, consider whether writing and executing this test is faster than just having a human do it. If you already have a test level set up to verify that when your character jumps, it triggers the jump sound, and all your QA testers must make the character jump[10] in the normal course of their testing, you probably don't need to spend the time on that test. But if there are ten characters to choose from, the player can change the characters' shoes, and there are twenty different kinds of terrain, you're probably going to save a lot of time and avoid a lot of human error by automating validation of that code.

13.3.2 Write Enough Tests (But Not Too Many)

It's easy to get carried away and write many tests through the course of the development process. It's also common to encounter developers, leaders, and teams who just won't get on board with writing tests for their code. Often, these two extreme viewpoints collide and jeopardize everyone's common goal: shipping a sufficiently bug-free game on time and without breaking the team in the process. Ensuring your codebase has enough tests, but not too many, is often more of an exercise in social engineering than software engineering.

13.3.2.1 100% Test Coverage Is a Non-Goal

It's surprising how many developers approach automated testing assuming that 100% test coverage is a goal. It's not, and doing so would waste huge amounts of time.[11] Instead, you can use the criteria for writing good tests in the previous section to determine whether writing a test is going to add value to your test suite. Then, periodically go through your existing tests and reevaluate them to see if they're still useful. As mentioned before, tests are code, and code requires maintenance. Keeping your test suite appropriately lean will help you catch regressions while avoiding bloat. Avoiding bloat is not just good code hygiene, it also helps avoid run-ins with misguided folks who are looking for any excuse to do away with tests.

13.3.2.2 Negotiating with Non-believers

Speaking of which, some folks just don't or won't value automated testing. Common excuses include:

- If we have to write tests for all of our code, it takes too long to write the code.

- We hired smart programmers, and we trust them to write good, bug-free code.

- We have QA for testing, we don't need to write our own tests.

Many coders and leaders of coders are concerned with code development velocity for good reason. They want to work quickly and efficiently because it feels good and because it's good for the bottom line. The US Navy SEAL saying[12] "slow is smooth, smooth is fast" applies here. Just because you're coding quickly doesn't mean you're spending less overall time on that code. If you've appropriately covered your code with automated tests, you will most likely spend less time on that code over the course of your project. Code without automated tests is more likely to cause bug hunts when integrated into a larger system, and bug hunts simply take longer than finding the cause of a broken test.

Unfortunately, we only have hindsight to prove this. If you have a past project where you can approximate the time spent on a portion of the codebase that was covered with automated tests versus a similar portion that wasn't, you may be able to provide some data to argue for or against automated testing. But most likely, you'll have to lead by example and use your *current* project as evidence for a future project. If your game is on a long enough timeline, you might be able to find two existing systems to compare before you ship and turn the tide for your team, project, and company.

There's another fallacy embedded in this excuse: "if we have to write tests for **all** of our code..." You *don't* have to write tests for all of your code. 100% test coverage is not the goal. Improved stability (and therefore improved development velocity by way of fewer bug hunts) is the goal.

Many leaders pride themselves on their teammates' ability to write good code and think of automated testing as an unnecessary time sink and a challenge to their abilities. The reality is that people who write code write bugs. People who write tests for their code commit fewer bugs to the codebase. Likely, many of those "good coders who don't need to write tests" have their own system for validating their code, they just don't share it with the rest of the team, or nobody ever asked.[13]

Many game teams rely solely on human QA testers to ensure their game is shippable. QA folks are amazing, and their efforts help us make better games by providing qualitative feedback on gameplay, sound, and visuals. But any human's ability to exhaustively test each system of a game is limited by time, energy, and attention, not to mention that we intentionally obfuscate many game systems to provide an immersive experience for players. So, any bug reports we get are inherently superficial and rarely point directly at the broken code. As we showed earlier in the chapter, we can exercise a function, class, or entire system with hundreds or thousands of inputs in a matter of seconds with automated tests. When one of those tests fail, they usually point directly at the bit of code that broke. So not only do we save QA tester time by having a machine do this kind of testing, but we also save programmer time by narrowing down the cause of a regression before the bug report is generated.

13.3.2.3 Organic Methods

One approach to adding tests to a test suite is to let them appear organically. Sometimes it's obviously helpful to write tests for some new code while you're developing it. For example, if you're writing a voice manager, it's likely you won't be able to immediately hook it into your audio system so you can hear the result. This is a great time to employ some test-driven development methodology.[14]

1. Stub in your API.

2. Write some tests that exercise that API. These tests will fail at first.

3. Implement your system until the tests pass.

Another helpful approach is to write tests when you get a bug report. The process tends to look like this:

1. Manually reproduce the bug and narrow down the cause.

2. Write a test that reproduces the bug. This test should fail if you were successful.

3. Attempt to fix the bug until the test passes.

4. Commit the fix and the test at the same time.

If that same code breaks again in a similar way, your test should catch the regression and narrow down the cause for the next fixer.

13.3.3 Run Your Tests Often (But Not Too Often)

You can put together the most beautiful, lean, and effective test suite for your code, and it won't have any impact if you don't run the tests enough and at the right time. You may ask, "when should I run my tests?" It works a lot like the concept of sample rate in digital audio. The more often you run the tests (higher sample rate), the smaller the set of changes (samples being interpolated or truncated) that could have caused a regression signaled by a test failure. There are a few common ways to schedule test runs:

• Periodic: Tests run hourly, nightly, weekly, etc.

• Commit: Tests run on every commit.

• Triggered: Tests run when a set of conditions are met.

Periodic test runs are the most common, because most game studios schedule nightly or weekly builds of the game for testing anyway. The length of the period determines the number of changes that could possibly have caused a test to fail, so a shorter period is better for automated test purposes. But build resources are often limited, and test runs are often the first thing on the chopping block if a build engineer needs to save resources. If you only have a dozen or so commits every day, this might be a good option. But if you're at a large studio with hundreds or thousands of commits a day, you'll have a lot of changes to wade through to bisect a test failure.

Running tests on every commit is a great option if you have a small codebase, or if you have enough build resources to handle a test build and run on every commit. But in most game development studios, this is going to be too resource-intensive to be feasible, and your build engineers will stand over your shoulder until you turn your tests off.[15]

Many build systems have ways to trigger a job if certain conditions are met. If you don't mind getting your hands dirty and negotiating with your build engineers, this is often the best option. Depending on your build system you could trigger your tests on any number of conditions, including:

- When the code under test has been changed.

- When a dependency of the code under test has been changed.

- When build configuration has been changed.

- When a release build is made.

The ideal scenario is that your tests run whenever anything has changed that might change the behavior of the code under test. Some more sophisticated build systems like Buck2[16] assemble a nice dependency graph that can be used to trigger tests. The reason this is ideal is that your tests *only* run when a commit could have caused a regression, and no more than that. This can help you appease the non-believers, or at least stay off their radar.

13.4 EXISTING AUTOMATED TESTING FRAMEWORKS

There are several automated test frameworks that can be used in game development. Some even come integrated into commercial game engines. Which one you use will be specific to the environment you're using. Here are some of the popular ones, grouped by development environment:

- Unreal Engine

  - Unreal Automation Testing Framework (for engine- and game-level testing)[17]

  - Catch 2 (for low-level testing without the whole engine)[18]

- Unity

  - Unity Test Framework (for C# code)[19]

- Godot

  - Godot Unit Test Framework (GUT)[20]

- C++

  - Google Test[21]

  - Catch 2[22]

13.5 ONWARD!

Hopefully this has given you enough tools to help your team make great game audio systems with less stress. Just like any technology, automated testing is constantly evolving. In particular, machine learning, reinforcement learning, and other AI-assisted automation appear to be on the horizon for testing of games and other interactive media. Many of the specifics of this chapter may not survive this kind of progress, but hopefully most of the concepts will translate to future methods of testing audio software. Just remember, the whole point is to let both the humans and the machines do more of what they're good at.

NOTES

1. (Khorikov 2020), p. 6.
2. In fact, I have witnessed tens of thousands of test cases execute on a code review in a matter of minutes while working on audio system code at Facebook, circa 2020.
3. A test suite is all the tests for your system or application.
4. https://github.com/google/googletest
5. This happens surprisingly often and is caught embarrassingly slowly.
6. For more detail, see Wikipedia contributors (2024). You can see an example of an implementation in a game engine by searching the Unreal Engine source for "PSNR". The source code can be found at https://github.com/EpicGames/UnrealEngine
7. (Khorikov 2020), p. 8.
8. This list is adapted from "The Four Pillars of a Good Unit Test" in (Khorikov 2020).
9. "A change made to the internal structure of software to make it easier to understand and cheaper to modify without changing its observable behavior" (Fowler 2018).
10. And they don't have the sound disabled!
11. This is a topic of much discussion, so rather than link you to a single book or article, I recommend just searching for "100% test coverage" and following the more credible sources to learn more.

12. The origin of the phrase is debated, and could come from ancient Rome, Japan, or China.
13. I had a great "aha" moment working with a very senior engineer when he was asked to improve test coverage for my team's codebase and he almost immediately committed some tests he, "had lying around to make sure he didn't break things".
14. I don't, however, subscribe to wholesale adoption of TDD. I think I've covered my reasoning enough with all of the "100% test coverage" talk.
15. I've sabotaged myself this way, and my tests were all disabled without anyone telling me. The next time I got a bug, I asked, "why didn't the tests fail?" and learned that they would have if they had been running.
16. https://buck2.build/
17. https://dev.epicgames.com/documentation/en-us/unreal-engine/automation-test-framework-in-unreal-engine
18. https://dev.epicgames.com/documentation/en-us/unreal-engine/low-level-tests-in-unreal-engine
19. https://docs.unity3d.com/Packages/com.unity.test-framework@1.4/manual/index.html
20. https://docs.godotengine.org/en/stable/contributing/development/core_and_modules/unit_testing.html
21. https://google.github.io/googletest/
22. https://github.com/catchorg/Catch2

REFERENCES

Benington, Herbert D. 1956. "Production of large computer programs." *Proceedings of the Symposium on Advanced Programming Methods for Digital Computers*, June 28–29: 15–28.

Fowler, Martin. 2018. *Refactoring: Improving the Design of Existing Code.* 2nd ed. Boston, MA: Addison-Wesley.

Khorikov, Vladimir. 2020. *Unit Testing: Principles, Practices, and Patterns.* Shelter Island, NY: Manning Publications.

Wikipedia contributors. 2024. "Peak Signal-to-Noise Ratio." *Wikipedia, The Free Encyclopedia.* September 22. Accessed April 6, 2025. https://en.wikipedia.org/w/index.php?title=Peak_signal-to-noise_ratio&oldid=1247121104

CHAPTER 14

An Algorithmic Approach to "Max Within Radius" Virtualization

Guy Somberg

14.1 INTRODUCTION

In offline audio mixing, there is a rule called the "Law of Two and a Half", coined by Walter Murch through his work on the film *THX-1138* (Murch 2005). This law can be summarized as the statement that one or two sounds playing at the same time must be in sync with their triggers, but if there are any more than that, then any sync point is as good as any other.[1] We translate this psychoacoustic effect into the realm of realtime game mixing through a feature called Max Within Radius.

The Max Within Radius feature generalizes Walter Murch's Law of Two and a Half into a game mix, where the mix must be reactive to the world, and where the player (rather than the game developer) has control over what is being heard at any moment. The way it works is that every Event that participates in the system has either two (or three) properties set on it:

- **Max Count**: The maximum number of instances of this Event that can be played within the given radius.

DOI: 10.1201/9781003519119-18

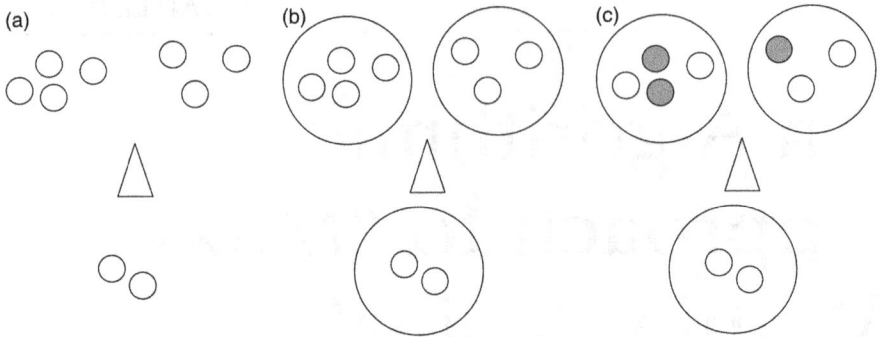

FIGURE 14.1 Simplified view of the Max Within Radius feature. (a) The listener and sound sources. (b) Radius around the sound sources creating three clusters. (c) Each cluster of sounds has been limited to two playing sounds (hollow) with the remainder (shaded) being virtualized.

- **Radius**: The radius to search for nearby Events within the same group.

- **Group**: All Events within the same group are counted toward the Max Count. This parameter is optional. If it is set, then it overrides the group name. If it is not set, then each Event gets assigned to its own unique group. This parameter allows multiple different Events to be considered a part of the same Ggroup.

Figure 14.1 shows a simplified view of this feature in action. The triangle is the listener and the small circles are sound sources in the same group, where the **Max Count** is two within the given **Radius**. We end up with three clusters of sounds and are able to cut out all but two sounds within each cluster.

14.2 A FIRST-PASS ALGORITHM

A naïve approach to implementing Max Within Radius would iterate over each Event in the group every time that we ask whether we've hit the max count for the group. If it has hit the limit, then virtualize the Event. This will function, but has a few problems:

- It is highly inefficient. Every Event is performing the same calculations (distance to members of the same group) over and over again.

- It does not necessarily select the best Events to be virtual. Events will be evaluated in arbitrary order, and it is that order that ends up selecting which Events will end up virtualized.

- It is focused on a single Event at a time, and doesn't acknowledge the nature of the feature as examining the entire corpus of currently playing Events in the group.

We can do better.

In order to do better, though, we must define how we expect the system to work. In the second bulleted point above, we refer to the "best" Event, but there isn't really a definition of what we mean by "best". We know that we're unlikely to get it from the naïve algorithm, but not what it actually is.

14.3 DEFINING "BEST"

Let us now dive a little deeper and define what result we want to achieve. Given two different configurations of virtualization selection for a set of input sounds, how do we evaluate which one is better than the other? To answer this, we need to consider what our final result should be, which leads us to the following rubric: we would like to fill as much of the sound field as possible with as few sounds as we can.

As an example, say we have a cluster of three sounds in the same group with a **Max Count** of two. Two of the sounds are close together and a third is further apart. In this case, we should prefer to keep the sound that is further apart along with one of the two that are clustered together, rather than selecting the two that are clustered together. Figure 14.2 shows an example of this situation. In this example, we should prefer to virtualize either sound A or B, as in Figure 14.2b or c, rather than sound C as in Figure 14.2d.

This naturally leads us to the question of how to decide between the sound A and sound B. On the surface, they are equivalent, so how do we differentiate between them? The feature that distinguishes the two sounds from each other can only be their distance to the third sound (C). Sound A is slightly farther away, which means that we will fill more of the sound field if we select it than if we select sound B (the closer sound). In our example from Figure 14.2, we would therefore select (c) rather than (b).

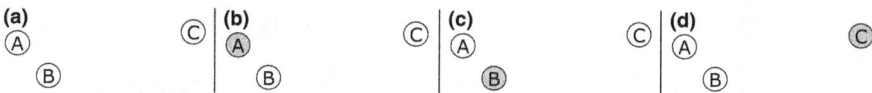

FIGURE 14.2 A situation with three sounds. (a) The locations of the sounds. (b) and (c) One of the sounds clustered together is virtualized. (d) The farther sound is virtualized.

So far, our algorithm seems to favor selecting sounds with farther neighbor distances, which will help us to satisfy the "fill as much of the sound field" portion of the rubric. What about the "as few sounds as we can" portion? In order to address that, we should prefer to play sounds that are in larger clusters – that is, sounds with more neighbors within range.

All of this leads us to the following algorithm:

1. Calculate all of the distance pairs between members of the group. This is an $O(N^2)$ operation, but our expectation is that N (the number of sounds in the group) is relatively small.

   a. For each sound in the group, track which other members are within the **Radius** (*"Neighbors"*), as well as the maximum distance of the sound to the Neighbors.

2. Sort the data by number of Neighbors, then by maximum distance to Neighbor.

3. Iterate over the sorted data. For each entry:

   a. If the entry has fewer nonvirtual Neighbors (*"Marks"*) than the **Max Count**, then the sound is nonvirtual, and add a Mark to each of its Neighbors.

   b. Otherwise, the sound is virtual.

14.4 EXAMINING THE ALGORITHM

Let's see how well this algorithm stacks up. We won't be doing a rigorous proof of optimality or correctness or anything like that here. Rather, we'll throw a few examples at it and make sure that we're getting results that make us happy and which also follow the rules.

14.4.1 Example 1

We'll start with the layout in Figure 14.3. Here we can see a few clusters of sounds: **A** and **B**, with maybe **D** depending on how close it is; **E**, **F**, and **G**; and then **C** off on its own. Let's go through our algorithm and try it out.

The first step is to measure all of the distances. Table 14.1 contains the full matrix of distances between the sounds. Note that this matrix is symmetrical across the diagonal – that is, the upper-right half of the matrix is identical to the lower-left.

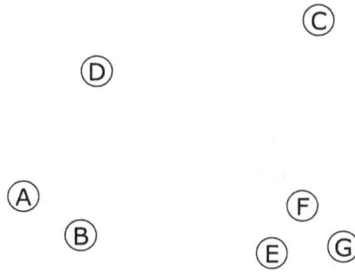

FIGURE 14.3   An example layout of sounds.

Now that we have calculated all of the distances, we go through every sound and keep track of all of their Neighbors (those sounds that are within the **Radius**), as well as the maximum distance to those Neighbors. We do need to define what our **Radius** is for this example, so we will say that it is 10 units. Table 14.2 summarizes this data. We also care about the count of the Neighbors, so the table includes that information. In practice, we will store the list of Neighbors and use the size of the list rather than storing a separate value, but we will list it out explicitly in the table for convenience.

Next, we sort the list of sounds by Neighbor count, then by max distance to Neighbor. Once we have that, we can go through and start to assign sounds as virtual or nonvirtual. For each sound, we make it virtual if it has a number of Marks (nonvirtual Neighbors) greater than or equal to the **Max Count**. If it has fewer Marks, then we make it nonvirtual and add a Mark to each of its Neighbors.

In this example, our sorted list is **A, E, G, F, D, B, C**. Let's start doling out virtualness and Marks for a **Max Count** of two:

- **A** has no Marks, so it can be nonvirtual, then **B** and **D** each get one Mark.

TABLE 14.1   Distances between All of the Sounds in Figure 14.3

	A	B	C	D	E	F	G
A	0	3.1	25.7	9.4	18.2	20.1	23.7
B	3.1	0	23.7	10.9	13.0	15.7	18.8
C	25.7	23.7	0	16.0	17.0	12.8	16.2
D	9.4	10.9	16.0	0	18.1	17.6	22.2
E	18.2	13.0	17.0	18.1	0	2.2	3.4
F	20.1	15.7	12.8	17.6	2.2	0	2.3
G	23.7	18.8	16.2	22.2	3.4	2.3	0

TABLE 14.2   Neighbors, Neighbor Counts, and Maximum Distance to Neighbor for Each Sound in Figure 14.3, Assuming a Radius of 10 Units

	A	B	C	D	E	F	G
Neighbors	B, D	A		A	F, G	E, G	E, F
Neighbor Count	2	1	0	1	2	2	2
Max Distance to Neighbor	9.4	3.1	0	9.4	3.4	2.3	3.4

TABLE 14.3   Virtualization Assignments and Marks for the Sounds in Figure 14.3, Assuming a Max Count of 2

	A	E	G	F	D	B	C
Virtualness	NV	NV	NV	V	NV	NV	NV
Marks	XX	X	X	XX	X	X	

- **E** has no Marks, so it can be nonvirtual, then **F** and **G** each get one Mark.

- **G** has one Mark, so it can be nonvirtual, then **E** gets one Mark and **F** gets one additional Mark.

- **F** has two Marks, which is the **Max Count**, so it is virtual.

- **D** has one Mark, so it can be nonvirtual, then **A** gets a Mark.

- **B** has one Mark, so it can be nonvirtual, then **A** gets another Mark.

- **C** has no Marks, so it can be nonvirtual. It has no Neighbors, so no Marks are added.

This leaves us with the results in Table 14.3. In this table, NV means nonvirtual, V means virtual, and we add an X for each Mark.

But wait! We have a problem here. Look at **A** – we have a sound that is nonvirtual, but it also has two Marks. Each Mark represents one non-virtual neighbor, and since **A** is also nonvirtual, that means that we have three nonvirtual sounds playing within the **Radius** of each other. Our **Max Count** in this example is two, so we can't have that.

14.5 FIXING THE ALGORITHM

Fortunately, we can fix our algorithm with a simple tweak (in bold and italics):

1. Calculate all of the distance pairs between members of the group.

   a. For each sound in the group, track the Neighbors and the maximum Neighbor distance.

2. Sort the data by number of Neighbors, then by maximum Neighbor distance.

3. Iterate over the sorted data. For each entry:

   a. If the entry has fewer Marks than the **Max Count**, *and each neighbor has fewer than (Max Count – 1) Marks*, then the sound is nonvirtual, and add a Mark to each of its Neighbors.

   b. Otherwise, the sound is virtual.

With this one tweak to our algorithm, we prevent a sound from being selected as nonvirtual if it would cause an already nonvirtual sound to have too many nonvirtual neighbors.

14.5.1 Example 1 Again

Let's apply this updated algorithm to Example 1 from Section 14.4.1. Tables 14.1 and 14.2 remain unchanged, but we need to make a change to Table 14.3. The updated values are in Table 14.4. We also include the values for a **Max Count** of 1, just to see what the difference would be. For the **Max Count** of two, the only change from our first attempt at the algorithm is that sound **B** is now virtual, but we can see that in all circumstances, the nonvirtual sounds have zero or one Marks.

Figure 14.4 shows the same configuration as Figure 14.3 with the virtual sounds shaded in gray.

14.5.2 Example 2

Let's go through one more example (Figure 14.5) before we get to the code. This time the sounds are clustered very differently. We have one central sound (**E**) and several clusters of individual or paired sounds: **A** and **F**, **C** and **G**, then **B** and **D** are relatively far apart and may or may not form a cluster. Let's go through the exercise again. Table 14.5 shows the distances

TABLE 14.4   Virtualization Assignments and Marks for the Sounds in Figure 14.3 Using the Updated Algorithm

	A	E	G	F	D	B	C
Virtualness (Max Count 2)	NV	NV	NV	V	NV	V	NV
Marks (Max Count 2)	X	X	X	XX	X	X	
Virtualness (Max Count 1)	NV	NV	V	V	V	V	NV
Marks (Max Count 1)			X	X	X	X	

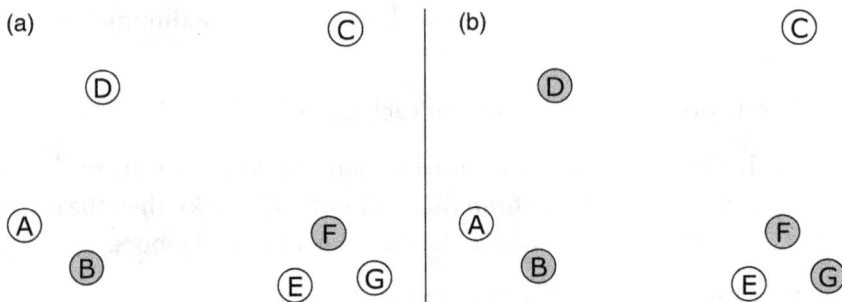

FIGURE 14.4 Sounds configuration from Figure 14.3 with virtual sounds shaded in gray. (a) Max Within Radius of 2. (b) Max Within Radius of 1.

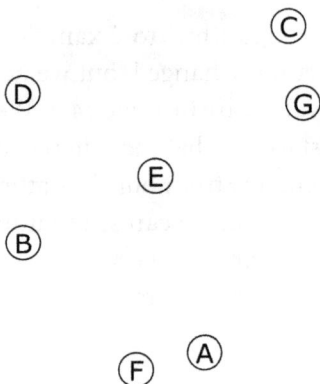

FIGURE 14.5 An example layout of sounds.

TABLE 14.5 Distances between All of the Sounds in Figure 14.5

	A	B	C	D	E	F	G
A	0	10.6	22.5	20.6	11.1	2.8	17.2
B	10.6	0	22.4	8.4	8.4	9.9	20.4
C	22.5	22.4	0	17.5	12.2	25.2	3.4
D	20.6	8.4	17.5	0	8.9	19.5	17.8
E	11.1	8.4	12.2	8.9	0	11.8	9.8
F	2.8	9.9	25.2	19.5	11.8	0	20.5
G	17.2	20.4	3.4	17.8	9.8	20.5	0

TABLE 14.6 Neighbors, Neighbor Counts, and Maximum Distance to Neighbor for Each Sound in Figure 14.6, Assuming a Radius of 10 Units

	A	B	C	D	E	F	G
Neighbors	F	D, E, F	G	B, E	B, D, G	A, B	C, E
Neighbor Count	1	3	1	2	3	2	2
Max Distance to Neighbor	2.8	9.9	3.4	8.9	9.8	9.9	9.8

TABLE 14.7 Virtualization Assignments and Marks for the Sounds in Figure 14.5

	B	E	F	G	D	C	A
Virtualness (Max Count 2)	NV	NV	V	V	V	NV	NV
Marks (Max Count 2)	X	X	XX	XX	XX		
Virtualness (Max Count 1)	NV	V	V	NV	V	V	NV
Marks (Max Count 1)		XX	X		X	X	

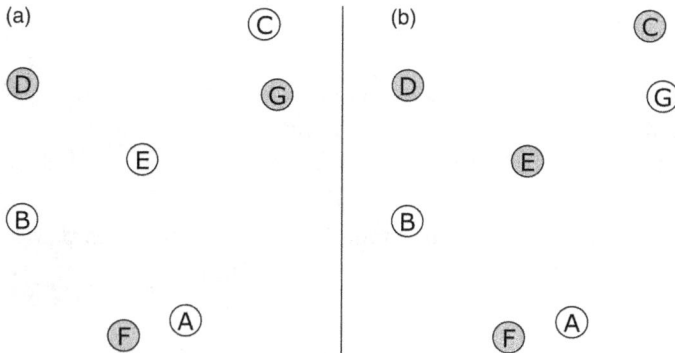

FIGURE 14.6 Sounds configuration from Figure 14.5 with virtual sounds shaded in gray. (a) Max Within Radius of 2. (b) Max Within Radius of 1.

in this second example, Table 14.6 shows the Neighbor counts and max distances with a **Radius** of 10 units, and Table 14.7 shows the resulting virtualness selection for a **Max Count** of both 2 and 1. Figure 14.6 shows the configuration with the virtual sounds shaded in gray.

This all looks good. We've got quite a successful algorithm! Let's go ahead and dive into the code.

14.6 THE CODE

There is a lot of infrastructure that we need to build in order to really take advantage of this algorithm. We will need some mechanism to group sounds together, track the minimal set of which groups need to be updated, and then combine the virtualization results from multiple groups together in order to apply virtualization changes to individual events.

We are going to skip most of that because it is largely mechanical and will vary greatly from engine to engine and from game to game. Instead, we'll look at the basic data structures that we'll be using and then dive straight into the actual algorithm.

14.6.1 Data Structures

Our first two data structures are placeholders that we'll be using to represent the data that the system understands about the Max Within Radius feature. These are more or less what you'd expect to see, but production code may differ for pragmatic reasons.

```cpp
// The data for a Max Within Radius group
struct GroupSettings
{
  // The name of the group - usually either the GUID of the
  // Event or a user-specified name.
  std::string GroupName;

  // The maximum number of sounds in the group that we would
  // like to have playing within the Radius.
  unsigned int MaxCount = 0;

  // The Radius that we would like to limit sounds within.
  float Radius = 0.0f;
};


// A collection of sounds within a single Max Within Radius
// group
struct GroupEntry
{
  // Constructors
  GroupEntry() = default;
  GroupEntry(GroupSettings&& Settings) :
    Settings(std::move(Settings))
  {}

  // The settings for the group.
  GroupSettings Settings;
```

```
  // List of Event Ids that belong to the group.
  std::vector<int> EventIds;
};
```

Those two data structures are the inputs to our algorithm. Our next two data structures are part of the output and the internal workings of the code.

```
// Our output structure containing a list of virtual and
// nonvirtual Event IDs for the group.
struct VirtualizationResult
{
  std::vector<int> VirtualEvents;
  std::vector<int> NonvirtualEvents;
};
```

```
// Internal working data structure
struct GroupEntryContext
{
  // Constructor to fill in the necessary data from the
  // Event Id.
  GroupEntryContext(int EventId) :
    EventId(EventId)
  {
    EventLocation = GetEventLocation(EventId);
  }

  // Our Event ID
  int EventId;

  // Location of this Event
  Point3 EventLocation;

  // Our list of neighbors within the Radius
  using GroupContextIt =
    std::vector<GroupEntryContext>::iterator;
  std::vector<GroupContextIt> NeighborsWithinRadius;

  // The maximum distance to each of our neighbors
  float MaxDistanceToNeighborWithinRadius = 0.0f;
```

```
// Our count of nonvirtual neighbors. These are our
// "Marks"
unsigned int NonVirtualNeighbors = 0;
};
```

One thing to note about the `GroupEntryContext` is that the `NeighborsWithinRadius` member is a `vector` of iterators to a `vector` of `GroupEntryContexts`, which in this case is itself the backing store for the `GroupEntryContext` structures. In other words, these are effectively internal pointers to the contents of the structure. We must therefore be very careful about the lifetime of these iterators; any operation that has the potential to change the contents of the `vector` or resize it can potentially invalidate all of these iterators. For example, part of our algorithm requires us to sort the collection, but doing so will reorder it, which will invalidate the iterators. As a result, our code will create one collection for the `GroupEntryContexts` themselves, and then another collection of iterators that can be sorted and operated on independently. We will see this in action in the next section.

14.6.2 Algorithm Code

We'll start with our main function that is a high-level description of the algorithm, then dive into the detail functions.

```
VirtualizationResult ResolveDirtyGroup(
  const GroupEntry& Group)
{
  // Start by constructing the contexts for all of the
  // Events in the group.
  auto Contexts = MakeGroupEntryContexts(Group);

  // Fill in the matrix of distance pairs.
  CalculateDistancePairs(Group, Contexts);

  // Get an array of iterators so that we can operate on
  // it without invalidating up the internal iterators.
  auto ContextIterators = GetContextIterators(Contexts);

  // Sort the iterators by Neighbor count and max distance
  // to Neighbor.
  SortIterators(ContextIterators);
```

```
  // Assign out the virtualization.
  return AssignVirtualization(Group, ContextIterators);
}
```

This function breaks down our algorithm into nice bite-sized chunks that we can approach one at a time. We'll start with the straightforward process of creating the contexts, which we can implement with a simple copy operation.

```
std::vector<GroupEntryContext> MakeGroupEntryContexts(
  const GroupEntry& Group)
{
  std::vector<GroupEntryContext> Contexts;

  // Reserve memory to limit allocations.
  Contexts.reserve(Group.EventIds.size());

  // Copying the IDs into the contexts will call the
  // appropriate constructor.
  std::ranges::copy(
    Group.EventIds, std::back_inserter(Contexts));
  return Contexts;
}
```

We now have a collection of GroupEntryContexts, so the next step is to fill in the matrix of distance pairs:

```
void CalculateDistancePairs(
  const GroupEntry& Group,
  std::vector<GroupEntryContext>& Contexts)
{
  auto RadiusSquared = Square(Group.Settings.Radius);

  // Calculate all of the distance pairs.  We're using an
  // iterator loop to save us the trouble of converting back
  // to iterators from an algorithm that dereferences
  // iterators under the hood.  Also, we've got a double
  // loop that we want to start in the middle, so having the
  // iterators already available makes that process simple.
  auto ContextsEnd = Contexts.end();
  for (auto FirstEntry = Contexts.begin();
```

```
      FirstEntry != ContextsEnd; ++FirstEntry)
{
  if (FirstEntry->EventId == -1)
    continue;

  const auto& FirstLocation = FirstEntry->EventLocation;

  // Inner loop starts at one past FirstEntry so that we
  // don't duplicate work.
  for (auto SecondEntry = FirstEntry + 1;
       SecondEntry != ContextsEnd; ++SecondEntry)
  {
    if (SecondEntry->EventId == -1)
      continue;

    const auto& SecondLocation =
      SecondEntry->EventLocation;

    // Calculate the squared distance between the entries.
    auto DistanceSquared =
      FirstLocation.DistanceSquaredTo(SecondLocation);

    // These two members of the group are outside of the
    // MWR radius, so they don't affect each other.
    if (DistanceSquared > RadiusSquared)
      continue;

    // Set the maximum distance on both entries if it's
    // longer than the current distance.
    FirstEntry->MaxDistanceToNeighborWithinRadius =
      std::max(
        FirstEntry->MaxDistanceToNeighborWithinRadius,
        DistanceSquared);
    SecondEntry->MaxDistanceToNeighborWithinRadius =
      std::max(
        SecondEntry->MaxDistanceToNeighborWithinRadius,
        DistanceSquared);

    // Make sure that each entry knows that the other is
    // a Neighbor.
    FirstEntry->NeighborsWithinRadius.push_back(
```

```
          SecondEntry);
      SecondEntry->NeighborsWithinRadius.push_back(
          FirstEntry);
    }
  }
}
```

For all that this is over a page of code, it is fairly straightforward: we loop through our elements and collect the neighbors within range, storing the maximum distance as we go. We could also write this as a two-pass operation where the first pass calculates the neighbors and the second pass does a `std::max_element()` on the neighbors to get the maximum value. Although that has some nice properties in terms of separation of concerns, it does also mean that we are calculating the squared distance multiple times for each neighbor. That won't end up being a huge cost, but we've kept the calculation inline here.

Now that we have our context objects and filled in our matrix, we can no longer touch the original **vector** in order to avoid invalidating the iterators. What we do, therefore, is make an array of iterators that we can operate on. That turns out to be a simple **transform** operation:

```
// Using declaration to use a terser name
using GroupContextConstIt =
  std::vector<GroupEntryContext>::const_iterator;
std::vector<GroupContextConstIt> GetContextIterators(
  const std::vector<GroupEntryContext>& Contexts)
{
  std::vector<GroupContextConstIt> ContextIterators;

  // Resize to our desired size.
  ContextIterators.resize(Contexts.size());

  // Transform each entry into an iterator to that entry.
  std::ranges::transform(Contexts, ContextPointers.begin(),
    [&Contexts = std::as_const(Contexts)]
    (const GroupEntryContext& Context)
    {
      // Because std::vector is contiguous, we can guarantee
      // that this distance() call will return the correct
      // distance from the beginning of the vector.
```

```
            return Contexts.cbegin() +
               std::distance(Contexts.data(), &Context);
        });
    return ContextPointers;
}
```

The final step before we can select whether each sound is virtual or not is to sort the collection.

```
void SortIterators(
    std::vector<GroupContextConstIt>& ContextIterators)
{
    // Sort the list of iterators.
    std::ranges::sort(ContextIterators,
        [](const GroupContextConstIt& Left,
           const GroupContextConstIt& Right)
        {
            // Primary key is the number of Neighbors.
            auto LeftNeighborCount =
                Left->NeighborsWithinRadius.size();
            auto RightNeighborCount =
                Right->NeighborsWithinRadius.size();

            // If the Neighbor counts are the same, then we
            // prefer the ones with a longer max distance.
            if (LeftNeighborCount == RightNeighborCount)
                return
                    Left->MaxDistanceToNeighborWithinRadius >
                        Right->MaxDistanceToNeighborWithinRadius;

            // Sort by larger Neighbor counts before smaller
            // neighbor counts.
            return LeftNeighborCount > RightNeighborCount;
        });
}
```

And that's all of the prep work that we have to do! We are now ready to decide whether each sound should be virtual or not. This is a straightforward process of iterating over the collection of iterators (which is now in the correct order), and then using the NonVirtualNeighbors count (a.k.a. Marks) to decide whether it can be virtual.

```cpp
VirtualizationResult AssignVirtualization(
  const GroupEntry& Group,
  const std::vector<GroupContextConstIt>& ContextIterators)
{
  VirtualizationResult ReturnValue;

  // With our context pointers sorted by most Neighbors,
  // then by max distance to Neighbor, we can now iterate
  // over each entry and decide which ones should be virtual.
  for (auto& Context : ContextIterators)
  {
    // Assume that we should be virtual, then check to see
    // if we can be nonvirtual.
    bool bVirtual = true;

    // If the nonvirtual Neighbor count has not yet reached
    // the Max Count for the group (in other words, the max
    // within radius has not been hit for this cluster of
    // sounds), then this entry might be nonvirtual.
    if (Context->NonVirtualNeighbors <
        Group.Settings.MaxCount)
    {
      // We've got nonvirtual Neighbors to spare, which
      // means that this sound can probably be non-virtual.
      // Before we can guarantee that, though, we need to
      // check that we wouldn't be making one of our
      // nonvirtual Neighbors go over the limit.
      auto bAllNeighborsHaveRoomToSpare =
        std::ranges::all_of(Context->NeighborsWithinRadius,
          [&](const auto& Neighbor)
          {
            return Neighbor->NonVirtualNeighbors <=
                   (Group.Settings.MaxCount - 1);
          });

      // If all of our Neighbors have at least one slot
      // available for a nonvirtual Neighbor, then we can
      // go ahead and be nonvirtual.
      if (bAllNeighborsHaveRoomToSpare)
        bVirtual = false;
    }
```

```
  if (bVirtual)
  {
    // If we are going to be virtual, then we add the
    // event to the list of virtual events.
    ReturnValue.VirtualEvents.push_back(Context->EventId);
  }
  else
  {
    // For a nonvirtual event,  we will need to go to
    // each Neighbor and apply a Mark to it indicating
    // that there is a nonvirtual Neighbor sound playing.
    for (auto& Neighbor : Context->NeighborsWithinRadius)
    {
      Neighbor->NonVirtualNeighbors++;
    }

    // ...before adding it to the list of nonvirtual
    // events.
    ReturnValue.NonvirtualEvents.push_back(
      Context->EventId);
  }
}
return ReturnValue;
}
```

14.7 CONCLUSION

Walter Murch's "Law of Two and a Half" is a valuable mixing tool in general, and the way that we bring it into the real time mixing context is with the Max Within Radius feature. On the surface, it is a simple operation, but taking a deeper look and stepping back to examine the feature leads us to an algorithm that has some depth and complexity. While the algorithm is quite efficient, it remains so only as long as the number of concurrently playing sounds in a group is kept small enough that the $O(N^2)$ portion – calculating the Neighbors and max distances – remains unproblematic. If there is some code that is spawning many instances of sounds concurrently, then some pre-filtering will be necessary to keep it in check.

All of the code in this chapter must be part of a larger system that tracks the group membership of playing sounds, and which identifies when a particular group might need to have its Max Within Radius virtualization recalculated. And that system, in turn, must be part of a system that is tracking and evaluating the virtualization state of all of the sounds. Nevertheless, this core is an invaluable piece of that whole structure.

NOTE

1. This pithy summary is sufficient for the purposes of this chapter, but doesn't really express the full intent of the law. The entire article is quite long and well worth the read. I encourage you to go read it!

REFERENCE

Murch, Walter. 2005. *Walter Murch*. April 1. https://transom.org/2005/walter-murch/

V
Music

CHAPTER 15

Synchronizing Music to Gameplay to Create Music Moments

Fiach O'Donnell

15.1 INTRODUCTION

The marriage of gameplay and music has been used so effectively in the modern video game era that its subtleties are often difficult to discern. In recent times, synchronization has come to the fore of game audio, which has helped to create highly immersive musical experiences tailored to each player's actions. Games like *Doom* (2016) (id Software 2016) feature sprawling soundtracks, where tracks have multiple verse and chorus variations, and song sections are parsed into smaller parts – all of which are available to be swapped out at runtime to time with player input. In *The Legend of Zelda: Breath of the Wild* (Nintendo 2017), game combat music is more aleatoric, with percussion and piano sounds playing on the next appropriate music beat after the player lands a hit on their enemy (Scruffy Music 2019). In the midst of all this action, the average player might be unaware that these musical moments so perfectly align with their inputs. But there's a subconscious feeling: *this is satisfying.*

In Walder (2019), Colin Walder outlines tooling for synchronizing action-based gameplay to music. This approach makes use of Wwise callbacks for bar, beat, and grid timings, alongside predictive synchronization to match animation, AI, and VFX with music. I highly recommend

DOI: 10.1201/9781003519119-20

reading Colin's chapter, as the tooling outlined in this chapter will discuss similar concepts. It's also a fascinating read!

In this chapter, we'll examine the principles behind developing a music moment system and take an inverse approach: synchronizing important musical beats to prescheduled in-game events. Depending on the user settings, this can create either a subtle or a more maximalist effect: stretching and contracting the music timeline to match powerful beat timings with in-game events, all while maintaining the musical key and structure. This approach may also be more suitable for cases where event timings are inflexible.

We'll achieve this outcome through the use of music callbacks and time-invariant pitch-shifting mechanics. As such, it's necessary to understand the pitch shifter and its uses.

15.2 THE PITCH SHIFTER

15.2.1 A Brief History

Simply put, pitch shifting is a technique used to modify the pitch of a sound. Pitch shifting was originally used in music recording, and was achieved by manually varying tape speeds, so that sections of a recording track could be pitched up or down. Speeding up or slowing down the tape would either raise its frequency (thereby reducing its duration) or lower its frequency (increasing its duration).

Like many modern recording techniques, we owe the popularity of pitch shifting to the musical ingenuity of The Beatles. The band famously used this method of pitch shifting in 1966 when recording their hit song "Strawberry Fields Forever" (Emerick and Massey 2007). Though perhaps a bit antiquated by today's standards, their method spliced two versions of the same track together: an original recording and an orchestral score recorded at a faster tempo and higher key. Increasing and decreasing the speeds of the two separate versions compensated for their differences in key – and in doing so, the band was also able to manipulate John Lennon's vocals to capture the slurred, dream-like quality that became indicative of their psychedelic sound.

The practice of pitch shifting grew in popularity in the mid-1970s after Eventide Inc. released the H910 Harmonizer: a digital effects processor widely considered as the first commercially available pitch changer (Eventide Audio n.d.). The rise of samplers in the 1980s not only provided the means to sample any sound, but also the ability to wield real time pitch control over it. From there, it wasn't long until pitch shifting entered the modern digital plugin space.

15.2.2 Time-Invariant Pitch Shifting in FMOD Studio

Advancements in digital signal processing have since allowed us to overcome the core resampling constraint where pitch change is affected by playback speed. This process, known as time stretching, is a core concept of this chapter. Time stretching is defined as changing the speed of an audio signal (in our case, the music) without affecting its overall pitch. We will use FMOD Studio and the underlying FMOD Core API to handle the application of our pitch-shifting mechanics based on music timeline callbacks. However, these steps should be easily reproducible in other audio environments with similar features.

In FMOD Studio, we have two pitch modifiers at our disposal (Figure 15.1). Event master tracks have a pitch control property that adjusts the sample rate of the event instruments. This value is in semitones, and we can consider it our *event instance pitch property*. FMOD also offers a Pitch Shifter plugin that can be added to any track; it expresses its pitch value as a floating-point between 0.5 and 2. These values represent one octave down and one octave up, respectively, from the standard baseline of no pitch change (represented by a default value of 1.0).

Instruments whose properties have been altered by any Pitch Shifter plugins will be summed together with the event instance pitch property, so determining the relationship between these values is fundamental to our system. Adjusting the event instance property affects the playback speed

FIGURE 15.1 Pitch Shifter plugin (Left) and Event Instance Pitch Property as part of the Event Macros (Right) in FMOD Studio.

of the event, but adjusting the plugin value changes the pitch of the event without affecting the playback speed. This is a *time-invariant* pitch shift.

By using both properties simultaneously with the right values, we can benefit from an increase or decrease in playback speed while maintaining the same pitch (i.e., a pitch-invariant time shift). The event instance value controls the track length, or tempo, but both pitch values will effectively cancel each other out. In the FMOD API, the pitch multiplier for an event instance is expressed in linear units in the range of [0, inf],[1] with the default value as 1. Depending on the value applied to the Pitch Shifter DSP/plugin, we can calculate the percentage at which to set the pitch instance value.

```
constexpr float OurNewDSPValue = 0.9f;

// Change the Pitch Shifter DSP value
PitchShifterDSP->setParameterFloat(
  FMOD_DSP_PITCHSHIFT_PITCH, OurNewDSPValue);

// Change the Event instance pitch value
EventInstance->setPitch(1.f / OurNewDSPValue);
```

This is easily verifiable in FMOD Studio, but one should note that the event instance pitch value here is in semitones. We can convert our event instance percent value (x) to cents using the formula:

$$c = 1200 \cdot \log_2(x)$$

The above example translates to approximately 182.4 cents, or 1.82 semitones, which, with the corresponding Pitch Shifter plugin value of 0.9, will speed up the event while maintaining its pitch.

15.3 PREPARATIONS

Now that we're familiar with what's required at a base level, there are some setup prerequisites we need to implement before we can begin programming our music moment system.

15.3.1 FMOD Studio Prerequisites

To start, we need a means of defining which audio events react to our tech. Assigning a user property for these events in FMOD Studio is best for

FIGURE 15.2 FMOD Studio Event Setup. (a) User Property, (b) Tempo Marker, (c) Pitch Shifter plugin.

tagging purposes, so the audio engine is aware of which events react to changes. The system will operate on the basis of timeline callbacks, so it is crucial to ensure that the music event track has the appropriate tempo marker(s) and time signature(s) assigned. The example in Figure 15.2 uses a 134 bpm 4/4 looping track, but we'll soon see that the tooling can easily account for other time signatures.

Finally, we'll assign a Pitch Shifter plugin on the master track with the value of 1 so that no pitch change is applied by default. (This last step is somewhat optional – we can also check for the DSP existence at runtime and create a new one if required.)

15.3.2 Beat Callback Prerequisites

The audio engine needs a map of read-writable data structures containing information about the music events – namely, the start time of the next bar and the total duration of a full bar. We'll call this data structure

`MusicProperties`. We'll also need a container to cache all the event IDs that we're synchronizing to music (`MusicMomentIDs`). Constructing the engine context goes well beyond the scope of this chapter, but for our purposes, let's assume that we already have:

    a. An interface for retrieving this engine context.

    b. An event lookup mechanism.

    c. A means of retrieving the current game time.

```
struct MusicProperties
{
  float TimeOfNextBar = 0.f;
  float BarDuration = 0.f;
};

class AudioEngineContext
{
public:
  // Engine context functions
  static AudioEngineContext& GetEngineContext();
  AudioEvent* GetAudioEvent(int EventId);
  const float GetCurrentTime() const;

  // Music Moment setup
  const MusicProperties* GetMusicProperties(
    int EventId) const;
  void SetMusicProperties(int EventId,
    const MusicProperties& NewMusicProperties);

  std::unordered_map<int, MusicProperties>
    MusicMomentIDProperties;
  std::vector<int> MusicMomentIDs;
}

const MusicProperties* AudioEngineContext::
  GetMusicProperties(int EventId) const
{
  auto FoundMusicProperties =
    MusicMomentIDProperties.find(EventId);
  if (FoundMusicProperties == MusicMomentIDProperties.end())
```

```
    return nullptr;

  return &FoundMusicProperties->second;
}

void AudioEngineContext::SetMusicProperties(int EventId,
  const MusicProperties& NewMusicProperties)
{
  auto FoundMusicProperties =
    MusicMomentIDProperties.find(EventId);
  if (FoundMusicProperties == MusicMomentIDProperties.end())
  {
    MusicMomentIDProperties.insert(
      { EventId, NewMusicProperties });
    return;
  }

  FoundMusicProperties->second = NewMusicProperties;
}
```

In the audio event class, as part of the event instance start and stop callbacks, we'll register and deregister the moment events to our IDs container. These event instances will also need to register with a new callback: the `FMOD_STUDIO_EVENT_CALLBACK_TIMELINE_BEAT` callback, which gets called whenever the FMOD event timeline hits a beat in a tempo section.

```
class AudioEvent
{
public:
  // ...
  static FMOD_RESULT F_CALL EventCallback(
    FMOD_STUDIO_EVENT_CALLBACK_TYPE CallbackType,
    FMOD_STUDIO_EVENTINSTANCE* CastedEventInstance,
    void* CallbackParameters);

  void HandleMusicBeatCallback(
    const FMOD_STUDIO_TIMELINE_BEAT_PROPERTIES&
      BeatProperties) const;

protected:
  int EventId = -1; // Assumed initialized by constructor
```

```
}

FMOD_RESULT F_CALL AudioEvent::EventCallback(
  FMOD_STUDIO_EVENT_CALLBACK_TYPE CallbackType,
  FMOD_STUDIO_EVENTINSTANCE* CastedEventInstance,
  void* CallbackParameters)
{
  // Get the EventId from our CastedEventInstance...
  auto& AudioEngineContext =
    AudioEngineContext::GetEngineContext();
  auto* AudioEvent =
    AudioEngineContext.GetAudioEvent(EventId);
  if (AudioEvent == nullptr)
    return FMOD_ERR_EVENT_NOTFOUND;

  auto& EventDescription = AudioEvent->EventDescription;
  if (EventDescription == nullptr)
    return FMOD_ERR_EVENT_NOTFOUND;

  FMOD_STUDIO_USER_PROPERTY MusicMomentProperty;
  FMOD_RESULT MomentResult =
    EventDescription->getUserProperty(
      "MusicMoment", &MusicMomentProperty);
  bool bHasMomentProperty = (MomentResult == FMOD_OK);

  auto& MomentIDs = AudioEngineContext.MusicMomentIDs;
  switch (CallbackType)
  {
    case FMOD_STUDIO_EVENT_CALLBACK_STARTED:
    {
      if (bHasMomentProperty)
        MomentIDs.push_back(AudioEvent->EventId);
    }
    break;
    case FMOD_STUDIO_EVENT_CALLBACK_STOPPED:
    {
      if (bHasMomentProperty)
      {
        MomentIDs.erase(std::remove(MomentIDs.begin(),
          MomentIDs.end(), EventId), MomentIDs.end());
      }
```

```
    }
    break;
    case FMOD_STUDIO_EVENT_CALLBACK_TIMELINE_BEAT:
    {
      auto* TimelineBeatProperties =
        reinterpret_cast<
          FMOD_STUDIO_TIMELINE_BEAT_PROPERTIES*>(
            CallbackParameters);
      if (TimelineBeatProperties != nullptr)
        AudioEvent->HandleMusicBeatCallback(
          *TimelineBeatProperties);
    }
    break;
  }
  return FMOD_OK;
}
```

The HandleMusicBeatCallback() function is where updating the timings for the event's MusicProperties data structure occurs. This starts with calculating the number of beats left in the bar. It is important to decrement the current timeline beat property by one when subtracting it from the upper time signature in order to account for the time from the final beat in the bar to the first of the next bar. The next step is to calculate the number of beats per second based on the time signature. Taking the reciprocal of this value gives the seconds per beat, which is the metric we'll use to calculate the time of the next bar based on how many beats are left.

```
void AudioEvent::HandleMusicBeatCallback(
  const FMOD_STUDIO_TIMELINE_BEAT_PROPERTIES&
    BeatProperties) const
{
  int BeatsLeftInBar = BeatProperties.timesignatureupper -
    (BeatProperties.beat - 1);
  if (BeatsLeftInBar <= 0)
    return;

  float BeatsPerSecond = BeatProperties.tempo / 60.f;
  BeatsPerSecond *= static_cast<float>(
    BeatProperties.timesignaturelower) / 4.f;
  float SecondsPerBeat = 1.f / BeatsPerSecond;
```

```
auto& AudioEngineContext =
  AudioEngineContext::GetEngineContext();
float TimeOfNextBar = AudioEngineContext.GetCurrentTime() +
  (SecondsPerBeat * BeatsLeftInBar);

MusicProperties NewMusicProperties = { TimeOfNextBar,
  SecondsPerBeat * BeatProperties.timesignatureupper };
AudioEngineContext.SetMusicProperties(
  EventId, NewMusicProperties);
}
```

The last thing to do as part of any setup is to initialize and release the pitch shifter DSPs for the event instances from the start and stop callbacks. The code for this is relatively simple, but long, so I instead included it as pseudocode below. In our case, our music event already has a Pitch Shifter effect set up on the master track in FMOD Studio, so we just need to retrieve this from the channel group and cache it (as `PitchShifterDSP`). If the event isn't configured with this effect, then additional setup is required to create the DSP at runtime.

```
class AudioEvent
{
  // ...
  void InitializePitchShifterDSP();
  void ReleasePitchShifterDSP();
  FMOD::DSP* PitchShifterDSP = nullptr;
}

void AudioEvent::InitializePitchShifterDSP()
{
  // Find the FMOD_DSP_TYPE_PITCHSHIFT from the channel group
  // (or create a new DSP). Assign it to the PitchShifterDSP
  // object. Initialize pitch value to default 1 and add to
  // the channel group
}

void AudioEvent::ReleasePitchShifterDSP()
{
  // Remove PitchShifterDSP from the channel group and
  // release it
}
```

We now have a setup where music sync events are registered and deregistered within the audio engine, and event pitch shifter DSPs are properly initialized and released. We also created audio engine data structures containing the start time of the next bar, and the bar duration, which will update with each event's beat callback. It's a lot of preparation, but we now have everything we need to get started!

15.4 SYSTEM IMPLEMENTATION

For the first pass, we'll receive a notification from somewhere in our game engine that an event has been scheduled, which will include the time until the event occurs. In theory, this event could be anything: a player skill, a monster spawn, an important boss attack, etc. For our purposes, we'll assume that these in-game event timings are fixed and can't be canceled after the fact. Once we've received the event call, it's a certainty that it (whatever "it" is) will occur.

Initially, we will synchronize the start of an upcoming music bar to this event, *if possible*. This *if possible* is necessary to acknowledge, as we will need to define some system constraints. We don't want the music to always synchronize if it's going to sound bad (i.e., too fast or too slowed down). We'll start with bar synchronization, then work backwards and extend the code to account for other important and non-important beats, depending on the musical time signature.

15.4.1 Bar Synchronization

We need another data structure in our audio engine: `MomentSyncData`. This is the object that gets created once we've checked that we can synchronize the music to the game event. It will consist of the audio event ID, an integer representative of how many bars from now the beat will occur (0 meaning the next bar start, 1 meaning the bar after that, etc.), the current time left until the sync event, and the target pitch value that needs to be reached in order to sync the music to the game event. We'll also include an invalid flag for easy cleanup.

The details about how we calculate the target pitch value will be discussed further on in this chapter, but for now, let's add another container in our audio engine for these objects.

```
struct MomentSyncData
{
    int EventId = -1;
```

```
    int BarNumber = 0;
    float TimeUntilSync = 0.f;
    float TargetPitchValue = 1.f;
    bool bIsValid = true;
};

class AudioEngineContext
{
    // ...
    std::vector<MomentSyncData> MomentDataToUpdate;
}
```

Managing the pitch shift update itself can be done within the engine tick. Our pitch shift operations will operate at a fixed rate, so before each update, we want to continuously ensure that we can reach our target value at this rate.

```
constexpr float IsEqualThreshold = 0.01f;
void AudioEngineContext::Tick(float DeltaTime)
{
    // ...
    for (auto& SyncData : MomentDataToUpdate)
    {
        auto* Event = GetAudioEvent(SyncData.EventId);
        if (Event == nullptr)
        {
            SyncData.bIsValid = false;
            continue;
        }

        if (SyncData.TimeUntilSync <= 0.f)
        {
            SyncData.bIsValid = false;
            continue;
        }

        // Check that we can still reach the target
        if (!Event->CanHitPitchTargetAtMaxRate(
                SyncData.TimeUntilSync,
                SyncData.TargetPitchValue))
        {
```

```
    SyncData.bIsValid = false;
    continue;
  }

  Event->UpdatePitchShifter(DeltaTime, SyncData);

  // Update the time left until our moment sync
  SyncData.TimeUntilSync -= DeltaTime;
}

// Remove invalid entries for next update
MomentDataToUpdate.erase(
  std::remove_if(
    MomentDataToUpdate.begin(), MomentDataToUpdate.end(),
    [&] (const MomentSyncData& SyncData)
    { return !SyncData.bIsValid; }),
  MomentDataToUpdate.end());
}

class AudioEvent
{
public:
  // ...
  void UpdatePitchShifter(
    float DeltaTime, MomentSyncData SyncData);
  float GetCurrentPitchValue() const
  { return PitchShifterValue; }

protected:
  // ...
  float PitchShifterValue = 1.f;
}
```

Now it's time to do all the work! Let's start by defining some additional functions before completing UpdatePitchShifter() – which we'll soon see is relatively straightforward, as it just calls each of these:

- GetTargetBeatForMomentSync(): Finds the target beat to sync the music to. For now, this is the start of the next feasible bar – it will be extended in Section 15.4.2.

- **CanHitPitchTargetAtMaxRate()**: A utility function to check if we can hit a pitch target within a given timeframe. This is dependent on the max pitch change constraint (**MaxPitchChangePerSecond**).

- **OnMusicMomentChanged()**: The entry-point function to schedule a music moment when a notification about a scheduled in-game event occurs. This performs an initial check to see if we can synchronize the music with the event, and, if we can, add an entry to the audio engine container so it can be regularly updated.

```cpp
class AudioEvent
{
public:
  // ...
  float GetCurrentPitchValue() const
  { return PitchShifterDSPValue; }

  std::optional<MomentSyncData> GetTargetBeatForMomentSync(
    const AudioEngineContext& EngineContext,
    float TimeUntilMoment);

  bool CanHitPitchTargetAtMaxRate(float TimeUntilMoment,
    float PitchTargetValue) const;

  void OnMusicMomentChanged(
    AudioEngineContext& EngineContext,
    float TimeUntilMoment);

  const float MaxPitchChangePerSecond = 0.05f;
}
```

We need some sort of arrangement to find the best bar candidate, since we want to check for synchronization not only with the next bar but also with future bars, depending on the event time. For that, we need one additional data structure – **BeatTimeData**. This contains the same integer representative of how many bars from now the beat will occur, as well as the time until that beat. We only need this data for **AudioEvent::GetTarget BeatForMomentSync()** at present, but it will be required again later when beat synchronization comes into play. So, let's define the type in the audio engine context, instead of in the event class.

```
struct BeatTimeData
{
  int BarNumber = 0;
  float BeatTime = 0.f;
};
```

Let's implement those `AudioEvent` functions. One important thing to note for `AudioEvent::GetTargetBeatForMomentSync()` is that if the pitch is constantly being updated, we are now getting our regular beat callbacks at a faster rate, so the properties with our bar timings aren't accurate. This is because we're not considering the current pitch value when calculating these timings. We can compensate for this when calculating our `TimeUntilSync` value.

The valid beat candidates will contain any `MomentSyncData` objects with which the system can synchronize based on its settings. We can use a `while` loop here to increment the necessary bar, time, and new pitch value variables to perform the same checks against subsequent bars. If the new pitch value fits within the pitch shifter min and max value thresholds, then it can be considered. For our case, though, we'll just use a predicate to find the closest candidate time with which to synchronize.

```
constexpr float PitchShifterMinValueThreshold = 0.9f;
constexpr float PitchShifterMaxValueThreshold = 1.11f;
std::optional<MomentSyncData> AudioEvent::
  GetTargetBeatForMomentSync(
    const AudioEngineContext& EngineContext,
    float TimeUntilMoment)
{
  if (TimeUntilMoment <= 0.f)
    return std::nullopt;

  // Get the beat timeline data
  auto* MusicProperties =
    EngineContext.GetMusicProperties(EventId);
  if (MusicProperties == nullptr)
    return std::nullopt;

  // Check value is within thresholds and we can reach it at
  // max rate
```

```cpp
auto IsValidPitchValue = [&](const float InTimeUntilMoment,
  const float InPitchValue)
{
  if (InPitchValue < PitchShifterMinValueThreshold ||
      InPitchValue > PitchShifterMaxValueThreshold)
  {
    return false;
  }

  return CanHitPitchTargetAtMaxRate(
    InTimeUntilMoment, InPitchValue);
};

// The initial BeatCandidate is the start of the next bar
BeatTimeData BeatData =
  { 0, MusicProperties->TimeOfNextBar };

float CurrentTime = EngineContext.GetCurrentTime();
float TimeUntilSync = (BeatData.BeatTime - CurrentTime) *
  GetCurrentPitchValue(); // Compensate for callback rate
if (TimeUntilSync <= 0.f)
  return std::nullopt;

// The list of potential moment sync candidates we can hit
std::vector<MomentSyncData> ValidBeatCandidates;

float NewPitchValue = TimeUntilMoment / TimeUntilSync;
int BarNumber = BeatData.BarNumber;
while (NewPitchValue >= PitchShifterMinValueThreshold)
{
  if (IsValidPitchValue(TimeUntilMoment, NewPitchValue))
  {
    ValidBeatCandidates.push_back({ EventId, BarNumber,
      TimeUntilSync, NewPitchValue, true });
  }

  // Check to sync with this beat in the next bar
  TimeUntilSync += MusicProperties->BarDuration;
  BarNumber++;
  NewPitchValue = TimeUntilMoment / TimeUntilSync;
}
```

```cpp
  if (ValidBeatCandidates.empty())
    return std::nullopt;

  // Return the nearest sync candidate
  auto MinValuePredicate = [](
    const auto& Elem1, const auto& Elem2)
  {
    return Elem1.TimeUntilSync < Elem2.TimeUntilSync;
  };

  auto MinElement = std::min_element(
    ValidBeatCandidates.begin(), ValidBeatCandidates.end(),
    MinValuePredicate);
  if (MinElement == ValidBeatCandidates.end())
    return std::nullopt;

  return *MinElement;
}


bool AudioEvent::CanHitPitchTargetAtMaxRate(
  float TimeUntilMoment, float PitchTargetValue) const
{
  float PitchChangeForRemainingTime =
    MaxPitchChangePerSecond * TimeUntilMoment;
  return abs(PitchTargetValue - GetCurrentPitchValue()) <=
    PitchChangeForRemainingTime;
}


void AudioEvent::OnMusicMomentChanged(
  AudioEngineContext& EngineContext, float TimeUntilMoment)
{
  // Get a target beat if we can find one
  std::optional<MomentSyncData> NewTargetSyncData =
    GetTargetBeatForMomentSync(
      EngineContext, TimeUntilMoment);
  if (NewTargetSyncData.has_value() == false)
    return;

  EngineContext.MomentDataToUpdate.push_back(
    NewTargetSyncData.value());
}
```

We can now finally complete our `UpdatePitchShifter()` function, set-ting the values of the pitch shifter DSP and the event instance pitch value (which we saw previously in Section 15.2.2).

```cpp
constexpr float EqualToValueThreshold = 0.001f;
void AudioEvent::UpdatePitchShifter(float DeltaTime,
  MomentSyncData SyncData)
{
  if (PitchShifterDSP == nullptr)
    return;

  float CurrentPitchValue = GetCurrentPitchValue();

  // Apply the max defined pitch change we want to do
  // per frame
  float MaxPitchChangePerFrame =
    DeltaTime * MaxPitchChangePerSecond;
  if (SyncData.TargetPitchValue > CurrentPitchValue)
  {
    PitchShifterValue = std::min(
      PitchShifterValue + MaxPitchChangePerFrame,
      SyncData.TargetPitchValue);
  }
  else if (SyncData.TargetPitchValue < CurrentPitchValue)
  {
    PitchShifterValue = std::max(
      PitchShifterValue - MaxPitchChangePerFrame,
      SyncData.TargetPitchValue);
  }

  // Applying this truncate makes everything sound smoother
  float NewValue = round(PitchShifterValue * 10.f) / 10.f;
  if (NewValue <= 0.f ||
      abs(NewValue - 0.f) <= EqualToValueThreshold)
    return;

  // Set the DSP and event instance pitch values!
  PitchShifterDSP->setParameterFloat(
    FMOD_DSP_PITCHSHIFT_PITCH,
    NewValue);
  EventInstance->setPitch(1.f / NewValue);
}
```

The last step is to build the interface for the other game code so it can try and schedule a music moment. This calls `AudioEvent::OnMusicMomentChanged()` for any audio events that are registered as moment events, which we defined as part of our preparations in Section 15.3. I recommend exposing this function as a console/debug command for easy testing.

```
class AudioEngineContext
{
public:
  // ...
  static void SyncMusicMoment(const float TimeUntilEvent);
}


void AudioEngineContext::SyncMusicMoment(
  const float TimeUntilEvent)
{
  if (TimeUntilEvent <= 0.f)
    return;

  auto& EngineContext =
    AudioEngineContext::GetEngineContext();
  for (auto Id : EngineContext.MusicMomentIDs)
  {
    auto* AudioEvent = EngineContext.GetAudioEvent(Id);
    if (AudioEvent == nullptr)
      continue;

    AudioEvent->OnMusicMomentChanged(
      EngineContext, TimeUntilEvent);
  }
}
```

15.4.2 Beat Synchronization: Important and Non-important

The current implementation works, but it is limited for what we want to do. If many different event triggers come in at random times to schedule music moments, we'll occasionally get a synchronization with the start of a bar, but most of the time the triggers may fail depending on the max pitch change threshold and the pitch shifter min and max thresholds. Modifying these values would elicit more syncs, but then the effect starts to sound a lot more noticeable. Finding this balance with the composition is key, but let's also open things up to allow for synchronization with other beats.

The example demo track from Figure 15.2 starts with a 4/4 beat, which means typically having a strong accent on the first beat, then a secondary accent on the third beat. In this case, since we're already favoring the first beat with our bar synchronization setup, we can just consider the third beat as "important", and therefore the second and fourth beats as "non-important".

With some time signatures, establishing the important beat(s) becomes a bit more subjective. Is the important beat for a 7/4 time signature the 5th beat in the bar or the 4th beat? Does one subdivide this as a 4/4 and 3/4 combination (ONE two three four FIVE six seven), or as a 3/4 and 4/4 combination (ONE two three FOUR five six seven)? Identifying the stress of these beats might seem intuitive, but we need to consider syncopation as a possibility. Should we allow for synchronization with all of these cases, favoring some over others? Unfortunately, there's no catch-all rule here, other than "defer to your score".

Regardless, defining a mapping of important beats (in order of preference) to time signatures is required in the `AudioEvent` class. This effectively defines the non-important beats, which are every other unspecified beat.

(Note: using `std::pair<int,int>` as the key in a C++ `unordered_map` below will require a suitable hash function, which I have not included here.)

```
using TimeSignature = std::pair<int, int>;
using ImportantBeats = std::vector<int>;
const std::unordered_map<
  TimeSignature, ImportantBeats, PairHash>
    ImportantBeatsMap = {
      { { 3, 4 }, { 3 } },
      { { 4, 4 }, { 3 } },
      { { 5, 4 }, { 4, 3 } },
      { { 6, 4 }, { 4 } },
      { { 7, 4 }, { 5, 4 } },
      { { 11, 4 }, { 7, 4, 10 } },
      { { 4, 8 }, { 3 } },
      { { 6, 8 }, { 4 } },
      { { 7, 8 }, { 5, 4 } },
      { { 8, 8}, { 5, 3, 7 } },
      { { 9, 8 }, { 4, 7 } },
      { { 12, 8 }, { 7, 4, 10 } } };
```

This will require editing the **MusicProperties** structure to include the times of the next important and non-important beats, alongside the previously defined bar time. Containers for the **BeatTimeData** structure (which we defined in the audio engine earlier) will do the trick, provided we add another integer variable to represent the beat number.

```cpp
struct BeatTimeData
{
  int BarNumber = 0;
  int BeatNumber = 0;
  float BeatTime = 0.f;
};


struct MusicProperties
{
  std::vector<BeatTimeData> ImportantBeatTimes;
  std::vector<BeatTimeData> NonImportantBeatTimes;
  float TimeOfNextBar = 0.f;
  float BarDuration = 0.f;
};
```

Naturally, this will also involve setting the times of these beats in the audio event beat callback when setting the properties data. These timings can easily be calculated based on the bar time and seconds per beat variables from before. Once we look up **ImportantBeatsMap** based on the time signature data, we can determine which data should be considered important versus non-important by beat (again, ignoring the first beat which is just a bar sync and is considered important separately).

```cpp
void AudioEvent::HandleMusicBeatCallback(
  const FMOD_STUDIO_TIMELINE_BEAT_PROPERTIES&
    BeatProperties) const
{
  // ...
  float TimeOfNextBar = AudioEngineContext.GetCurrentTime() +
    (SecondsPerBeat * BeatsLeftInBar);

  std::vector<BeatTimeData> ImportantBeatTimes;
  std::vector<BeatTimeData> NonImportantBeatTimes;

  auto FoundImportantBeats = ImportantBeatsMap.find({
```

```
   BeatProperties.timesignatureupper,
   BeatProperties.timesignaturelower });

int CurrentTimelineBeat = BeatProperties.beat;

// Already accounting for beat 1 (bar start)
int StartBeat = 2;

for (int i = StartBeat;
     i <= BeatProperties.timesignatureupper; i++)
{
  int BarNumber = 0;
  float TimeOfBeat = 0.f;

  // If we've already passed (or are on) the beat in this
  // bar, set our timing for the next bar
  if (CurrentTimelineBeat >= i)
  {
    // Decrement beat number since we want the number of
    // intervals from the first beat
    TimeOfBeat = TimeOfNextBar +
      (SecondsPerBeat * (i - 1));
    BarNumber = 1;
  }
  else
  {
    TimeOfBeat = AudioEngineContext.GetCurrentTime() +
      (SecondsPerBeat * (i - CurrentTimelineBeat));
  }

  BeatTimeData NewBeatData = { BarNumber, i, TimeOfBeat };

  // Add this beat timing to either the important beat
  // array or non important beat array
  if (FoundImportantBeats == ImportantBeatsMap.end())
  {
    NonImportantBeatTimes.push_back(NewBeatData);
  }
  else
  {
    auto& ImportantBeatsArray =
```

```
      FoundImportantBeats->second;
    if (std::find(ImportantBeatsArray.begin(),
      ImportantBeatsArray.end(), i) !=
      ImportantBeatsArray.end())
    {
      ImportantBeatTimes.push_back(NewBeatData);
    }
    else
    {
      NonImportantBeatTimes.push_back(NewBeatData);
    }
  }
}

MusicProperties NewMusicProperties = { ImportantBeatTimes,
  NonImportantBeatTimes, TimeOfNextBar,
  SecondsPerBeat * BeatProperties.timesignatureupper };
AudioEngineContext.SetMusicProperties(
  EventId, NewMusicProperties);
}
```

After this, the biggest change required is how we find the target beat to synchronize with. This involves integrating important and non-important beats with the functionality in `AudioEvent::GetTargetBeatForMomentSync()`, but we may still want to give priority to bar syncs over these beats because bar syncs will usually sound more impactful to the listener.

We can change the function parameters to include a new **enum** type indicating the types of beats with which to try to synchronize. This means we can run this function multiple times inside `AudioEvent::OnMusicMomentChanged()` in order of preference. Once a target beat has been found, we can add the data to the audio engine container, as we did before.

```
enum BeatSyncType
{
  Bars,
  Important,
  NonImportant,
}

std::optional<MomentSyncData> GetTargetBeatForMomentSync(
  const AudioEngineContext& EngineContext,
```

```
  BeatSyncType SyncType,
  float TimeUntilMoment);

void AudioEvent::OnMusicMomentChanged(
  AudioEngineContext& EngineContext, float TimeUntilMoment)
{
  std::optional<MomentSyncData> NewMomentSyncData;

  // Prioritize bar sync
  NewMomentSyncData =
    GetTargetBeatForMomentSync(EngineContext,
    BeatSyncType::Bars, TimeUntilMoment);
  if (!NewMomentSyncData.has_value())
  {
    // Failing this, try to sync with an important beat
    NewMomentSyncData =
      GetTargetBeatForMomentSync(EngineContext,
        BeatSyncType::Important, TimeUntilMoment);
    if (!NewMomentSyncData.has_value())
    {
      // Failing this, try to sync with a non-important beat
      NewMomentSyncData =
        GetTargetBeatForMomentSync(EngineContext,
          BeatSyncType::NonImportant, TimeUntilMoment);
    }
  }

  if (NewMomentSyncData.has_value())
  {
    EngineContext.MomentDataToUpdate.push_back(
      NewMomentSyncData.value());
  }
}
```

The MomentSyncData structure now also needs to cache the beat number. We can then modify AudioEvent::GetTargetBeatForMomentSync() to finish off setting up synchronization with the new beats. Adding a switch statement based on the new enum parameter that's passed in gives us the closest immediate beat timings from the beat callback. We can then use the same while loop from before for checking resulting pitch values across future bars to find matches.

```cpp
struct MomentSyncData
{
  int EventId = -1;
  int BarNumber = 0;
  int BeatNumber = 0;
  float TimeUntilSync = 0.f;
  float TargetPitchValue = 1.f;
  bool bIsValid = true;
};

constexpr float PitchShifterMinValueThreshold = 0.9f;
constexpr float PitchShifterMaxValueThreshold = 1.11f;
std::optional<MomentSyncData> GetTargetBeatForMomentSync(
  const AudioEngineContext& EngineContext,
  BeatSyncType SyncType,
  float TimeUntilMoment)
{
  //...
  if (MusicProperties == nullptr)
    return std::nullopt;

  std::vector<BeatTimeData> BeatTimings;
  switch(SyncType)
  {
  case BeatSyncType::Bars:
  {
    BeatTimings.push_back(
      { 0, 1, MusicProperties->TimeOfNextBar });
    break;
  }
  case BeatSyncType::Important:
  {
    BeatTimings = MusicProperties->ImportantBeatTimes;
    break;
  }
  case BeatSyncType::NonImportant:
  {
    BeatTimings = MusicProperties->NonImportantBeatTimes;
    break;
  }
  }
```

```
if (BeatTimings.empty())
  return std::nullopt;

// ...

float CurrentTime = EngineContext.GetCurrentTime();

// The list of potential moment sync candidates we can hit
std::vector<MomentSyncData> ValidBeatCandidates;

for (auto& BeatData : BeatTimings)
{
  float TimeUntilSync = (BeatData.BeatTime - CurrentTime) *
    GetCurrentPitchValue();
  if (TimeUntilSync <= 0.f)
    continue;

  // The while loop check from before goes here, except
  // we'll also add BeatData.BeatNumber as part of our
  // object push_back
}

if (ValidBeatCandidates.empty())
// The rest of this function remains the same...
}
```

15.5 REMARKS AND CONSIDERATIONS

15.5.1 A Note on Logging

There's already a lot of code presented in this chapter, so some bells and whistles had to be omitted for brevity's sake. However, I would be remiss if I didn't mention logging. Adding logging at different points is critical for a system like this, so we can verify which beat is being synchronized to the event and check that the beat does, in fact, play close to the same time as the game event (depending on the composition, this isn't always as obvious as you might think!). Logging is also extremely beneficial for identifying why moment synchronizations pass or fail, and examining what target pitch values are being calculated in these cases. This can, in turn, influence threshold adjustments.

15.5.2 Next Steps and Considerations

We can always take things further! Some potential next steps might include:

- Adding a cooldown reset to slowly lerp our music pitch back to its default rate after hitting a moment sync, as well as a priority setup for sync requests. This latter step would prevent attempts to consistently override the current synchronization whenever we receive any new scheduling call from game events. The system outlined in this chapter is also based on the philosophy of proceeding at the fastest possible rate per frame for moment syncs. Further calculations to determine the optimum rate per frame could help create a more consistent "rising" effect right up to this point.

- Improving accuracy due to potentially inaccurate beat timings and clock drift. We can improve this through repeatedly querying the target beat, thereby consistently ensuring we can still make the sync point, or by querying the target beat again after we've reached the target pitch to get a more recent reading. Since our FMOD timeline beat callbacks don't include any data about the next beat, we're also (unfortunately) at the mercy of inaccurate important beat synchronizations prior to a time signature change.

- Utilizing other tools. Modifying the Pitch Shifter controls time stretching for the music, but for a more comprehensive system we might want to do this in conjunction with other effects or event property changes. Tweaking EQ settings would help minimize any potential pitch change artifacts, while applying a riser or stinger at the point of creation would help put even more emphasis on our music moment.

15.6 CONCLUSION

In this chapter, we established the potential to create powerful moments of music–gameplay synchronization through the use of timeline beat callbacks and time-invariant pitch-shifting mechanics. This method of shaping the music timeline to coincide with in-game events differs from other approaches which schedule game events to trigger alongside musical beats. While both methods produce unique audio outcomes, syncing music to gameplay offers the programmer more real time control over the musical components in order to match game event cues whose timings may be inflexible. This system engenders nuanced, atmospheric, and psychologically satisfying gameplay that enriches the player's overall sensory experience.

NOTE

1. Although the range is arbitrarily large (up to the precision of a float), FMOD will clamp the final combined pitch to the range [0, 100].

REFERENCES

Emerick, Geoff, and Howard Massey. 2007. *Here, There and Everywhere: My Life Recording the Music of the Beatles*. New York, NY: Gotham Books.

Eventide Audio. n.d. "H910 Harmonizer: First Digital Effects Processor." *Eventide Audio*. Accessed April 18, 2025. https://www.eventideaudio.com/rackmount/h910-harmonizer/

id Software. 2016. *Doom*. PlayStation 4. Bethesda Softworks.

Nintendo, EPD. 2017. *The Legend of Zelda: Breath of the Wild*. Nintendo Switch. Nintendo Co., Ltd.

Scruffy Music. 2019. "Invisible Sound Design in Breath of the Wild." *YouTube*. July 19. Accessed April 18, 2025. https://www.youtube.com/watch?v=Vgev9Gzybk8

Walder, Colin. 2019. "Synchronizing Action-Based Gameplay to Music." In *Game Audio Programming Principles and Practices 2*, edited by Guy Somberg, 345–360. Boca Raton, FL: CRC Press.

CHAPTER 16

Remixing Musical Loops in RealTime

David Su

Four bars forward is equal to six counterclockwise revolutions, which equals a full loop extraction.

—(GRANDMASTER FLASH, COLUMBIA
UNIVERSITY LECTURE)[1]

16.1 INTRODUCTION

Interactive music systems in video games are continually evolving to adapt to the challenges and opportunities presented by ever-shifting technologies. Increases in gameplay time as well as real time processing power afford – and often necessitate – semi-procedural approaches to music in order to achieve broad musical coverage without ballooning scope. One such approach is real time remixing, which involves adjusting properties of separate disparate musical phrases so that when combined they create a cohesive musical whole. Real time remixing is especially well-suited to music with a strong rhythmic emphasis and consistent tempo – styles such as contemporary pop, hip-hop, and electronic music (to name a few) tend to be a good fit for this technique.

Manipulating one fragment of music to match another in real time is a common DJ practice known as beatmatching, which dates back to the 1960s[2] and is considered an essential feature of modern DJ software. In the same way that video game music has built upon linear techniques such as looping and orchestration to pioneer interactive techniques such as

DOI: 10.1201/9781003519119-21

horizontal resequencing and vertical layering, it can be fruitful to consider how we might make use of beatmatching and remixing as a tool in our interactive music arsenal. Loop-based remixing also opens up additional ways for the player to experience music, such as spatialized stems, player-driven remixing, and more. One particularly motivating use case is that of diegetic musical elements that remain musically coherent when played over a variety of different background music tracks.

This chapter's code is written in C++ – custom classes and types created specifically for the chapter will be prefixed with `Gap` (short for "Game Audio Programming"), while classes or types without this prefix are assumed to be either classes provided by the underlying audio engine or built-in C++ types. I've aimed to keep the code relatively generic, as the general principles and techniques are applicable regardless of what specific language, game engine, and/or audio middleware you choose to use.

16.2 LOOPS, SONGS, AND PHRASES

16.2.1 Data Types

We begin by establishing the background music as a song, on top of which multiple loops (i.e., pieces of music that repeat) can play simultaneously in a musical fashion. Conceptually, loops and songs can both be thought of as musical phrases – as such, they both share some common properties that we can encapsulate in a musical phrase data type[3]:

```
class GapPhraseData
{
public:

   AudioEvent* PlayEvent = nullptr;
   AudioEvent* StopEvent = nullptr;
   float Bpm = 120.f;
   GapKeySignature KeySignature = GapKeySignature();
};
```

Loops require additional musical manipulation, so they will need some additional properties. To do so, we can create a loop data type with the pertinent properties for our purposes.

```
class GapLoopData : public GapPhraseData
{
   // Playback
```

```
    int32_t PlaybackInterval = 1;
    GapBeatDivision PlaybackIntervalUnit =
      GapBeatDivision::Bar;
    int32_t PlaybackOffset = 0;

    // Pitch/Key
    bool bPreservePitch = true;
    bool bMatchSongKey = true;
};
```

The loop data's `PlaybackIntervalUnit` property, represented in beat divisions, determines how often a loop should play. In our implementation we support bar, beat, and step divisions, following the common sequencer convention that a bar contains four beats[4] and a beat contains four steps. In Western classical terms, a step is equivalent to a sixteenth note, and a beat is equivalent to a quarter note.

```
enum class GapBeatDivision : uint8_t
{
  Step, // i.e. sixteenth note
  Beat, // i.e. quarter note
  Bar
};
```

The loop data's `PlaybackInterval` property determines how many beat divisions should elapse before we restart playback of our loop – it essentially represents the desired duration of the loop in musical time. For example, a 4-bar loop would have a playback interval unit of type `GapBeatDivision::Bar` and a playback interval of 4. The `PlaybackOffset` property allows us to define a "pre-roll" for our loop – our loop player will wait for the given number of beat divisions before commencing loop playback. Finally, the `bPreservePitch` and `bMatchSongKey` properties determine pitch-shifting behavior, which we'll discuss in Section 16.4.2.

For our purposes we won't actually be defining any song-specific properties, but in practice you might have properties such as music-related metadata (e.g., title or description) or gameplay-related associations (e.g., if a certain song is associated with specific environments or aspects of player progression through the game).

```
class GapSongData: public GapPhraseData {};
```

16.2.2 Song Playback

Before we get to loop playback, we need to set up playback of the actual song. Let's create a song player:

```cpp
class GapSongPlayer
{
public:

  void Play();
  void Stop();

  void BindLoopPlayer(GapLoopPlayer* InLoopPlayer);

  static void SongPlaybackCallback(
    CallbackType InCallbackType,
    CallbackInfo* InCallbackInfo);

  static void SongStopCallback(
    CallbackType InCallbackType,
    CallbackInfo* InCallbackInfo);

  void Initialize();
  void Deinitialize();

  int32_t GetPlayingId() const;

  // Returns a copy
  std::vector<GapLoopPlayer*> GetLoopPlayers() const;

  // --------

  GapSongData* Song = nullptr;

private:
  std::vector<GapLoopPlayer*> LoopPlayers = {};
  int32_t_t PlayingId = INVALID_PLAYING_ID;
};
```

The song player holds an array of loop players which are added via the `BindLoopPlayer()` function.

```
void GapSongPlayer::BindLoopPlayer(
  GapLoopPlayer* InLoopPlayer)
{
  LoopPlayers.push_back(InLoopPlayer);
}
```

When we play the song, we make sure to bind the song playback call-back to the playing event.

```
void GapSongPlayer::Play()
{
  if (auto* SongPlayEvent = Song->PlayEvent)
  {
    PlayingId = SongPlayEvent->PostOnGameObjectID(
      PLAYBACK_AUDIO_OBJECT_ID,
      nullptr,
      &SongPlaybackCallback,
      static_cast<void*>(this),
      PLAYBACK_CALLBACK_TYPE_ALL,
      nullptr);
  }
}
```

In `SongPlaybackCallback()`, the song player forwards callback notifications to each loop player, which handles the callbacks according to its own loop properties.

```
void GapSongPlayer::SongPlaybackCallback(
  CallbackType InCallbackType,
  CallbackInfo* InCallbackInfo)
{
  if (!InCallbackInfo)
  {
    return;
  }

  auto* Cookie = InCallbackInfo->Cookie;
  auto* SongPlayer = static_cast<GapSongPlayer*>(Cookie);
  if (!SongPlayer)
  {
    return;
  }
```

```
  // --------

  for (auto* LoopPlayer : SongPlayer->GetLoopPlayers())
  {
    if (LoopPlayer)
    {
      LoopPlayer->SongPlaybackCallback(InCallbackType,
                                       InCallbackInfo);
    }
  }
}
```

Now we'll take a look at the loop players themselves.

16.2.3 Loop Playback

Here's what the class declaration for our loop player looks like:

```
class GapLoopPlayer
{
public:

  GapLoopPlayer();

  void Play();
  void Stop();

  void SongPlaybackCallback(
    CallbackType InCallbackType,
    const CallbackInfo* InCallbackInfo);

  // --------

  UGapLoopData* LoopData = nullptr;

private:

  GapSongPlayer* GetSongPlayer() const;
  void BindToSongPlayer();

  void UpdateRealTimeParameters();
  void UpdatePlaybackSpeed(float InPlaybackSpeed);
```

```cpp
  void UpdatePitchShiftAmount(
    float InPlaybackSpeed,
    bool bInMatchSongKey,
    const GapKeySignature& InLoopKey,
    const GapKeySignature& InSongKey);

  bool DoesCallbackMatchPlaybackIntervalUnit(
    CallbackType InCallbackType) const;

  bool HasReachedPlaybackOffset() const;
  bool HasReachedPlaybackInterval() const;

  // --------

  AudioComponent* PlaybackAudioComponent = nullptr;
  int32_t PlayingId = INVALID_PLAYING_ID;
  int32_t NumCallbacksElapsed = 0;
};
```

It can also be helpful for the loop player to either implement or derive from another class that has a transform so that we can give it an in-world location. One particularly motivating use case for this is if we want the different stems of our song to play back diegetically – we can set up each stem as a loop player, and then position those loop players wherever we want in the world.

We've also set up our loop player to automatically bind to the song player upon creation, which prevents the user from having to manually bind the loop to the song.

```cpp
void GapLoopPlayer::Initialize()
{
  SetupPlaybackAudioComponent();
  BindToSongPlayer();
}

void GapLoopPlayer::BindToSongPlayer()
{
  if (auto* SongPlayer = GetSongPlayer())
  {
    SongPlayer->BindLoopPlayer(this);
  }
}
```

As with the song player, the bulk of the loop playback logic takes place in a playback callback function. Within that function, we check three primary conditions:

1. Whether the callback type we're responding to matches the loop data's playback interval (i.e., beat division)[5]:

```cpp
bool GapLoopPlayer::DoesCallbackMatchPlaybackIntervalUnit(
  CallbackType InCallbackType) const
{
  if (!LoopData)
  {
    return false;
  }

  switch (LoopData->PlaybackIntervalUnit)
  {
    case GapBeatDivision::Step:
    {
      return (InCallbackType == CallbackType::Step);
    } break;

    case GapBeatDivision::Beat:
    {
      return (InCallbackType == CallbackType::Beat);
    } break;

    case GapBeatDivision::Bar:
    {
      return (InCallbackType == CallbackType::Bar);
    } break;

    default:
    {} break;
  }

  return false;
}
```

2. Whether loop playback has reached the loop data's playback offset:

```cpp
bool GapLoopPlayer::HasReachedPlaybackOffset() const
```

```
{
  if (!LoopData)
  {
    return false;
  }

  // --------

  return (NumCallbacksElapsed >= LoopData->PlaybackOffset);
}
```

3. Whether loop playback has reached the loop data's playback interval:

```
bool GapLoopPlayer::HasReachedPlaybackInterval() const
{
  if (!LoopData)
  {
    return false;
  }

  const int32_t PlaybackInterval =
    LoopData->PlaybackInterval;
  if (PlaybackInterval < 1)
  {
    return false;
  }

  // --------

  const int32_t NumCallbacksSincePlayback =
    NumCallbacksElapsed - LoopData->PlaybackOffset;

  return (NumCallbacksSincePlayback % PlaybackInterval == 0);
}
```

If all of these conditions are met, we then proceed to play the loop:

```
void GapLoopPlayer::Play()
{
  if (!PlaybackAudioComponent || !LoopData)
  {
    return;
```

```
    }

    PlayingId =
      PlaybackAudioComponent->PostEvent(LoopData->PlayEvent);
}
```

Putting that all together, we get the following song playback callback function:

```
void GapLoopPlayer::SongPlaybackCallback(
  CallbackType InCallbackType,
  CallbackInfo* InCallbackInfo)
{
  if (!DoesCallbackMatchPlaybackIntervalUnit(InCallbackType))
  {
    return;
  }

  // --------

  if (HasReachedPlaybackOffset() &&
      HasReachedPlaybackInterval())
  {
    Play();
  }

  // --------

  NumCallbacksElapsed++;
}
```

This playback logic ensures that the loops will play at the correct musical time, based on the loop and song properties. However, you may have noticed a problem: just because a loop begins playback at the correct time doesn't mean it will actually make musical sense with the underlying song. For example, a loop in D# major at 79 BPM is unlikely to gel musically with a song that's in A minor at 101 BPM. The main incoherencies arise due to differing tempos and keys. As such, we'll need to do some additional work to reconcile those differences. Let's start with tempo.

16.3 TEMPO

16.3.1 Representing Tempo

Tempo refers to how fast or slow a piece of music is played, and is typically represented via beats per minute (BPM). In our `GapPhraseData` class, this is represented as a `Bpm` float, as shown in Section 16.2.1.

16.3.2 Beatmatching

In order to make the loop play "at the same tempo" as the song, we need to adjust the loop's playback speed to account for tempo differences between the loop and song. This is precisely the beatmatching process mentioned in Section 16.1, and the method for calculating the appropriate playback speed is simply to divide the song BPM by the loop BPM.

```
float CalculatePlaybackSpeed(float InLoopBpm,
                             float InSongBpm)
{
  return InSongBpm / InLoopBpm;
}
```

Taking our previous example of a loop at 79 BPM playing over a song at 101 BPM, in order to get the loop to play at 101 BPM, its playback speed is 101/79 = 1.278.

We can then take this value and pass it to a parameter that controls playback speed. The specific implementation details will vary here depending on your engine and/or middleware (e.g., some APIs will let you adjust playback speed directly, without binding to a parameter), but most audio engines and middleware will let you adjust playback speed at runtime.

```
void GapLoopPlayer::UpdatePlaybackSpeed(
  float InPlaybackSpeed)
{
  GetSoundEngine()->SetParameterValue(
    PARAM_PLAYBACK_SPEED,
    InPlaybackSpeed,
    PlaybackAudioComponent->GetGameObjectID());
}
```

Now that we've reconciled our tempo differences, let's take a look at key.

16.4 KEY

16.4.1 Representing Key

In the Western classical tradition as well as much of contemporary Western pop, a key signature (e.g., D# major, A minor) determines the set of notes that comprise a piece of music, providing a framework for its harmonic activity. A key signature is composed of a root note and a key quality. The key quality defines which notes are included (expressed as relative intervals from a given note), and the root note defines which note we measure those relative intervals from. For example, the key of A major contains the notes {A, B, C#, D, E, F#, G#}, whereas the key of A minor contains the notes {A, B, C, D, E, F, G}.[6] Both the root note (expressed as a pitch class) and key quality can be represented as enums,[7] with the key signature represented as a struct containing both.

```
enum class EGapPitchClass : uint8_t
{
  None = 0,
  A, As, B, C, Cs, D, Ds, E, F, Fs, G, Gs
};

enum class GapKeyQuality : uint8_t
{
  None = 0,
  Maj,
  Min
};

struct GapKeySignature
{
  GapPitchClass RootNote = GapPitchClass::None;
  GapKeyQuality Quality = GapKeyQuality::None;
};
```

Note that for pitch classes we represent all accidentals as sharps, using the character **s** instead of the # character in accordance with C++ identifier requirements.

16.4.2 Transposing Keys

At a high level, what we want to do is to transpose, or shift, the loop's key signature to match the song's key signature. This is a similar process to transposing two notes (or pitch classes), but with the added wrinkle of key qualities. For example, the key of A minor contains the notes {A, B, C, D, E, F, G} and C major contains the notes {C, D, E, F, G, A, B}. These two sets are actually composed of the exact same notes, just in a different order, so if the loop is in A minor and the song is in C major, no transposition is needed. This is known as enharmonic equivalence, and it's something we need to take into account when transposing keys. Any major key will be enharmonically equivalent to a minor key whose root note is 3 semitones lower than its own. Likewise, any minor key will be enharmonically equivalent to a major key whose root note is 3 semitones higher than its own. For example, C major is enharmonically equivalent to A minor (A is 3 semitones below C: C→B→A#→A), whereas C minor is enharmonically equivalent to D# major[8] (D# is 3 semitones above C: C→C#→D→D#).

With all of this in mind, we can transpose our loop key with a two-step process:

1. Match the loop and song key qualities.

2. Match the loop and song root notes.

Let's start with matching the loop and song key qualities, which amounts to converting both loop and song keys to enharmonically equivalent keys with the same quality. In practice, we can just convert one of the key qualities to match the other. Since we're manipulating loops, it feels sensible to convert the loop's key quality to match that of the song. For example, if the loop is in D# major and the song is in A minor, we can represent the loop key as A# minor (enharmonically equivalent to D# major) and the song key as A minor (unchanged).

```
GapKeySignature CalculateEnharmonicallyEquivalentKey(
    const GapKeySignature& InKey,
    GapKeyQuality InQuality)
{
    // Same quality (and thus same key) as original
    if (InKey.Quality == InQuality)
    {
        return InKey;
    }

    // Invalid quality; just return original
```

```
if (InKey.Quality == GapKeyQuality::None ||
    InQuality == GapKeyQuality::None)
{
  return InKey;
}

// --------

auto EquivalentKey = InKey;

// Maj ==> Min
if (InKey.Quality == GapKeyQuality::Maj &&
    InQuality == GapKeyQuality::Min)
{
  EquivalentKey.RootNote =
    CalculateTransposedPitch(InKey.RootNote, -3);
}

// Min ==> Maj
else if (InKey.Quality == GapKeyQuality::Min &&
         InQuality == GapKeyQuality::Maj)
{
  EquivalentKey.RootNote =
    CalculateTransposedPitch(InKey.RootNote, 3);
}

return EquivalentKey;
}
```

Note that `CalculateEnharmonicallyEquivalentKey()` makes use of a `CalculateTransposedPitch()` function, which performs the requisite math on the pitch classes as integers, then converts the result back to a pitch class.

```
GapPitchClass CalculateTransposedPitch(
  GapPitchClass InPitch, int32_t InTransposeSemitones)
{
  // Invalid pitch
  if (InPitch == GapPitchClass::None)
  {
    return GapPitchClass::None;
```

```
}

// --------

// Add semitones to pitch
const auto PitchInt = static_cast<uint8_t>(InPitch);
int32_t TransposedPitchInt =
  PitchInt + InTransposeSemitones;

// Collapse to 12-tone
TransposedPitchInt = TransposedPitchInt % 12;

// Convert negative values
if (TransposedPitchInt < 0)
{
  TransposedPitchInt += 12;
}

// Cast to pitch class
GapPitchClass TransposedPitchClass =
  static_cast<GapPitchClass>(TransposedPitchInt);

return TransposedPitchClass;
}
```

We can also define helper functions for getting a key's relative major and minor key.

```
GapKeySignature GetRelativeMajorKey(
  const GapKeySignature& InKey)
{
  return CalculateEnharmonicallyEquivalentKey(
    InKey, GapKeyQuality::Maj);
}

GapKeySignature GetRelativeMinorKey(
  const GapKeySignature& InKey)
{
  return CalculateEnharmonicallyEquivalentKey(
    InKey, GapKeyQuality::Min);
}
```

Now that the loop and song have matching key qualities, in order to match their root notes we can calculate how many semitones it takes to transpose the loop key's root note to match the song key's root note. For example, if the loop is in D# major and the song is in A minor (i.e., C major), it takes 3 semitones (D#→D→C#→C). Note that we want to find the shortest path between the two notes – if we were to shift D# in the other direction, it would take 9 semitones (D#→E→F→F#→G→G#→A→A#→B→C). For our purposes, we're interested in the smaller value, since we want to minimize the amount of pitch shifting (which leads to audible artifacting) that we perform.

```
int32_t CalculateSemitoneDifference(GapPitchClass InPitchA,
                                    GapPitchClass InPitchB)
{
  if (InPitchA == InPitchB)
  {
    return 0;
  }

  if (InPitchA == GapPitchClass::None ||
      InPitchB == GapPitchClass::None)
  {
    return 0;
  }

  // ---------

  const auto PitchAInt = static_cast<uint8_t>(InPitchA);
  const auto PitchBInt = static_cast<uint8_t>(InPitchB);

  // ----
  // Calculate upper and lower differences
  int32_t DiffUpper = (PitchAInt < PitchBInt) ?
                      (PitchBInt - PitchAInt) :
                      (PitchBInt - PitchAInt + 12);

  int32_t DiffLower = DiffUpper - 12;

  // ----
  // Choose the closer difference
  // (i.e. the difference with a lower absolute value)
```

```
  const auto AbsDiffUpper = std::abs(DiffUpper);
  const auto AbsDiffLower = std::abs(DiffLower);

  return AbsDiffUpper < AbsDiffLower ? DiffUpper : DiffLower;
}
```

Finally, we take that semitone difference and convert it to a pitch-shift amount, which tells us how much to pitch shift our loop by.

```
float CalculatePitchShiftAmount(float InTransposeSemitones,
                                float InPlaybackSpeed)
{
  // Playback speed compensation to preserve original pitch
  const float PlaybackSpeedCompensationAmount =
    12.f * std::log2f(1.f / InPlaybackSpeed);

  // Manual transposition
  const float PitchShiftAmount =
    PlaybackSpeedCompensationAmount + InTransposeSemitones;

  return PitchShiftAmount; // In semitones
}
```

Note that in some cases we may not actually want to match the loop key to the song key (e.g., for drum loops), so we don't need to perform that extra transposition and calculation. However, we may still want to preserve the pitch of the original loop, which will still require pitch shifting to compensate for playback speed adjustments. This is where the loop data's bPreservePitch and bMatchSongKey properties defined in Section 16.2.1 come into play: these properties allow designers to control the pitch-shifting behavior on a loop-by-loop basis. As such, our final pitch shift amount calculation will need to take into account both pitch preservation and song key matching.

```
void GapLoopPlayer::UpdateRealTimeParameters()
{
  if (!LoopData)
  {
    return;
  }
```

```
const auto* SongPlayer = GetSongPlayer();
if (!SongPlayer)
{
  return;
}


const auto& SongData = SongPlayer->Song;
if (!SongData)
{
  return;
}


// --------


const float LoopBpm = LoopData->Bpm;
const float SongBpm = SongData->Bpm;
const float PlaybackSpeed =
  GapLoopPlayer::CalculatePlaybackSpeed(LoopBpm, SongBpm);


const bool bPreservePitch = LoopData->bPreservePitch;
const bool bMatchSongKey = LoopData->bMatchSongKey;


const auto& LoopKey = LoopData->KeySignature;
const auto& SongKey = SongData->KeySignature;


// --------


// Update playback speed
UpdatePlaybackSpeed(PlaybackSpeed);


// Update pitch shift amount only if either we're
// preserving pitch or matching song key (or both)
if (bPreservePitch || bMatchSongKey)
{
  UpdatePitchShiftAmount(
    PlaybackSpeed,
    bMatchSongKey,
    LoopKey,
    SongKey);
}
}
```

The actual `UpdatePitchShiftAmount()` function (called in the last few lines of `UpdateRealTimeParameters()`) is implemented as follows:

```
void GapLoopPlayer::UpdatePitchShiftAmount(
  float InPlaybackSpeed,
  bool bInMatchSongKey,
  const GapKeySignature& InLoopKey,
  const GapKeySignature& InSongKey)
{
  // --------
  // Calculate transposition amount

  float TransposeSemitones = 0.f;

  if (bInMatchSongKey)
  {
    // Can be either major or minor, as long as they are the
    // same quality -- here we opt for major
    const auto LoopKeyMajor = GetRelativeMajorKey(InLoopKey);
    const auto SongKeyMajor = GetRelativeMajorKey(InSongKey);

    TransposeSemitones =
      CalculateSemitoneDifference(
        LoopKeyMajor.RootNote,
        SongKeyMajor.RootNote);
  }

  // --------
  // Calculate pitch shift amount

  const float PitchShiftAmount =
  CalculatePitchShiftAmount(
      TransposeSemitones,
      InPlaybackSpeed);

  // --------
  // Set pitch shift amount

  GetSoundEngine()->SetParameterValue(
    PARAM_PITCH_SHIFT_AMOUNT,
    PitchShiftAmount,
    PlaybackAudioComponent->GetGameObjectID());
}
```

As shown above, once we've calculated our pitch shift amount, we then set that value for a parameter, similar to what we did with playback speed. Again, the specific implementation details will vary depending on the tools and technologies you use, but most audio engines and middleware come with a built-in real time pitch shifter these days. In your own implementation you'll want to double check the API of your pitch shifter and make sure you're mapping the parameter value accordingly. For example, Wwise's Pitch Shifter effect (Audiokinetic n.d.) defines its pitch in cents (1 cent = 1/100th of a semitone) with a range of −2400 to 2400 cents, while FMOD's Pitch Shifter effect (Firelight Technologies n.d.) defines its pitch in octaves (1 octave = 12 semitones) with a range of 0.5–2.0 octaves. If you're interested in implementing your own pitch shifter, Stephan Bernsee's blog post "Pitch Shifting Using the Fourier Transform" (Bernsee 1999) may be a good starting point.

16.5 ADDITIONAL CONSIDERATIONS

And that's it! With a relatively small amount of code and setup we've created a pretty powerful and flexible system for real time remixing. With that in mind, let's take a look at some additional things we may want to consider when putting this into practice.

One area of improvement for our current implementation is in the handling of odd playback interval lengths. For example, if we have a 4-bar loop and a song that contains a 7-bar phrase, the loop and song will get out of sync. There are a few things we can do to mitigate this. One approach is to restart the loop every time we reach "bar 1" of a phrase in the song – for our current implementation, we can encode this information in custom markers, which we can then respond to via marker callbacks. A similar solution works for odd time signatures (also known as odd meters), using beats and steps rather than bars as the beat division interval. Alternately, we could define a custom time signature data structure and reconcile any interval length mismatches using that info.

Another area of improvement is the handling of real time key and tempo changes, in particular ramp-ups and wind-downs that involve smooth interpolation between two tempos. Currently our implementation assumes that a song maintains the same tempo and key throughout its entirety, which is not always the case. To handle real time changes at the song level, we first need to make sure those changes are represented on the song data and/or playback side. These tempo changes are where an audio engine or middleware's built-in interactive music capabilities can be useful. For example, Wwise and FMOD both expose their music timeline information via callbacks.

Once we receive these callbacks, we can then make sure on the loop side to recalculate our loops' playback speeds and transposition amounts at regular intervals (e.g., on each game frame)[9]. This may result in some drift for tempo ramps, especially for fast interpolations between two tempos (or frame rate fluctuations if the calculation is done on the game thread), but the good news is that because our callback-driven playback scheduling is still in place, once the loop restarts it will play at the right time (and of course can still continue updating playback speed throughout restarts).

Finally, we've looked entirely at real time processes for manipulating our musical material, but it's worth considering the benefits of offline and hybrid processes as well. For example, we can often get higher-quality time stretching with fewer artifacts via an offline process. As such, we could run a batch of time stretches per loop per bucket of tempos, and at run-time choose the source audio from closest bucket, performing real time time stretching as needed. Because the buckets span a range of tempos, our worst-case real time time-stretching amount will be lower than if we only had a single audio source (and thus a single tempo bucket) per loop. The same approach can be taken for keys with regards to pitch shifting, and can be thought of as analogous to multisampling in the realm of sample libraries. By reducing the amount of real time processing we have to perform on our loops' source audio, we can reduce artifacts and improve the quality of our loop playback.

Other potential considerations include seeking, starting in mid-phrase of the loop (e.g., if the song is already playing by the time we're to begin our loop), matching harmonic modes (e.g., changing a loop from major to minor or vice versa), and allowing loops themselves to be treated as songs.

16.6 CONCLUSION

By drawing inspiration from DJ techniques and adapting them for game audio, we're able to create interactive musical experiences that go beyond traditional game music approaches. It is my hope that this exploration of real time loop-based remixing in the context of games may serve as further inspiration for your game audio programming endeavors, and I look forward to seeing and hearing (and playing) how you put your own spin on things.

I'd like to thank Caleb Epps, Justin Smith, and the rest of the Brass Lion Entertainment audio team for their continued creativity, wisdom, and support in collaboratively building interactive music systems that push boundaries while staying true to their musical and cultural origins.

And the other side of a loop is a loop.

—FRANK OCEAN, SEIGFRIED (2016)

NOTES

1. From a guest lecture for Josef Sorrett's "Hip Hop at 50: Music, Politics, Religion" course (Muniz 2024).
2. Francis Grasso is commonly recognized as one of the first DJs to employ beatmatching. He began DJing in 1967, and in an interview with DJ History (Broughton 2016) he describes being "able to beat mix right away".
3. Notice that `GapPhraseData` contains a `KeySignature` member of type `GapKeySignature` – we'll discuss this key signature data structure in more detail in Section 16.4.1.
4. This doesn't account for odd time signatures, which we'll touch on briefly in Section 16.5.
5. In our example, there is a one-to-one relationship between beat division and callback type, which might make you wonder why we don't just use the callback type directly and forgo the beat division data type. One reason is that callback types vary across audio engines, which means that the exact matching conditions for each beat division will depend on what callback types are available. Another reason is that callback types often include non-music-related callbacks (e.g., callbacks for when an event has started or stopped playback), so for the purposes of reasoning about rhythm it can still be useful to have a data type dedicated to beat divisions.
6. That is, A natural minor contains those notes – natural minor is typically what we mean when we say "minor", but just know that there are also other minor keys such as the harmonic and melodic minor.
7. For more flexibility with the key qualities we could define additional harmonic modes and/or customizable key qualities defined as pitch class arrays, but since we don't need that level of harmonic granularity for most remixing scenarios (not to mention the fact that it would complicate our transposition calculations) we've opted to go with major and minor only. If you really wanted to you could represent the other Western modes by simply changing the root note so that the pitch set lines up – for example, D Dorian contains all the same notes as A minor. However, depending on the music content you might find that setting a loop's key to D minor can sound better in most cases, even if it's *technically* in D Dorian.
8. Technically we'd prefer the key to be E♭, since the E♭/D♯ note is the third scale degree of C minor (C, D, E♭, F, G, A♭, B♭), but since we're representing pitch classes solely using sharps we end up with D♯. That being said, D♯ as a pitch class is enharmonically equivalent to E♭, and thus so are D♯ major and E♭ major as keys.

9. Note that in our implementation we haven't actually defined exactly where, or how often, `UpdateRealTimeParameters()` gets called, as those decisions are highly dependent on context and use cases. For example, if we know that our song will maintain the same tempo and key throughout its entire duration, then we can essentially take a fire-and-forget approach to updating our pitch-shifting and time-stretching parameters, only updating them when a new song is played. On the other hand, real time tempo and key changes will require the additional measures we outline in this current section.

REFERENCES

Audiokinetic. n.d. "Pitch Shifter." *Wwise SDK*. https://www.audiokinetic.com/en/library/edge/?source=Help&id=wwise_pitch_shifter_plug_in

Bernsee, Stephan. 1999. "Pitch Shifting Using The Fourier Transform." *Stephan Bernsee's Blog: Gedanken About Digital Signal Processing*. September 21. https://blogs.zynaptiq.com/bernsee/pitch-shifting-using-the-ft/

Broughton, Frank. 2016. "Interview: Francis Grasso, NYC Disco DJ Pioneer." *Red Bull Music Academy*. November 15. https://daily.redbullmusicacademy.com/2016/11/francis-grasso-interview

Firelight Technologies. n.d. "Pitch Shifter." *FMOD Engine User Manual*. https://www.fmod.com/docs/2.03/api/effects-reference.html#pitch-shifter

Muniz, Matthew. 2024. "Hip-Hop at 50: Grandmaster Flash on Revolutionizing the Music World." *Columbia College*. February 9. https://www.college.columbia.edu/news/hip-hop-50-grandmaster-flash-revolutionizing-music-world

Ocean, Frank. 2016. "Seigfried". *Blonde*. Boys Don't Cry, August 20.

Index

Note: **Bold** and *Italic* page numbers refer to **tables** and *figures*. Please numbers followed by 'n' refer to notes.

For Product Safety Concerns and Information please contact our EU
representative GPSR@taylorandfrancis.com
Taylor & Francis Verlag GmbH, Kaufingerstraße 24, 80331 München, Germany